The Hermeneutics of Person, Belongingness and Diverse Philosophies

(An Anthology)

Dr. Stanley Uche Anozie

Copyright © 2022 Dr. Stanley Uche Anozie
Copyright © 2022 Generis Publishing

All rights reserved. This book or any portion thereof may not be reproduced or used in any manner whatsoever without the written permission of the publisher except for the use of brief quotations in a book review.

Title: The Hermeneutics of Person, Belongingness and Diverse Philosophies

(An Anthology)

ISBN: 979-8-88676-022-4

Author: Dr. Stanley Uche Anozie

Cover image: www.pixabay.com

Publisher: Generis Publishing
Online orders: www.generis-publishing.com
Contact email: info@generis-publishing.com

Table of Contents

General Introduction 7

Part I: African Hermeneutics of *IHE* (Being and Light), Person and Hope. 9

Chapter 1: *IHE* (BEING) in African Igbo Ontology/Metaphysics 10

Chapter 2: Contemporary African Philosophical Notion of the Person and Community: An Essential Perspective to Integrative Ethics of Globality.......... 29

Chapter 3: The Hermeneutics of Hope in African Igbo Ontology 55

Part II: African Hermeneutics of Culture and Spirituality/Esotericism. 73

Chapter 4: The Paradox of Non-Violent Religions and Violent Cultural Practices: Igbo Nigeria Africans 74

Chapter 5: The Nigerian Government War Against Boko Haram/Terrorism (an Ellulian Communicative Perspective).. 96

Part III: African Hermeneutics of Ethics and Political Belongingness (Applied Ethics). 147

Chapter 6: Advancing an African Cosmopolitanism and Political Philosophy of Patriotism (The Hermeneutics of African Political Philosophy of Patriotism) 148

Chapter 7: African (Igbo) Ethics of Rights' Discourse: Theory and Practice .. 179

Chapter 8: African Perspectives on Global Development 195

Chapter 9: African Hermeneutics of Illuminating Consciousness: The Intercultural Problem of Language and Hermeneutics--------------------------230

General Introduction

Philosophical hermeneutics has become central to my research and writings. It is my wish to build on the work I have done so far. In this book, I will present diverse essays that I have written in the course of my hermeneutical studies. It means that this book is an anthology.

I have chosen to entitle this book: *The Hermeneutics of Person, Belongingness and Diverse Philosophies (an anthology).* This is to help accommodate some of recent hermeneutical reflections on the person, social responsibility, political belongingness, political rights, rights to self-determination, justice, global development, cultural competence, the question of responsibility, just war theory, etc. Different essays addressed different topics or subject matters in philosophy, theology, human rights, public policy and governance. Some of the ideas ranged from indigenous African philosophy/African hermeneutic philosophy to Western/European perspectives on person, culture, ethics, human rights, governance and philosophy of diversities. I hope that the chapters below will present interesting themes for African scholars/researchers, non-Western and Western scholars.

Each essay has got its own specific introduction and conclusion. Each essay has been identified by the style and period of my philosophical research. This specific information is to help readers appreciate the context and content of my hermeneutical contributions. There is no general conclusion; the conclusion of each essay is suitable for understanding the book.

Here is the basic goal structure of the book:

Part I: African Hermeneutics of *IHE* (Being and Light), Person and Hope.

Part II: African Hermeneutics of Culture and Spirituality/Esotericism.

Part III: African Hermeneutics of Ethics and Political Belongingness (Applied Ethics).

Part I:
African Hermeneutics of *IHE* (Being and Light), Person and Hope

Chapter 1
IHE (BEING) in African Igbo Ontology/Metaphysics

Stanley Uche Anozie

(Philosophy Department, Boston College, Chestnut Hill, MA, USA, 2021)

Abstract. As a pace-setter in his own right, Professor Pantaleon Iroegbu's approach to African Igbo Ontology or Metaphysics as the *Kpim* of philosophy is challenging as well as invigorating. For him, "Kpim" is an African Igbo word for 'the kernel', the substance, the essence of a thing, the reality or the most real of reality; like *Hypo-kaimenon* (Greek for underlying entity), etc. In an attempt to revive and advance the philosophical richness of Iroegbu's contributions to African Igbo Ontology or Metaphysics (or science of being and Being-itself), as a former student of Iroegbu, I will articulate an equivalent to his *Kpim* (the kernel, the substance, the core of a thing, etc.). This new equivalent to *Kpim* is African Igbo word *Ihe* (Thingness/Substance/Essence). A common saying in African Igbo lifeworld summarizes this new equivalent: *Ihe kwuru, ihe akwudobe ya* or *Ihe bu ihe di* or *Ihe mere ihe oji buru ihe obu*. (Only being makes a thing possible or Being makes a thing what it is). In understanding African Igbo ontological concepts of *Ihe* and *Mmadu*, it is only Being-itself that makes the "being of personhood" possible.

Keywords: Being, *Ihe, Kpim, Chi*, African, Igbo, Metaphysics/Ontology.

Introduction

In this work, I will attempt some critical reflections on "Being" in African Ontology. *Being* (Greek: *Ousia, Hypo-kaimenon* or Latin: *Substantia*) is equivalent to "Kpim" or "Ihe" in African Igbo ontology or metaphysics. *Kpim* is

Ihe. Igbo people say: "Ihe mere ihe oji buru ihe"---meaning "what makes a thing what it is or what makes one who he/she is."

African Igbo language expresses Being as "Ihe". African Igbo people often say: *Ihe mere ihe* (meaning--What makes a thing what it is). Without *Ihe* (being) there is *nothing*. There is a similarity of meaning between Being (*Ihe*) and Light (*Ìhè*)/or beauty. African Igbo metaphysics or ontology will use "Ihe" for-- Essence/Substance/Whatness, while "Ìhè" for--Light (as in openness, presence or radiance). *Ìhè* (light, openness or presence, radiance, disclosure) makes *Ihe* (substance or what is or essence) to be manifested or disclosed.

Human being or person, as a disclosure of being (*Ìhè* —light, beauty, radiance), is an instance of Being itself (Ihe). This instance reflects in Martin Buber's Hebrew ontology of person. The person is disclosed through his/her relationship to other beings/persons.[1] In African Igbo Ontology, *Mmadu* (Person), *Chi/chi* (Personal guardian) and *Ihe* (as Being and as *Ìhè*-- Light or Beauty) are all necessary in understanding *Ihe* or *Kpim* (Reality). I will take a look at *Ihe* (Being) in African Igbo Ontology and language.

African Igbo Language: *IHE* as "Being"

In my recent work on *The Hermeneutics of African Igbo Ontology of Hope*[2], I elucidated on three generative themes. They are: a) Hope as *Ìhè* (Light of Hope. Light as Hope. A light at the end of the tunnel) (ontological hope), b) Hope as *Nkuzi* or a part of *Nkuziology* (Life's teaching or social learning, the experience of life that forms humanity) (epistemological/pedagogical hope), and c) Hope as *Nchekube/Nchekwube*[3] or *Olileanya* (including Igbo names like *Nchekubechi/Nchekwubechi*, *Chekwubenachi*, *Olileanyachi*, *Echi-di-ime*--- tomorrow has promises, tomorrow is a day of hope or is a day to be hopeful) (anthropological hope).[4] For the purpose of this work, focused on *Ihe* (Being/Substance/Essence) in Africa Igbo Ontology, I will explain *Ihe* as Being and the diverse ways of understanding *Ihe* in African Igbo lifeworld.

---

[1] For Martin Buber, we are relational beings.
[2] This is another developing research project under the central theme of African Igbo Ontology/Metaphysics. I have carefully chosen to retain or repeat some of my reflections here to allow for more profound or thoughtful considerations by a diverse audience.
[3] African Igbo dialect difference but same essence or meaning (*Ku* or *Kwu* are interchangeable).
[4] I have sometimes considered adding "futuristic" to anthropological hope in order to emphasize the place of time to hope or the fulfilment of one's essence. This could be described as "anthropological/futuristic hope".

Within African Igbo lifeworld, Professor Pantaleon Iroegbu is a pace-setter in terms of African Igbo Ontology or Metaphysics. He identifies *Being/the Innermost Essence* or underlying entity as the *Kpim* of philosophy. Metaphysics or Ontology is what an individual person undertakes or does.[5] For Iroegbu, "Kpim" is African Igbo word for "the kernel", the substance, the essence of a thing, the reality or the most real of reality; like *Hypo-kaimenon* (Greek for underlying entity),[6] etc. In an attempt to advance the philosophical richness of Iroegbu's contributions to African Igbo Ontology or Metaphysics (or science of being and Being-itself), I will articulate and advance a hermeneutical equivalent to Iroegbu's *Kpim* (Igbo word for the kernel, the substance, the *core* of a thing, etc.) to another Igbo word *Ihe* (Being/Thingness/Substance/Essence/Ultimate Entity). *Ihe* has got 2 distinctive and interrelated connotations.

These 2 distinctive and interrelated connotations mutually sustain the understanding of *Ihe* or Being. The *first connotation* is: *Ihe*—means—'Being', 'Whatness', 'Quiddity', 'Essence' of a thing, the really real or the real thing, or reality itself. For instance, in African Igbo language expression: *Ihe mere ihe oji buru ihe obu*—meaning—'What or that which made a thing what it is' or 'What/That which really makes a thing a thing or whatever it is'. The *second connotation* is: *Ìhè* (Light, Disclosure, Openness, the Ability to be known, and Transparency/transparent)—could be related to 'disclosure' or revealing nature (a liberal interpretation could be like German--*Dasein*—as part of *Sein, Existenz* (revealed)). *Ìhè* ('light' or 'reveal-ness' or becoming known) is intrinsic to understanding *Ihe* (as Being or beingness or the kernel of a thing or Greek's *Ousia*. *Ìhè* (Light) is directly and epistemically tied to *Ihe* (Being, Essence, Substance or Whatness). It is only *Ihe* (Being, Quiddity or Essence or Reality) that is strictly associated with *Ìhè* (Light/Disclosure/Transparency). Without *Ìhè* (Light—Disclosure), the disclosing/transparent nature of *Ihe* (the kernel, substance or essence) will be impossible to comprehend or be encountered.

In this inevitable association between *Ihe* (the kernel, substance or being) and *Ìhè* (light or disclosure), I will discuss the significance of *Ìhè* (Light of Hope. Light as Hope. A light for direction or revelation of being or truth)- as an essential aspect of the hermeneutics of hope in African Igbo Ontology. The idea of Hope could be communicated through an English expression like the "light at the end of the tunnel" or "reality" that truly reveals itself, while "Hopelessness"

---

[5] Pantaleon Iroegbu, *Metaphysics: The Kpim of Philosophy*, Owerri, International University, Press, 1995, p. 325.
[6] Stanley Uche Anozie "The Problem of Evil in Plato and Gadamerian Plato", *Revue Roumaine de Philosophie*, 66, 1, București, 2019, pp. 116-129.

depicts darkness, failure, disappointment, etc. I will take a look at some African Igbo expressions in relation to explaining *Ìhè* (light, disclosure) as important to understanding African Igbo Ontology.

IHE (BEING) and Hope[7]

In African Igbo world, people often say: *Ihe kwuru ihe akwudebe ya*—meaning—"When a thing stands, then another things stands by it." (This also means that without a substance, a source, a real thing; then there can be nothing else close to it. *Ihe*—keeps anything in being. It makes a thing possible or capable of being. It is like the word substance (Latin, *Substantia*) or (Greek, *Hypo-kaimenon* or *Ousia*). Substance is something that is underneath or the underlying entity. As is a common saying, it is strictly on something that another thing can stand upon. Nothing is super-imposed on nothing. On nothing "nothing" else stands. "Nothing" is not an underlying entity.[8] One could relate this to my earlier works on African Igbo notion of 'Mmadu' (Person) as the beauty of life[9], and *The Problem of Evil in Platonism and Gadamerian Plato*.[10] Without substance there will be no shadow. Shadow is an accident. It is totally supported by substance or being. Accident (not a road mishap) does not exist in itself.[11]

Another enlightening concept is *Ìhè* in *Ihe-eke*—meaning—The Light that creates. *Ihe-Chukwu*—The light of God---this could be considered to be the 'action' or 'activity' of Being itself. God (although religiously used does imply the Being that truly exists in itself, by itself, and for itself. Without this God or Being, nothing else has existence or being. There is also a Christianized utterance of "Ìhè si na Ìhè." (The Un-caused Cause, Causality itself or from reality itself).

A third consideration of *Ihe* points to something unique in African Igbo Ontology. *Ihe-anyi* or *Ihe-anyi-chukwu*--meaning—"Nothing is impossible to God." The point of this African Igbo ontological/metaphysical expression is that

---

[7] I am inclined to relate Jean-Paul Sartre's *Being and Nothingness: an essay on phenomenological ontology* to "Being and Hope" (Igbo--*Ihe* [Being] and *Ìhè* [Hope]).
[8] Non-thing can hermeneutically be an Ultimate Entity or Being. That is the difference between "Nothing" and "Non-thing". Non-thing is not a physical object.
[9] Stanley Uche Anozie, *Hans-Georg Gadamer and African Hermeneutic Philosophy*, Chisinau, Generis Publishing, 2020, p. 169.
[10] S. U. Anozie "The Problem of Evil in Plato and Gadamerian Plato", pp. 116-129.
[11] *Ibidem*, pp. 116-117.

"Ihe" is actuality, Being, becoming to being, etc. The actuality or the becoming of the real is also the becoming of hope and hopefulness. The presence of the real reveals or would eventually reveal the most real. That which is eventually revealed is the real that becomes, or the becoming-being. (ontological hope).[12]

Epistemologically speaking, we know a thing in a limited manner, in potentiality, and truly know in actuality. There is nothing that is fully known in actuality in the physical world (Igbo: *Uwa nkea*). The most real is the most 'true' and the most present. To be present, or this 'presence', is understood as that which eliminates the un-truthful or 'hopelessness' on the truth. It is important to understand the dynamism of reality and to be confident in the unfolding of reality in reality's own time. Human beings (*Mma ndu*--the beauty of life) are part of this unfolding of reality. Unfolding of reality is the actualization of the fullness of human becoming (anthropological hope).

BEING as *IHE NKUZI* (Being as Didactic)

The African Igbo people of Ngwaland (Southeastern Nigeria) have a common saying: *Obu otu ihe nu* or *Obu otu ihe uwa nu* or *Obu otu ihe uwa di* -- meaning—"That is how reality is or things are" or "That is how the world is" or "such is the world/reality." I will relate this to epistemological/pedagogical/didactic notion of *Ihe* (Being) known through *Nkuzi*—Life's teaching/experience of reality. Life as part of *Ihe* is series of enlightening or illuminating experiences teach us about reality or truth about actualized reality. *Nkuzi* does not take place in the false or fake. Life crafts us in the truth, not in the false or fake. Life makes us or cultivates us.[13] I consider this "cultivation" through *Nkuzi* as part of our actualization of the fullness of being (understanding our *Ihe*/Whatness/Essence). African Igbo people express this reality in heuristic wise-sayings like *Onye Ije ka onye isi awomma* (A traveler is better experienced than the untraveled elderly person or better put life is the best teacher).

As a scholar that has been shaped by the experiences of life (Ihe uwa or Ihe ije uwa), Iroegbu adumbrates that *Nkuzi* or *Paideia*/teaching aligns with the *Kpim* of education. *Kpim* "is the quintessence, which is the thingness of a thing

---

[12] I have taken some time to develop these nuances in my work on *The Hermeneutics of Hope in African Igbo Ontology*. These nuances include: ontological hope, anthropological hope, epistemological hope, pedagogical hope, etc.
[13] S. U. Anozie, *Hans-Georg Gadamer and African Hermeneutic Philosophy*, p. 99.

and the somethingness of something (Iroegbu, 2002:17)."[14] In this sense, for me, the African Igbo words *Ihe* and *Kpim* are related to *Nkuzi* (teaching or cultivating) in African Igbo worldview or *Bildung* in German socio-cultural world. In Benson Peter Irabor and Okikiola Oludare Olufowobi's essay, 'An Exploration of Pantaleon Iroegbu's Pedagogy of Nkuziology for Contemporary Africa,' Iroegbu's view is emphasized:

> *Nkuzi* means to knock, hit, strike aright or to repair, to shape to required proportion. On a piece of iron that is crooked or rugged, one hits with a harmer to straighten it, to make it fine. The same word is used for the verb, to teach, *nkuzi*. In this transferred, but very real sense, to teach is to knock, straighten or shape the pupil, student or subject aright.[15]

I would like to add here that 'Nkuzi' (*N-kuzi*) does not imply violence. It is all about cultivating a morally-balanced person. Like the verb 'kuzi', it means hermeneutically to put to the right path or direction, to align properly, to put on the good state or good character. *Nkuzi* (as teaching, education or transmission of knowledge) does not promote falsity or that which in fake or unreal. *Nkuzi* illuminates, and does not take place in an environment that leaves any human person disillusioned or in the dark. I appreciate the resources and quotations attributed to Iroegbu in Irabor and Olufowobi's work. For instance, "Nkuziology therefore, is the balanced upbringing, knocking aright, the teaching of the person to be balanced, good and respectful to order and goodness (Iroegbu, 1995, 264)."[16] The message of the statement above affirms my own understanding of Iroegbu's articulation of *Nkuzi* (teaching) or my advancement of *Nkuzi* in promoting *Nkuzi* as balanced upbringing, crafting a balance person, etc. For the sake of clarity and implications to post-colonial narratives on mono-source

---

[14] https://www.academia.edu/43644897/An_Exploration_of_Pantaleon_Iroegbu_s_Pedagogy_of_Nkuziology_for_Contemporary_Africa (accessed on 13 August 2021). See Pantaleon Iroegbu, *Kpim of Theodicy Proving the Existence of God Via Hermeholiontica*, Ibadan, Hope Publications, 2002, p. 17.

[15] https://www.academia.edu/43644897/An_Exploration_of_Pantaleon_Iroegbu_s_Pedagogy_of_Nkuziology_for_Contemporary_Africa (Accessed on 13 August 2021). See Pantaleon Iroegbu, and M. A. Izibili, *Kpim of Democracy Thematic Introduction to Socio-Political Philosophy*, Benin City, Ever-Blessed Publishers, 2004, p. 13.

[16] https://www.academia.edu/43644897/An_Exploration_of_Pantaleon_Iroegbu_s_Pedagogy_of_Nkuziology_for_Contemporary_Africa (accessed 13 August 2021). See Pantaleon Iroegbu, *Metaphysics: The Kpim of Philosophy*, Owerri, International University Press, 1995, p. 264.

epistemology, I have chosen to avoid using the term "Nkuziology" because of the linguistic dominance of Westernized education.

In light of *Ihe* and *Nkuzi* relations, *Nkuzi* is a thought pattern, a logical approach, a study, a science or a systematic knowledge approach in its own right. *Nkuzi*, as a thought pattern or study, focuses on information for self-development through communication. It is about acquiring the basic skills for a genuine and fulfilling existence. *Nkuzi* (teach/teaching) is about knowledge of the truth, the eternal truth, and the truth of life.[17] *Nkuzi* makes it possible for the manifestation of a life of purpose, a life in accord with one's *Chi*. The manifestation of a life of purpose is same with the 'manifestation' of *Ihe* (*Ìhè* — light or direction or substance or essence—that discloses itself). This "manifestation" of essence (*Ihe*), and in the light (*Ìhè*), authenticates the role of personal mentor or guardian or *chi onye*. In Irabor and Olufowobi's work, it stated:

> Thus, Iroebgu[Iroegbu] (2005a:221) avers that knowledge given in teaching has three basic foci: information, formation and reformation. It is information in that it is a communication of ideas and facts that are meant to be used to achieve some goals. It is Formation in that those facts given in information are destined to constitute the mental and personality structure of the recipient.[18]

My goal above is to associate **IHE** to ***Nkuzi*** (from Being/Reality to *Nkuzi*) in order to identify this pedagogical aspect of **IHE as *Nkuzi*** (life's teaching or social learning). For *IHE as Nkuzi*, it means that life teaches every one of us. Life teaches 'life' (how to live) or the art of living. The experiences of life are parts of our human becoming or actualization of self (as a part of reality) and reality. One African saying adds: "If one does not chew water he does not know that water has bones." (It means that one who has not experienced life's ups and downs does not know that life is hard or what life is). Another African Igbo proverb states: *Agbisi gba otule, ya amuru ako*--meaning--When the black

---

[17] There is no desire for that which is false or fake in African Igbo notion of *Ihe* and *Nkuzi*. *Nkuzi* is always for the truth, the truth of life. This truth of life is reality itself or *Ihe*.
[18] https://www.academia.edu/43644897/An_Exploration_of_Pantaleon_Iroegbu_s_Pedagogy_of_Nkuziology_for_Contemporary_Africa , accessed 13 August 2021. See Pantaleon Iroegbu, "Philosophy of Education: Ethics of Teaching profession", in P. Iroegbu, A. Echekube, (eds.), *Kpim of Morality: General, Special & Professional,* Ibadan: Heinemann Educational Books, 2005, p. 221. See Pantaleon Iroegbu, and M. A. Izibili, *Kpim of Democracy Thematic Introduction to Socio-Political Philosophy*, p. 13.

ant stings the buttocks, next time the [buttocks] learns wisdom. (It means that if things have not happened to a person, he/she does not develop wisdom or, simply put, experience is the best teacher). What makes a man thin also makes him stout. (It means that what a man suffers greatly to obtain is valuable to him. What challenges a person brings the person his/her true becoming or wellbeing). This simply is the dialectics of life (Being is Becoming). The challenges or tragedies of life are not ends-in-themselves. They are rather life's teaching moments for human experience, true human becoming, en-wisdomization (enwisdomizing experience, to-make-wise experience), for transformation and for the better. The experiences of life are for our becoming or continuity of beingness. *To be* is *to exist* with the goal that one's fullness of being is a task that should be accomplished. It implies that:

a) Being or *Ihe* is that which is present, temporally distant, and beyond. *Ihe* or Being has no temporal restrictions.

b) Being-in-fullest is the aspiration of all beings. An aspiration fulfilled through *Nkuzi*/Education/*Paideia*.

Nkuzi/Education/*Paideia*, like any other human activities, cannot escape the realm of ontology/metaphysics or being. Ontology/Metaphysics, the issue of ultimate reality or innermost essence, is central to any concept of education because it is important that any educational program be based upon fact and reality rather than on fancy, illusion, or mere imagination. As earlier pointed out, I am of the view that there is an ontological desire for truth in us. The quest/desire of the truth through knowledge is the same for rational beings. In African Igbo world, *Nkuzi* is always about and for the truth, the truth of/about life. *Nkuzi* is focused on the life or *Ihe uwa or Ihe ndu* (Realities of life). I will take a brief look at *Ìhè* (as light, radiance and beauty) in relation to *Mmadu* (personhood, the beauty of life) in African Igbo Ontology.

IHE as Light, Radiance and Beauty: African Igbo Ontology of Person

African Igbo ontology of person (*Mmadu*—Igbo word meaning—*the beauty of life*) could be appreciated within the richness of the ontology or metaphysics of beauty. At the core of the concept of beauty or the beautiful is disclosure, light, radiance, truth, reality, etc. In African Igbo language 'mma' (*mara mma*—beautiful)[19] is associated with disclosure, light, radiance, truth, reality and hope (to be and continue to be real). The notion of *Mmadu* (the beauty of life) is related to disclosure, truth or reality. The beautiful makes life worth-living, fulfilling and radiant. The beautiful is a pointer to Beauty itself, and Beauty makes 'the beautiful' possible.

The Greek word for the beautiful is "kalon". Beauty could be expressed in German as "schön"--adjective for beautiful, "die Schönheit"--noun for beauty. For these different languages, the essence (the inner meaning) of the beautiful is expressible or communicable by the respective languages in their own ways. That means there is an inner dimension to language. Our languages express reality or being (language is ontology as well as ontological). Like Hans-Georg Gadamer the being that is understood is language. Language speaks us. Language or the ability to language comes through *Nkuzi* (teaching, education, cultivate/cultivating, discipline, upbringing, awareness creation, etc.) One knows the truth about *Mmadu* (person, the beauty of life) through *Nkuzi* or learning. Without Nkuzi, it will be difficult to comprehend the relevance of language to understanding *Being* or *Mmadu* (person) captured in the notion that language (*Okwu* in Igbo)[20] comes through *Nkuzi*. One truly knows 'being' through, and in, language. Language reveals this being of things.

Language is understood through *Nkuzi*. *Nkuzi* is possible through language. Language (Okwu) and *Nkuzi* are indissociable. *Nkuzi* makes reality become truly present. This present-ness of reality is the realization of being of a thing. In light of the above, *Nkuzi* discloses understanding and meaning of reality, truth, knowledge of African Igbo notion of "Ihe". The *Ihe* in a human being or person is truly known through *Erlebenis* (German for "to live out"—*erleben/leben*—or as meeting/encounter with other human beings/persons), not merely as *Erfahrung* (German for experience), and *Bildung* (German for education/social education). In *Hans-Georg Gadamer and African Hermeneutic Philosophy*, I explained "Bildung" as "formation or education in the development of human culture and understanding of self. 'Bildung' points to a continual process or movement..."[21]

This formation or education in the development of human culture and the self is anchored on encounter. The encounter between persons that reveal being

---

[19] See my reflection above on African Igbo notion of the person as the beauty of life (mma , mma ndu, mmadu).
[20] Okwu Igbo (Igbo language), Okwu Bekee (English or White person's language), and Okwu ndi obodo ozo (a foreign language). Okwu is also 'word' or 'logos' or 'being' or 'reality.'
[21] S. U. Anozie, *Hans-Georg Gadamer and African Hermeneutic Philosophy*, p. 99.

(*Ihe*) is foundational to African Igbo Ontology of person (*Mmadu*, as an encounter/*Erlebnis* of Being-itself). For me, Martin Buber's Hebrew humanism/non-African ontology of person as a being of encounter or a relational being helps to express the intercultural similarities of understanding reality (Being-itself and the being of person). I will explain African Igbo and Buber's Hebrew ontology of person below.

African Igbo Ontology of Person and Martin Buber's Ontology of Person

In Ronald Gregor Smith translation of Martin Buber's view, he notes as:

> To man the world is twofold, in accordance with his twofold attitude. The attitude of man is twofold, in accordance with the twofold nature of the primary words which he speaks. The primary words are not isolated words, but combined words. The one primary word is the combination I-*Thou*. The other primary word is the combination *I-It*; wherein, without a change in the primary word, one of the words He and She can replace It. Hence the I of man is also twofold. For the *I* of the primary word *I-Thou* is a different *I* from that of the primary word *I-It*. [22]

The above comments of Buber are on the two-twofold world reflecting the twofold attitude of man/person. In his twofold attitude man/person speaks or relates to reality around him. Buber further makes a distinction from what he called the three spheres of relations: *I-Thou*, *I-It* and *I-Thou* (in terms of Eternal *Thou*). For a clear discourse considering the importance of the *I-Thou* relation (direct person to person relation), the three relations will be discussed in this order: The *I-* [Eternal] *Thou* relation, the *I-It* relation and the *I-Thou* relation.

The *I-* [Eternal] *Thou* relation, according to Buber is, "our life with spiritual beings. There the relation is clouded, yet it discloses itself... We perceive no *Thou*, but none the less we feel we are addressed and we answer-- forming, thinking, acting. We speak the primary word with our being, though we cannot utter *Thou* with our lips."[23] The Eternal *Thou* is the source of *Thou*- relation that is individually grounded in the *I-Thou* relation. According to Wood,

---

[22] Martin Buber, *I and Thou*, translated by Ronald Gregor Smith, New York, Charles Scribner's Sons, 1958, p. 3.
[23] M. Buber, *I and Thou*, p. 6.

meeting in the I- [Eternal] *Thou* (God) "is that which binds the moments of Thou-relation into the world of *Thou*."[24] The relation with one another is basic to persons and person's individual relation with the Eternal *Thou*. Buber's Eternal *Thou* is same as Aristotle's First Cause. The Eternal *Thou* is God based on Buber's religious background. Although we will not dwell much on the Eternal *Thou*, Buber states that the being of each person is genuinely based on the being of the Absolute, which is the source of all beings—Being *qua* being. This means that every *I-Thou* relation is the loving relation between person and person and the *Thou* of God is reached through the *I-Thou* relation.

The *I-It* relation exists between "our life with nature…. Creatures live and move over against us."[25] It is the experience and utility form of relation, e.g., the relation to an object. The *I-It* relation should not exist between person and person. However, a relation can move from *I-Thou* to *I-It* and better from *I-It* to *I-Thou*. According to Buber this is possible through change of attitude that establishes a mode of existence.[26] This mode of existence for the I-It relation is about perception, sensation and experience of objects or things. He adds:

> The life of human beings is not passed in the sphere of transitive verbs alone. It does not exist in virtue of activities alone which have some *thing* for their object. I perceive something. I am sensible of something. I imagine something. I will something. I feel something…. The life of human beings does not consist of all this and the like alone. This and the like together establish the realm of *It*. But the realm of *Thou* has a different basis.[27]

The *I-It* relation is based on experience, perception and sensation, while the *I-Thou* relation is based on intimate encounter. With the brief explanations of the *I-* [Eternal] *Thou* and *I-It* relations let us discuss the *I-Thou* relation. The *I-Thou* relation is essential in the integration of persons and interpersonal community. Buber's discourse on the *I-Thou* concept and *I-Thou* relation took a gradual development. Many philosophers influenced Buber. One of them was Ludwig Feuerbach who inspired Buber on the use of this concept I-Thou. As Wood points out:

---

[24] Robert E. Wood, *Martin Buber's Ontology: An Analysis of I and Thou*, Evanston, Northwestern University Press, 1969, p. 42.
[25] M. Buber, *I and Thou*, p. 6.
[26] *Ibidem*, p. 3.
[27] *Ibidem*, p. 4.

Buber's reading of Feuerbach...gave a "decisive impetus' to the young man's thought. That impetus was twofold. In the first place, Feuerbach placed philosophical anthropology, the question of man, at the center of the philosophic enterprise....Feuerbach centers upon man in his totality. In the second place, for Feuerbach, man himself is located, not in individuals, but in the relationship of man with man, in the I and the Thou. It was Feuerbach who, for the first time, made the *I-Thou* relation the very center of his philosophizing. This was to form the center of Buber's own thought: ...But at this stage it remains an impetus, not yet the center.[28]

Following Feuerbach's influence and use of the *I-Thou*, Buber later made the I-Thou relation the center of his socio-philosophy. The *I-Thou* is about human relation. It is "our life with men,"[29] meeting and in dialogue with fellow-persons. Buber writes about the primary words of *I-Thou* as that which

do not signify things, but... intimate relations. Primary words do not describe something that might exist independently of them, but being spoken they bring about existence. Primary words are spoken from the being. If *Thou* is said, the *I* of the combination *I-Thou* is said along with it.... The primary word *I-Thou* can only be spoken with the whole being.[30]

The *I-Thou* relation is the existential and concrete relation between person and person. It also has an ontological side to this relation because of the nature of the being of person. Buber's initial use of the *I-Thou* relation had more of a psychological meaning with respect to the relation between two people. In the course of Buber's reflections and works, he has in some ways shifted from the psychological interpretation of this relation to more refined (existential) relation. Friedman explains that "in *Ich und Du* (1922)[31] it is used to illustrate the *I-Thou* relation, an event which takes place between two beings which none the less remain separate."[32] Buber tries as much as possible to remain concrete and existential in his philosophy. Even if there could be a mystical dimension in the

---

[28] R. E. Wood, *Martin Buber's Ontology: An Analysis of I and Thou*, p. 5.
[29] M. Buber, *I and Thou*, p. 6.
[30] *Ibidem*, p. 3.
[31] German translation of Buber's *I and Thou*-- written in 1922.
[32] Maurice S. Friedman, *Martin Buber: The Life of Dialogue*, New York, Harper and Row Publishers, Inc., 1960, p. 49.

relation, Buber refuses to base this philosophy on the mystical, suprasensible, or *noumenal* world of Plato. Wood admits that:

> Buber wants to remove all psychologizing tendencies which would interpret away the essential character of the act; relation, he insists, is not psychological so much as it is ontological, i.e., a relation to the being of the Other. But he likewise wants to preclude the kind of mystical absorption in which the self and Other seem to melt together... For Buber... is a realm which is neither objective nor subjective nor the sum of the two.[33]

Buber in his *I-Thou* socio-philosophy indicates that the *I-Thou* relation involves the wholeness of being of person. It is not totally the psychological, mystical, but the existential wholeness of being and living. Buber notes that the primary word *I-Thou* "can be spoken only with the whole being...the whole being can never take place through my agency, nor can it ever take place without me. I become through my relation to the *Thou*; as I become *I*, I say *Thou*."[34] This means that *I-Thou* relation is really about concrete living and meeting.

For Buber the *I-Thou* relation, which involves living and meeting, truly includes accepting and affirming the otherness of each individual—as person. He explains:

> But what the genuine saying of 'Thou' to the other in the reality of the common existence basically means—namely, the affirmation of the primally deep otherness of the other, the affirmation of his otherness which is accepted and loved by me---this is devalued and destroyed in spirit through just that identification. The teaching of identity not only stands in opposition to the belief in the true being of a common logos and a common cosmos; it also contradicts the arch reality of that out of which all community stems—human meeting.[35]

In the above, Buber affirms the common beingness of all human being. For all human beings within the community there is meeting and affirmation of the *Thou* of the other person. The *I-Thou* is the basis of the world of relation between persons. Buber explains, "In this meeting each of the two certainly does

---

[33] R. E. Wood, *Martin Buber's Ontology: An Analysis of I and Thou*, p. 41.
[34] M. Buber, *I and Thou*, p. 11.
[35] M. Buber, *The Knowledge of Man*, p. 96.

not say to himself, 'He over there is you', but perhaps each says to the other, 'I accept you as you are.' Here first is uncurtailed existence."[36] The *I-Thou* relation opens one to the other person. Only in *I-Thou* relation is true human existence possible and he enters into a life of dialogue with others. Without this meeting, living and dialogue, it becomes an *I-It* relation based on experience or use. Buber clarifies:

> I do not experience the man to whom I say *Thou*. But I take my stand in relation to him, in the sanctity of the primary word. Only when I step out of it do I experience him once more. In the act of experience *Thou* is far away. Even if the man to whom I say *Thou* is not aware of it in the midst of his experience, yet relation may exist. For Thou is more than It realizes. No deception penetrates here; here is the cradle of the Real Life.[37]

Buber's distinction of *I-Thou* relation and the *I-It* relation is unique and essential in his description of the ontology of interpersonal relation. The *I-Thou* relation is accurately described with the German word *Erlebnis*-which is "to live out," than with experiencing and experience (*Erfahrung*). He distinguishes the use of *Erfahrung* (experience) and *Erlebnis* (to live out) to describe the *I-It* and *I-Thou* relations respectively: Wood elaborates:

> This is what founds the world of It. Buber terms it "experience" (*Erfahrung*) and then plays on the etymological root of the term in *fahren*, "to travel." To travel is precisely to experience only the surface of life, since real intimacy is possible only through a mode of prolonged dwelling with the Other. Buber uses another term for experience to describe the I-Thou relation: *Erlebnis*, from *leben*, "to live", signifying authentic human living.[38]

The distinction between *I-It* and *I-Thou* relations is clearer in terms of "to live" (*Erlebnis*) because it is in living, in true meeting, that a person's uniqueness and genuineness are manifested. In living through *I-Thou* relation a person matures and becomes truly a person. Buber emphasizes that in the *I-Thou* relation "He who gives himself to it may withhold nothing of himself."[39] Thus the *I-Thou* relation is the genuine relation that should guide life and other activities in an interpersonal community. The *I-Thou* relation means relating

---

[36] *Ibidem*
[37] M. Buber, *I and Thou*, p. 9.
[38] R. E. Wood, *Martin Buber's Ontology: An Analysis of I and Thou*, p. 40.
[39] M. Buber, *I and Thou*, p. 10.

with others as, "ends in themselves."[40] This notion of "end in themselves" aligns with Buber's idea of person (not even as *means* to God, but end in himself even before the Eternal Thou[41]—God).

Having presented a short overview on Buber's Ontology of person or human being, one already appreciates the features of connections between African Igbo Ontology of person as being (*Ihe*---whatness/essence and as a being that discloses itself) and Buber's views. In African Igbo Ontology/Metaphysics, this *Ihe* (Being) and *Ìhè* (Light/Disclosure) are related to *Ihe* and *Chi* (the Creative Being or Force). Each person (as *Ihe*---being or human being) has its own *Chi* (better put as *chi* or *chi onye*) manifested through Buber's interpersonal encounter with other people (the actualization of being).

African Igbo Ontology of Person in *IHE* and *CHI* (Creative Being)

The dynamism of *Ihe* essentially aligns with African Igbo notion of 'Chi' (God) or 'Chi-onye' or 'chi' (personal guardian). One's *chi* or *Chi* itself determines the 'essence of beingness' (nature of being) of the person. This essence or form of beingness is related to 'Ihe' (light or the disclosure of the individual person or group). This *Ihe* aligned with *Chi* is truthfulness that gets fully fulfilled in African Igbo worldviews and proverbs. Here are some African Igbo proverbs with *Chi* (as creative being/force or fate) that resonate with Hope or Hopefulness. For instance,

a) *Chi onye adighi n'izu ma mmadu egbuna ya* (meaning--If one's *Chi* [fate or destiny] is not in agreement, nobody can kill him). This means that 'Chi' (Fate, Creative Force or God) does not conspire against us or undermine our essential nature or self-actualizations. There is hope of success as long as the creative force or fate is on our side.

b) *Omere ma chi ekweghi ndi uta atala ya* (meaning--Whoever that has tried his/her best should not be blamed.) *Chi* (fate or creative force) guarantees that one cannot accomplish more than he/she is destined for.

---

[40] M. S. Friedman, *Martin Buber: The Life of Dialogue*, p. 200. Friedman explains, "For Buber the concern for the other as an end in himself grows out of one's direct relation to this other and to that higher end which he serves through the fulfillment of his created uniqueness."
[41] M. Buber, *I and Thou*, p. 6.

On chapter fourteen of Achebe's *Things Fall Apart* a proverb was used. It says, "[I]f a man said yea his *chi* also affirmed."[42] This proverb illustrates the double aspects of human existence. The double aspects are the divine and the human aspects of existence. For a person to accomplish anything in African Igbo worldviews he/she must live in accord with his/her destiny or fate and learn from the experience in line with his/her destiny. Existence is facilitated by the divine (*Chi okike* or creative being). Some African Igbo people associated this *Chi okike* or *Chi-ka* (He who is the greatest. He is the greatest being that guarantees hope) to *Osebuluwa/Oliseburuwa* (The Being/He who holds the world/universe).[43] Existence involves an unpredictable aspect, which implies that a person has to first accept that he/she is capable of accomplishing a task before one's *Chi* (personal god or guardian) concurs with the same task.

A further discussion of the role of *Chi*[44] in African Igbo worldviews is necessary because of *Chi*'s place in their proverbs and in the events that happen in people's life. A subtle but important distinction to note here is that *Chi* is started with a capital letter to associate it with Igbo religion (as respect to the divine or a higher being or source of being).[45] However, I will retain the use of *chi* (starting with small letter) as is in Achebe's book. They both mean the same thing. For the Igbo, according to Christian Anieke, *Chi* is an important concept in traditional society. It is defined as personal destiny or personalized providence "of the individual which shapes their history and destiny. Some see *Chi* as a divine emanation from…which is responsible for the individual's fate or destiny."[46] The complexity of meanings about the specific role of the *Chi* is still present in the statement made above. But *Chi* involves element of both fate and faith (personal duty blessed by one's *Chi*),[47] in terms of the support one receives from the gods in order to succeed or in hope to succeed in one's

---

[42] Chinua Achebe, *Things Fall Apart*, Canada, Anchor Canada edition, 2009, p. 131. See Chinua Achebe, *Things Fall Apart*, London, Heinemann, 1958, p. 165.

[43] Professor Ikechukwu Kanu brought this to my attention. He translated it as 'He who holds the world.'

[44] S. U. Anozie, *Hans-Georg Gadamer and African Hermeneutic Philosophy*, pp. 237-243.

[45] I chose to capitalize '*Chi*' considering its religious connotation in African Igbo thought. The role of *Chi* or fate is essential in Okonkwo's tragedy.

[46] Christian Anieke, *Problems of Intercultural Communication and Understanding in Achebe's Representation of the Igbo and their Culture*, Enugu, Mbaeze Printing Press, 2008, p. 34. See Pauline Aligwekwe, *Continuity of Traditional Values, The Igbo of Nigeria*, Owerri, 1991, p. 173. See Elizabeth Isichei, *A History of the Igbo People*, London, The Macmillan Press, 1976, p. 75.

[47] Raphael Okechukwu Madu, *African Symbols, Proverbs and Myths: The Hermeneutics of Destiny*, New York, Peter Lang, 1996, p. 183.

individual task. It is in this sense that *Chi's* role could also imply the task of a mediator (a personal guardian[48]).

One's relationship to the Supreme Being (God) is determined by one's relations to his/her *Chi*. Since *Chi* is only an individual relationship, rather than universal, there could be a lucky person (with a good luck *Chi* [*Chioma*] or even a bad luck person (with bad luck *Chi* [*Chiojoo*]). This reminds us about the place of proverbs among African Igbo. For example: *Omere ma chi ekweghi ndi uta atala ya* (He/She that has done his/her best should not blame his/herself if there are failures). It means that we all have our limitations of success. Our hope is always to put in our own and unique best. Another African Igbo proverb says: *Onye kwe ma chi ya ekweghi, o ga-egbu onwe ya?*[49] (It means if one says yes and his/her *Chi* disagrees, should one commit suicide? It also means that one should be positive-minded and hopeful). The second aspect of the proverb above: "*o ga-egbu onwe ya?*" (meaning--Should one commit suicide?) aligns with the culture of hope and hopefulness. There is always a possibility that each person's *Chi* (personal god or guardian) could help reverse a tragic situation to become a fulfilling or hopeful one.

In African Igbo lifeworld, *Ihe-bu-ihe* means entity, main thing, the essential being or ultimate entity. *Ihe-bu-ihe* reflects looking forward to, 'expecting positive results or outcomes' based on the fact that the most real or the necessary being makes the real possible. This could be related to Necessary Being and Contingent beings' discussions. The Necessary Being (*Chi, Chi-na-eke, Oseburuwa*) makes hope possible for contingent beings. It is the hope that emerges at the culmination of our historical beingness, within the universal history (that includes the African Igbo historical consciousness).

In summary, an unfolding narrative history of a particular people- in this case-the African Igbo people on *Ihe* or Being is a part of the unfolding of universal history of Being or the fully-actualized reality.

---

[48] S. U. Anozie, *Hans-Georg Gadamer and African Hermeneutic Philosophy*, p. 237.
[49] *Ibidem*, p. 242.

Conclusion

At the influence of Achebe, Iroegbu and Buber, I have articulated African Igbo ontology of being as best captured by the concept of *Ihe*. Using the concepts of: a) *Ìhè* (Light or Disclosure/Transparency), and b) *Ihe* (Being). *Nkuzi* makes reality become truly disclosed or present. This present-ness of reality is the realization of being. *Nkuzi* makes the real. *Nkuzi* crafts that which becomes before us as *Being/Ihe di adi*. *Nkuzi* is the realization of self/personhood and reality through experience (not merely through experimentation) as living or living it out. Our existential humanity is part of the unfolding of the totality of reality (*Ihe*---Reality and *Ìhè*---the Light that reveals Reality). The unfolding of reality is the actualization of the fullness of humanity or the fullness of human becoming. *Kpim* is Being. *Ihe* is Being. *Mmadu* (Person) is the beauty of life. It is an instance or a presence of *Ihe* (Being).

Reference List

Achebe, Chinua, *Things Fall Apart*, Canada, Anchor Canada edition, 2009.

Anieke, Christian, *Problems of Intercultural Communication and Understanding in Achebe's Representation of the Igbo and their Culture*, Enugu, Mbaeze Printing Press, 2008.

Anozie, Stanley Uche, *Hans-Georg Gadamer and African Hermeneutic Philosophy*, Chisinau, Generis Publishing, 2020.

---------"The Problem of Evil in Plato and Gadamerian Plato", *Revue Roumaine de Philosophie*, 66, 1, 2019, pp. 116-129.

Buber, Martin, *Between Man and Man*, translated by Ronald Gregor Smith, London, Collins Clear-Type Press, 1947.

----------*I and Thou*, translated by Ronald Gregor Smith, New York, Charles Scribner's Sons, 1958.

----------*I and Thou*, translated by Walter Kaufmann, New York, Charles Scribner's Sons, 1970.

----------*The Knowledge of Man: A Philosophy of the Interhuman*, New York, Harper Torchbooks, 1965.

Friedman, Maurice S, *Martin Buber: The Life of Dialogue,* New York, Harper and Row Publishers, Inc., 1960.

Iroegbu, Pantaleon, *Metaphysics: The Kpim of Philosophy*, Owerri, International University Press, 1995.

----------*Kpim of Theodicy Proving the Existence of God Via Hermeholiontica*, Ibadan, Hope Publications, 2002.

Iroegbu, Pantaleon; Izibili, M.A, *Kpim of Democracy Thematic Introduction to Socio-Political Philosophy*, Benin City, Ever-Blessed Publishers, 2004.

Iroegbu, Pantaleon, "Philosophy of Education: Ethics of Teaching profession", in Pantaleon Iroegbu; A. Echekube, (eds.), *Kpim of Morality: General, Special & Professional*, Ibadan, Heinemann Educational Books, 2005, p. 221.

Lindfors, Bernth, "The Palm-oil with which Achebe's Words are Eaten", in Francis Abiola Irele (ed.), *Chinua Achebe Things Fall Apart (Authoritative Text, Contexts and Criticism)*, New York, W. W. Norton & Company, 2009, pp. 560-561.

Madu, Raphael Okechukwu, *African Symbols, Proverbs and Myths: The Hermeneutics of Destiny*, New York, Peter Lang, 1996.

Wood, Robert E, *Martin Buber's Ontology: An Analysis of I and Thou*, Evanston, Northwestern University Press, 1969.

Chapter 2
Contemporary African Philosophical Notion of the Person and Community: An Essential Perspective to Integrative Ethics of Globality

Stanley Uche Anozie

(Philosophy Department, William Paterson University, Wayne, New Jersey, USA, 2016)

Abstract. In global ethics or integrative ethics of globality, what should be central is that every individual person or relational being of beauty demands dignity, equity, freedom, justice, peace, tolerance, respect, common good and happiness or satisfaction (flourishing). These concepts are at the heart of Igbo Nigeria Africans' communitarian ethics of common good or African hermeneutical philosophy of person/community but we have to arrive at them through the exercise of epistemologies and interpretations of values. We are required to merge these values in order to provide content for contemporary global ethics'. Achieving this goal clearly demands a thorough systematic and holistic nudging—that is a continual ethics process.

Keywords: Igbo Nigeria Africans, Hermeneutical Philosophy, Human Person, Individual Person, Community, Common Good, Humanity.

Introduction

It is important to consider contemporary Igbo Nigeria Africans' philosophical notion of the person and community in order to see what contributions it does provide to understanding ethics of globality. The ethics of globality, for me, is not different from the course of studies in relation to advancing global human well-being. In an emerging world of interconnectivity and necessary interrelationships, we are evaluated, tasked, held accountable from a more global sense. In this light, we need to live by and our actions be justified through the principle or hermeneutics of political belongingness and the doctrine of our common humanity. It is of glowing insight to know that Igbo Nigeria Africans' worldviews on person and community have strong roots in social ethics that encourages the emergence of an integrative ethics of globality. The Igbo Nigeria Africans' concept of the person, as a unitive concept, in my analysis, has two lineal aspects/views (horizontally considered) that are mutually inclusive: (i) Person as the beauty of life, and (ii) Person as relational--"I am because we are." These contributions from Igbo Nigeria Africans' interpretive worldviews or hermeneutics are very relevant to current projects in ethics of globality. Some of these views I have developed in my other works. Presently, I will undertake a brief project on developing an integrative global ethics in contemporary world (multicultural society and very itinerant citizenry).

i). Person as the Beauty of Life

Like most African communities and nations, the Igbo, a major ethnic group in Southeastern Nigeria, uses the terms "human being" and "person" interchangeably. Being called a 'human being' is the same as being called a person, and vice versa. The Igbo language considers person as *Mmadu* (Mma-du), which is the combination of *Mma* (Beauty) and *Ndu* (Life). The concept of person is the concept of the beauty of life; indeed the concept of the 'beauty of all created things' in their totality. Human beings make the world beautiful and meaningful. Another Igbo Nigeria Africans' expression that connects to beauty of life is: "mmetuko ahu bu uto ndu" (the beauty of life is in mixing up with others). Life is truly beautiful when human beings live or mix up with other persons. The Igbo Nigeria African notion of the person as the "beauty of life" evokes in philosophers the traditional doctrine of the "transcendentals", the essential properties of being (the essential perfect prototypes that is the cause of all things in the universe), to which the beautiful is counted (next to the one, the true, and the good). Thomas Aquinas, a Medieval philosopher, offers us some resourceful materials on the transcendental (on the nature of Substance—the One). Beauty, for him, is one of the transcendental forms. Plato, in the *Symposiums* (4th Century BC), makes reference to the "beauty of one form" (beautiful forms and beauty in every form is one and the same) (Solomon and Higgins, 2013, p. 365). Beauty is its own truth, even when that which is not beautiful per se is the real truth. Beauty and truth and reality do not always exist or co-exist in One Single subject or object.[50]

In the Modern philosophy, Kant relates beauty to nature and its grandiosity. Nature is life *qua tale*. Nature is what is 'bio', life, living (Latin, *vivus*), 'what is alive', etc. The beauty of life is extended as the beauty of nature, which suggests the purposiveness of nature. The beauty of nature—the beauty in nature—is because nature is a continuum, continuity, being-in-existence. Being-in-existence is to be essentially purposive/ purposeful. Without purpose, there is no existence. I relate this to the idea of purposiveness of existence as well as that 'nature' is purposive and "hospitable to our ends". (Rohlf, Michael. 2016. Immanuel Kant. Accessed November 5, 2017. http://plato.stanford.edu/entries/kant/#UniNatFre). This "our ends" is same as the "disclosure of purpose." This point relates to Friedrich Nietzsche's view that life is "artful." It means that a "well-lived life is itself a work of art" (Solomon and Higgins, 2013, pp. 363-364).

In this section, I argue along the direction *of* or *from* beauty—to purposiveness—to purposeful agency—to purposeful action (being, agency and habitation to improve capacity to agency). I consider this narrative in terms of the link between existence, purposiveness, and beauty as same as that which is essential in understanding "Cosmic Consciousness" (merely used here as the 'Intelligence' or the higher 'Mind' that brings everything into a meaningful or purposeful wholeness-the higher Mind, 'Welt Geist', the 'Nous' of all meanings/meaningfulness).[51] In this sense, strictly speaking, can one appreciate the ontological richness between person as the beauty of life and the capacity to have a purposeful agency in order to actualize this "moral beauty" or "beauty" as a moral good in every aspect of the moral being/the moral person? (So the wholeness experienced is cosmic as well as moral. It is moral because it is cosmic—as integrated, whole, merged, harmoniously merged or as harmony).

This harmony which is vividly drawn from the notion of person as the beauty of life (as moral beauty) is a pertinent notion of our *Zeitgeist*. I think this

---

[50] John Keats, 1795-1891 ("Beauty is truth, truth beauty—that is all/Ye know on earth and all ye need to know.") See Solomon and Higgins (2013), p. 364. When Shakespeare refers to human beings as "a piece of work..." it reflects this beautiful one, this art-work that is purposeful. See Shakespeare's *Hamlet*, Act II, Scene 2.
[51] I will like to bring in here Richard Bucke's thought on *Cosmic Consciousness* which, although is said to emerge among us, but no, it has always been with us. Cosmic Consciousness is not an end or goal that is arrived at or accomplished, but a point of consciousness, of holistic awareness.

aspect is significantly absent in Western philosophical tradition, or better put, it was neglected or underemphasized. Of course, there are footprints of "person-with-the-other" form of ethics, especially after the 16th/17th Century philosophy. The basis of Western philosophical tradition is tainted with emphases on material-ness[52], material well-being (giving rising to economic domination and competition). The West also focused on materiality of painting, what is enjoyable, fictional, and imaginational and ideal (idyllic, arts and ideals, without blemish). In such a competitive framework, it is difficult to see through existence as much of "beauty," and human beings as the "beauty" of this totality of existence, the totality of reality (what is truly real). The notion of beauty is clearly present in Western philosophical thought.[53] In Robert Solomon and Elizabeth Higgins' views, "[T]hroughout most of Western history, reality itself, created by God, was conceived of as beautiful" (Solomon and Higgins, 2013, p. 365), but it seems materialistically rather than holistically (mind, body, and soul) considered.

As a matter of fact, in Africa (among the Igbos), culturally speaking, there is an intrinsic connection between person and beauty. The beautiful is understood as what which reveals itself. In the description of the person as the beauty of life we recognize something of the Heideggerian notions of being (Sein) and of the human being (Da-sein): being reveals, manifests, and discloses itself through, in, and to others. It is through human being (Dasein) that being (Sein) discloses itself. A person's essence is in disclosedness. Something similar is expressed in the word "Existenz"-'to stand out'; the idea of person means standing out and disclosure of (the human) being through its beauty. The notion of person as the beauty of existence is common among Africans, but not exclusively. Richard C. Onwuanibe, former Associate Professor, Cleveland State University, Ohio elaborates that for the Igbo: "[T]rue personhood, as pure subject, is not something that can be analyzed into anything… Personhood is a manifestation or presence" (Onwuanibe, 1984, p. 186).

---

[52] Material-ness or materiality is fully metaphysical and so not "material" in the sense of "perishable" or "physical", or "corporeal." In this footnote section, this is the second or third level of application and abstraction. In my paper, 'material' is of the first level of application and abstraction.

[53] I have tried to articulate this topic in my philosophy class on "beauty." The evolving nature of understanding beauty in the West seems to be narrowed down to "corporeal" beauty. Much of this is driven by the cosmetic and fashion industries. According to Robert Solomon and Elizabeth Higgins, "Plato and Confucius (and many other thinkers) have taken the ultimate good in human life to be characterized by its beauty" (Solomon and Higgins, 2013, p. 363).

Onwuanibe underscores the metaphysical, transcendent dimension of the person, which is an essential topic among African philosophers. [Could we consider this as part of the remnant of atrophying civilization or in the sense of nostalgia of Africanity, Memory and Belongingness? Is beauty a concept that is ad rem to thoughts of developing people who live in squalor, dirt, and in 'the lack' of the beautiful things of life? I relate this thought to that of a very progressive world that gained some of its richness from Africa.] Person has a physical (material or bodily) and a spiritual (transcendent) aspect. African philosophical thought conceives of person as a totality of spirit (soul) and body. There is something similar in Senegal (West Africa), for instance, in Wolof, the main language of Senegal, spirit is translated as "xel, sago, or degal," while matter or body is "lef" (thing) or "yaram" (body.)

These ideas/concepts show that in African hermeneutical philosophy (including Igbo Nigeria Africans), a person has to be thought of as a subject, rather than a mere object–if we accept Onwuanibe's distinction. Onwuanibe states, "Object-oriented thinking aims at controlling and exploiting the other, while subject-oriented thinking feels the demand of the freedom of the other" (p. 186). Being a subject rather than an object, the person is not to be used, abused, and exploited. It does not matter if the 'individual' person is aware or not aware of the abuses/exploitations. As person, the 'individual' human being is an end in him/herself with dignity and freedom to actualise his/her actual agency. This is where the notion of ethics clearly shows itself.

ii). Person as Relational—"I am because we are"

Igbo Nigeria African thinkers try to develop a notion of person in which traditional African elements as well as the idea of an individual human being with rights are respected. In this notion, concepts like: person, mutuality, and interpersonal community need to be balanced (that is, carefully articulated and based on a sound meeting point). African philosophy of the person centers on "I am because we are, and since we are therefore I am." The African philosophical paradigm for thinking about the person is the paradigm of "I-We"; i.e., it strives for a dialectical balance between "I" and "we". The person is an 'individual' human being in a community of persons (within a space of balanced or ethical diet that is measured in genuine solidarity). African society puts more emphasis on the community rather than on the individual human beings. A community is based on persons' solidarity rather than on human individuality. Scholars and philosophers like William Sweet, Richard Onwuanibe's *Igbo Metaphysics of*

Person, Pantaleon Iroegbu's *'Kpim' Metaphysics*, etc, who have done research on the African philosophical notion of person and socio-political thought, would commonly call the African notion of person 'communitarian.' The "kpim" or "kernel" or "essence" of the person is to be unique (distinct) as well as communitarian (relational). [Late Prof. Pantaleon Iroegbu was one of the scholars that introduced me to the "kpim" or "kernel" of person philosophy (Kpim Metaphysics) as 'being-with'. See also Iroegbu, Appropriate Ecclesiology, 1996, p. 92. Iroegbu describes this community based understanding of person as "Umunna" or in terms of "being-with-the-others."]

The Igbo Nigeria Africans' communitarian notion of person does affirm unique, distinct, independent rational beings and also insists on the intrinsic relational nature of the person, who is connected to other persons in the community—in a web of connectivity (not collectivity). In Martin Buber's person philosophy, the notion of person and collectivity is somehow clouded, especially when he allowed the translation of communitarian to collectivistic (collective) as interchangeable. I do not see them to be closely alike. Communitarian refers to the relationship between persons in a community, while collectivistic is the relationship between individuals (including rational and irrational animals in a group or class). They both are rather very distinctive from each other. May I introduce a similar distinction in regard to the relation between mutuality and reciprocity?

In my earlier published work, I noted that "the notion of *mutuality* [of rights] guarantees a level of protection or security in the face of the changeableness of human needs…. The use of the principle of *reciprocity* seems to be very peculiar; it does not provide for a real community of rights in some African communities…*reciprocity* means that one is required to grant to others goods of a certain value because one has received goods and vice versa. …The person using *reciprocity* only helps those who helped him/her. …the idea of *mutuality* entails that people's rights are respected in that they are duly given, by those who are able to give them, the goods to which as prospective agents they have a right but which they cannot obtain by their own efforts" (Anozie, 2016, p. 93). In reflecting truly on Igbo Nigeria African hermeneutical notion of person, words like collective and collectivity are terms we must carefully weigh for their implications. Ours is a notion of person as a human being (not an individual) within a community—and must be part of a community. I have avoided using "an individual" so as to keep us from mixing this understanding up with person or human being. In a way, Buber's and Boethius' notions of person are not quite good examples of Igbo Nigeria African hermeneutical notion of person, although much of Buber, in terms of the *I-Thou/I-We*, and Boethius, in this line, could be related to African hermeneutical views on person. Buber uses concepts like the "I-Thou", "I-it", and "I-We" relationships are similar to the core principles of Igbo Nigeria Africans' consideration of person as a relational being. But back to the specific point about "collectivity," it is not a part of African hermeneutical philosophy of person/community. Like some other Western philosophers, Buber uses individuals and persons interchangeably. I have tried to steer away of such muddled usage of these concepts for an effectively pointed assertion of what African hermeneutical philosophy of person is all about. One could also ask how African views on a rational being in a community different from Boethius, or even related to Jacques Maritain's.

Boethius and Maritain: Person and Individual

In Boethius' view, person is "an individual substance of a rational nature (est naturae rationabilis individua substantia)" (Boethius, 1953, pp. 84-85). The person as a rational nature has also consciousness. Consciousness is an essential element in understanding a person. Boethius' person philosophy presents persons as "singular," "singularity," and "individuality," probably immersed in the search for self-survival in his/her isolated-ness. These notions have prevailed in Western philosophical thought. John Coates alludes to the relationship between person and freedom and the rights of private property in Maritain's personalism philosophy. There seems to require a revolution to find control through the state as a social organization in charge of individuals' well-being. In traditional individualism, the idea of isolated individuals without links to a social whole is one of the worst concerns of humanity. Coates adds, "Maritain's distinction between the person and the individual.... It is based, first of all, on a recognition that because man has a need of his fellows to perfect his specific activity, he is on that account an individual part of a city or community, so that a submission of his own to the larger good, where the two conflict, is called for by reason" (Coates, 1949, p. 12).

Jacques Maritain himself clearly addresses the metaphysical distinctiveness between the concept of individual and the concept of person. He clarifies:

> [T]here is not in me one reality, called my individual, and another reality, called my person. One and the same being is an individual, in

one sense, and a person, in another sense. Our whole being is an individual by reason of that in us which derives from matter, and a person by reason of that in us which derives from spirit.... No doubt, each of my acts is simultaneously the act of myself as an individual and the act of myself as a person (Maritain, 1965, pp. 22-23).

Maritain says that individuality and personality (person) "are the two metaphysical aspects of the human being" (p. 22). Maritain considers individual as matter, person as spirit. Africans see them as distinct, and of same quality, together. Igbo Nigeria Africans' see the individual as a holistic materialistic view of human being, within his/her conditions. Being a person is ontological indissoluble, it is never lost in a human being except through the moral actions of the particular human being in question. You are either a person or an individual. Both are not 50-50 percent contained in one single human being. The individual is a numerical figure for rational and irrational beings. 'Individual person' is my concept in this paper to express a 'singular' person. It is a way of describing person as 'numerical' being but an individual does not truly exist. To be an individual is to lose the human capacity to existence (the essence of existence, the metaphysical distinctiveness that makes a being possible) as a person.

African Scholars: Some Critiques

A person's individual interest is not more than the community's. The person ought to be at the service of the common good of the community. He/she is incomplete without the community. (Dzobo, 1992) The Latin word for person—*persona*—relates to the mask worn by an actor, the role or the character of an actor, or to an individual. Gradually, it has come to mean or imply "something which is self-existent," "something in its own right" (Kant's end-in-itself). Personhood is now perceived in the sense of relation, being-with others. Personhood implies being in human community. For one to be in a human community is to live with the challenges of the lifeworld which are parts of a true personhood. The community determines some of what happens in its relation to an individual or single person. For most Africans:

> the reality of the communal world takes precedence over the reality of individual life histories, whatever these may be. And this primacy is meant to apply not only ontologically, but also in regard to epistemic accessibility. It is in rootedness in an ongoing human community that

the individual [person] comes to see himself as man, and it is by first knowing this community as a stubborn perduring fact of the psychophysical world that the individual [person] also comes to know himself as a durable, more or less permanent, fact of this world (Menkiti, 1984, pp. 171-172).

I introduced 'person' to emphasis my point on 'individual person' as expressing a 'singular' person, a numerical being, not individual –which is for me loses its essence of existence as human being. In my view, Ifeanyi A. Menkiti clearly expresses his point on the role of the community but lost much of the credit by mixing up individuals for persons. The community is the ontological bond of persons—a community of persons, not a collectivity of individuals.

The dominant emphasis on the community in the African notion of person has been criticized by people like Kwame Gyekye, a Ghanaian philosopher and a Visiting Professor of African-American Studies at Temple University, Philadelphia, Pennsylvania; and Francis O. C. Njoku. They are concerned that the individual dimensions of the person's well-being are neglected. The overbearing precedence of community over the 'individual' person calls for some individualist alternatives. The concern is that this communitarian notion of person may limit or undermine the inviolable rights/dignity of the person, especially when it focuses on the rights of the community or associates the rights of the 'individual' person as subordinate to that of the community (as in I am because We are). The concern is to ensure against the community interfering with an individual person's responsibility and hence prevent his/her freedom and well-being from being sacrificed to a presumed higher common goal. Among other African philosophers, Gyekye criticizes the African notion of person because of its implications for human well-being. He states:

> it is possible for people to assume offhandedly that with its emphasis on communal values, collective good and shared ends, communitarianism invariably conceives the person as wholly constituted by social relationships; that it tends to whittle down the moral autonomy of the person; that it makes the being and life of the individual person totally dependent on the activities, values, projects, practices and ends of the community; and consequently, that it diminishes his freedom and capability to choose or question or re-evaluate the shared values of the community (Gyekye, 1992, p. 102).

In the later part of the above quote, Gyekye emphasizes the individual's freedom and ability to be critical of the shared values of one's community, one understands that that there is an obvious obstacle to individual person's freedom and well-being but the desire to question the values of the community is part of the ongoing discourse between individual person's and their communities for a better society. Peaceful existence, freedom and human rights are subject matters that will always be part of any developing and developed society. The difference for these societies is that in a developing society the agitations and the dialogue for change go on. In the developed society, the agitations and dialogue are directed at maintaining and securing the democratic principles to sustain freedom, rule of law and citizen mind. This is why critical or reflective thinking should be a part of every human organization, even when it is denied or the opportunity is frustrated. The demand for well-being should be at the core of political agitation (leading to consideration of political personhood in a community).

African philosophers have expressed concerns about the repercussions of the African notion of person on the 'individual' political person. Many Africans share the conviction that the idea "I am because we are" (I-We) is apt to express and justify their notion of community; but that this idea may have negative implications for individual persons as members of the community. The community sanctions the protection of individual person's well-being and encourages this political notion of person. A political notion of person recognizes person as the product of a social agreement- a member of a community. The person is totally dependent on the community to have rights and freedoms. This applies to African communities that only recognize the social rights of the person as long as they are in accord with the good of the community. Njoku adds, "[E]vidently, the community in the African sense presents itself as the greatest infallible judge and distributor of resources for social living. Rights are then community-sanctioned" (Njoku, 2004, pp. 154-155). It is easy to notice the devaluation of the person as an ontological and irreplaceable being in this situation. The ontological notion of person emphasizes that the person is an incommunicable entity with rational soul. The person is an 'end in itself.' A person is a being with free essence and dignity through creation.

Considering the above, it is difficult to hold on to the "I-We" person view as conceived by contemporary African philosophical thought. If one looks at the ontological and the political notions of person separately, then the "I-We" person will be different, but to separate the ontological and the political does not mean much in African worldview. In fact, the ontological and the political are inseparable because the real world of being (spiritual) and physical world are somehow connected. There is always continuity from one level of being-ness to the other, and vice versa. However, Bénézet Bujo, an African and Professor Emeritus of Moral Theology at University of Fribourg, Switzerland, in defense of "I-We" person and community philosophical thought, explains that:

> Because there is interdependence between the community and the individual, the community must not subordinate what is particular, but should promote and support it, because without the individuality of the single members it would totally disintegrate. Interaction, within the African context, makes it clear that the individual is an incomplete being who is basically dependent on the community (Bujo, 1998, p. 148).

Bujo also talks about "cognitus sum, ergo sumus" (I am known, therefore we are) as the central principle of African ethics. This principle is very different from the Cartesian principle of "I think, therefore I am) which is at the basis of Western liberal individualism. For Bujo and other African scholars, person is strictly considered in terms of a relational being within a community. Africa philosophical ethics focuses on developing the common good values like: hospitality, friendship, dialogue with the members of other ethnic groups, and co-operation among communities in mutual respect. "One who is not a member of my own group is ultimately also the 'property' of the other just as I myself am, and this means that I owe him respect and esteem. Thus one is ultimately related to all human beings" (Bujo, 2001, pp. 5-6).

In Bujo's view, African ethics is for everyone and includes "indeed even those not yet born constitute an important dimension" (Bujo, 2001, p. 5). In light of our main theme on integrative ethics of global, there is need for ethical pluralism, without contradictions (Bujo, 2001, p. 12). For a globalized world, ethical rules are in context and with cultural condition. We are always in a continual search for moral truths or values for integral well-being (Bujo, 2001, p. 8). My aim here is to underscore or advance an African perspective as a moral actor in support for an integrated ethics of being. This integrated ethics of being will help lay down the "norms and for ethical conduct as a whole" (Bujo, 2001, p. 5). I will now proceed to discuss the tenets of an integrative global ethics and emphasize on community, especially in light of Léopold Sédar Senghor's pre-emptive contributions to ethics of our times.

In Defence of Community: the 'We' and Community Ethics

The view of Senghor remains relevant here when he describes this "I-We" as "essentially relations with others, an opening out to the world, contact and participation with others" (Senghor, 1966, p. 46). This concept of the "I-We" as Senghor further clarifies is based on dialogue and reciprocity (my mutuality). Senghor again explains that ethnologists have often praised the "unity, the balance, and the harmony… founded on dialogue and reciprocity, the group had priority over the individual without crushing him" (Senghor, 1966, p. 50). The main criticism against the African concept of person and community is that it sometimes devalues the individual person's well-being and is unable to guarantee a protecting-community (I-We community).

The concept of the 'I-We' community or communal-mutuality is based on co-dependence and mutuality (not necessarily reciprocity). Ethnologists and other writers recognize the unity, the balance, and the harmony that ideally exists between the community and the person. The community has "priority over the individual without crushing him, but allowing him to blossom as a person" (Senghor, 1966, p. 50). But the question that needs to be addressed is: if the interest of one collides with the other what happens? Can the person lose his status as an 'end-in-itself', a subject? Following my earlier comment about Igbo Nigeria African hermeneutical philosophy of person, it considers person as a subject rather than an object, it is the community that determines what and whose interest ought to be protected when there is a collision of interests. The community arbitrates between the two 'individual' persons. The interest of an elder is much more important than that of a younger person. The interest of an elderly person who is closer to the ancestors and gods is considered more than that of an ordinary member of the community. Protecting the interest of an elderly person must be allied with the common interest of the community at large (Anozie, 2016, p. 90). In my work above, I noted that protecting the interests of others in line with common interest is a way of "guaranteeing the provision of necessary resources/conditions that permit the common good and well-being of the people, especially for those unable to provide these rights or well-beings for themselves" (Anozie, p. 98).

The interests of the chief priests of the gods of the land are considered more than any other person in the community. The particular interest of a pregnant woman (because of her situation) is more than that of a man or a young person because the baby (life in her) could be a respected ancestor reincarnating or coming back to life (still closer to the ancestral world). The interest to be served could be determined by what is best for the supernatural world (of cosmic unity) rather than the physical world. [Bujo has a similar notion that sees the world from cosmic, anthropocentric and religious perspectives]. What is best in light of cosmic unity/consciousness is for the community to continue to be in genuine existence. The continuity of community is quintessential to authentic existence of the 'individual' person. Whenever the continuity of community is antagonistic to genuine essence and existence of the individual person, then that community is on its way to ontological obliteration. The well-being of the community must reflect in the well-being of individual persons in such a community. They both mutually mirror the purposes for their presence. As we recall, although the community has the final say and any individual person's interest is relatively secondary to the primary vision/interest of the community, however, whatever interest that is protected, the individual person is directly and indirectly served through that of the community. The 'individual' person is an end-with-the-community or Others (is an end-in-alliance-with-the community). The individual person is not an end-in-itself without the I-We community. The relevance of the concept of "I-We" is in seeking and maintaining a balance between person and community. The community ceases to exist without the individual persons. The essential "We" is as important as the "Thou"—"person."

The 'essential We' or a genuine 'I-We' community means there has to be an authentic recognition of the other as a *Thou* or person with dignity and potential. Within the community, the individual person relates with others in the context of the common good required for actualizing a genuine "I-We" community (healthy, non-oppressive community). The common good is not a contingent good (non-intrinsic) but an essential good for an 'essential I-We'. The common good, in this case of Igbo Nigeria Africans' I-We community, is not against human rights, but could be difficult to understand in Western liberal individualistic notion of human rights (or a universalizing claim of Western morality which is at the heart of colonialism/Western Christianity). The 'I-We' community (and common good) is designed to developing a moral personhood. That is the goal for character-based Igbo Nigeria African ethics. I will later discuss this character ethics. This notion of person (moral person—it is the goal of African ethics to impart the individual being to becoming a person. A person is what one develops oneself to become) is at the heart of the nature of ethics that is not based on religion but on developing a human person with an individual person's relations in a community (communitarian ethics of duty). The process of becoming a person is affected by the family, which is the basic unit of a community. The community is first a family. I now will consider the role of family in the formation of character and the emergence of ethics of globality.

Africa: The Role of Family

In this subsection, I will like to further advance my views in *African Esotericism* (an essential aspect of developing African ethics in a working democratic society) which is relevant at this stage of this paper. The process of establishing a working democratic structure is a way of solidifying a sound ethical community, where justice continually reigns. African community, as in other communities, is naturally constituted by individual family units. The family remains the main basic unit of society –a necessary point of departure for ethical transformation of our world.

Africans, over the years, have maintained a relatively secured form of family structure. The fact of this point is not determined by the riches or wealth shared by African families but rather measured by socio-cultural and philosophical principles/norms that make it imperative, in most case, for families to be valued. Of course, in Western philosophy and cultural reflections, there exist family ties. In comparison to other societies (thought civilizations), the West's emphasis on individuality undermines the conditions for the emergence of communal-oriented family. Within the Igbo Nigeria African world, the notion of the beauty of life and the relational relevance in the definition of a person do help to cement or strengthen the transformation via thought to actualization of a relational world.

According to Igbo Nigeria African traditions, the desire to belong to the class of guardians help sustain youth ethical discipline. The family (parents) encourage their young ones to join cultural groups to access these moral trainings or embrace communal ethical skills. In my paper on *African Esotericism*, in support of family and development of personhood and the moral cult of guardians, I made reference to Anozie Onyema, who explains that, "[F]or one to qualify to belong to this class of guardians one needs to excel in great human and humane qualities"(Onyema, 1999, p. 174). Onyema adds:

> [T]o qualify as 'Oji Ofo'[title for ethical knowledge and being], one must be known by the community as a person of probity of character, one who is impeccable, whose honesty glaringly is beyond dispute, one

who is not easily bent to the whims and caprices of the time, one who sees dignity more valuable...one who values his name more than what he has. Hence the Igbo is wont to say, 'aha oma kariri ego'—good name is worth more than money...Ofo though a little piece of wood has more because of its religious symbolism (Onyema, 1999, pp. 174-175; Ejizu, 1986, p. 2).

As I noted above, the notion of person as a relational being implies belonging and being rooted "in an ongoing human community" (Menkiti, 1984, pp. 171-172). The ongoing human community takes precedence over the individual person without necessarily obliterating the person's dignity. In the community the individual person genuinely thrives. Bujo argues that the "I-We" person and community philosophical thought "makes it clear that the individual [person] is an incomplete being who is basically dependent on the community" (Bujo, 1998, p. 148). To be is to be completed. The concern is that Igbo Nigeria African communitarian notion of person may limit or undermine the inviolable rights and dignity of the person as a unique human being (Gyekye, 1992, p. 102); (Njoku, 2004, pp. 154-155).

Despite family conflicts, societal crises, etc, I argue that some of these crises do come from the clash of cultures, unethical technologies mixed and promoted with civilizations, etc. These situations do not totally distort the relevant notions of African hermeneutical philosophy on person, family, and community of mutual existence. The place of family in the community of mutual existence is the basis of our ethics, at least domestic ethics. "[T]he basis of morality was fulfillment of obligation to kinsmen and neighbors, and living in amity with them" (Wilson, 1971, p. 98). These facts remain central in the ethical life of the people and formulation of moral principles they communicate to younger generations (Hoegberg, 2011, p. 146). One has to decipher if these moral principles are religious- or humanistic-driven.

Religion and African Ethics

The rise of moral decadence in Igbo Nigeria African society could be linked to failures to connect our values to inner purposefulness for common good and promotion of human dignity. Socio-political values, moral and cultural dynamism, and human dignity are at the center of African philosophical and religious thought. The ancestors, the gods, the one God, etc are there for developing moral values for the good of the living. Although religion plays a very significant role in the life of Igbo Nigeria Africans, but religion does not necessarily determine everything about African moral life. As Gyekye notes African ethical principles and values are not founded on religion. Why? African traditional religion and spirituality is a non-revealed form of religion. God (as a sole moral giver) is not at the centre of African traditional religion, but humanism or good of humanity is. Whatever affirms this humanistic dimension on Igbo ethical lifeworld is considered as necessary to Igbo people. As Cole and Aniakor puts it, "[T]he concept of ikenga[symbol of authority] reverberates throughout much of Igbo life" (Cole and Aniakpor, 1984, p. 24). Religion is at the serves of humanism. For this reason, Igbo Nigeria Africans' consider religion as a utilitarian project. Igbo Nigeria Africans' hermeneutical ethics is not dependent on African religions but they mutually support each other in metaphysical subtlety. This explains the place of person as an ethical cum relational being. Igbo Nigeria Africans' ethics is non-revealed and non-individuality based ethics. It is thus an ethics based on solidarity, political belongingness/well-being, and deep in human understanding. P. Iroegbu calls this form of African ethics –the ethics of "Umunna" (kinsmen and the good for kinsmen, tied to the family) — that naturally leads to ethics of our common humanity.

Common Humanity and Shared-values Philosophy

I will develop this idea in light of relational being. The ethics of common humanity explores the riches of shared values, share-existence, shared-beingness, etc. Of course, as I pointed out, there could be various reasons to see failures of individual person in recognizing these common humanity and shared values in words and actions. One thing so clear about the integrity of African ethics is that the foundations are similar to Aristotelian Virtue ethics or ethics of character.

Ethics as character-based is an important point in African ethics. Ethics does not imply perfection in actions. It is much of practicing, nudging, reviewing, and re-engineering. What we do is acquired through time, through practising, and through observing respected people in the community. Most of these respected people in the community are members of social groups, cultural groups, age-grade groups that positively influence the lives of the young.[54] For

---

[54] See my work on Okonko, Okoroshi group in Stanley Uche Anozie, 'The Paradox of Non-violent Religions and Violent Cultural Practices' in The Root Causes of Terrorism, edited by

instance, Igbo Nigeria African will say "Onye agwa ojo"—meaning—a person with bad characters. For a person to be unethical is to be without good characters or to have no character. (Yoruba, Nigerians call it "Ewe." Igbo, Nigerians call it "Agwa" or "Mmeso oma").

Character and Loss of Personhood in African Ethics

In contributing to global ethics, Africans understand that the intercultural situation between their culture and that of Europeans shaped the new perspectives on life. The situation has also shown the demand for a new mode of existence that is part of the common unfolding history of our time. Chinua Achebe's attention is drawn to narrating the story of this cross-cultural encounter, especially in a positive and productive light and from the perspective of an Igbo Nigeria African person. It is this honorable goal that makes Achebe's narrative a great opportunity for unity and recognition of cultural diversity. The cross-cultural interaction is a form of comparative study, the relation of the peoples and cultures. It also does not overlook the complexes, the "crossroads of cultures" that are natural to such fusion of perspectives or cultures. In his later writings, Achebe was critical of what he considered as the moral failures of Igbo peoples' individualistic ethics. For me, Achebe's use of individualistic ethics for the Igbo Nigeria Africans seems awkward and should be looked at as practices of a later development considering long years of communalism/communitarianism. Individualistic ethics could also spring from structural reactions to years of socio-economic neglect and abuse of the fundamental rights of the people. [My reading of Chinua Achebe suggests his concern for the problem of individualism in Igbo African societies. See Achebe, The Trouble with Nigeria, 1983), p. 58, p. 60, p. 62.] Gyekye explains that "[T]he type of social structure or arrangement evolved by a particular society seems to reflect –and be influenced by –the public conceptions of personhood held in the society" (Gyekye, 1992, p. 101). It is a form of losing personhood when a people digress from their valuable socio-philosophical practices. Now I take look at Gyekye's contributions to African ethics and my explanations on the loss of personhood because of loss of moral character (unethical behaviors).

Gyekye's essay on 'African Ethics' and its relation to the idea of "individual" and "person" are laudable. I will also address the development of a

---

Mahmoud Masaeli and Rico Sneller (UK: Cambridge Scholars Publishing, 2017), pp. 258-279.

moral person, the notions of human being and individual (not the same as an individual person as I used above). There is a clear distinction between the moral or ethical person and the non-ethical individual.

The individual is that human being who persists in a series of bad practices (unethical behaviors) and does not recognize the dignity of the other person. However, this individual does not lose his/her essential personhood based on the mere bad or ill wishes of the other who wants it so, rather one becomes an individual by continually participating in inhuman actions (One can relate this to Hannah Arendt's discourse on Adolf Eichmann in her book— Eichmann in Jerusalem: A Report on the Banality of Evil—on Eichmann's evil actions following Hitler's commands). Was Eichmann naturally evil (unethical subject)? No. Did he commit some atrocities? Yes, as convicted! In Igbo Nigeria African ethics, there is a distinction between a moral person (truly a person), a human being (children, sick fellows, mentally challenged people, intellectually challenged people) and an individual (evil and unethical subject). As Gyekye notes, "it does not imply at all that an individual considered 'not a person' loses his rights as a human being or as a citizen or that people in the community should cease to demonstrate a moral concern for him or display the appropriate moral virtues in their treatment of him; only that he is not considered a morally worthy individual" (Gyekye, Kwame. African Ethics. 2010. Accessed November 5, 2017. http://plato.stanford.edu/entries/african-ethics/).

African Ethics is helpful for imparting ethical ideas of Africans to young generations of Africans, especially in the context of our integrative /globalized communities and our common humanity (this topic I plan to further develop in my work on *political belongingness and well-being*). Our ethics are influenced by the concrete realities of our *Lebenswelt* (world of lived experience). It is only within these socio-cultural-economic-political-religious conditions that life is truly meaningful. No ethical being operates with moral principles that are not constitutive of his/her life world. However, being constituent of one's moral world could involve issues one may not yet be conversant with. The implication is that as time goes on, through intercultural experiences and encounters, people from different cultural worlds could agree to fashion out a common framework that is appropriate to global needs of their time. This is why an integral global ethics is a necessity in our co-mutually-existent world. It is also why Igbo Nigeria African hermeneutical ethics (as part of African hermeneutical philosophy) is worth consulting and advancing in order to achieve a comprehensive approach to all moral issues that impact our genuine living. Bujo has criticised the mono-cultural hegemony or 'global monoculture' of Western ethics. We have to go beyond the assumptions that Western ethical claim is the universal foundation for all forms of ethics (Bujo, 2001, p. xii). It is clear that what we need is a dialogical approach with other philosophies/civilizations. For this paper, I will briefly focus on Africa and China (a new global economic relationship that provides a background for consideration on the framework for an integrative global ethics).

Global Ethics: African/Chinese Economic Collaboration and Global Development

Following the dynamics of business development and economic cooperation, Africa and China have charted a new way to pursue mutual economic development. According to BBC Website information on the ideological, commercial and economic relationship between Africa and China: "China's relationship with Africa goes back at least 40 years. Once the connection was ideological, today the pair are bonding over commerce and capitalism. China is now the largest investor in Africa with over $200bn [billion] of investments circulating on the continent" (BBC. 2015. How Does Africa Get on With its Biggest Investor, China? Accessed November 5, 2017. http://www.bbc.com/news/business-33653673). Despite the level of collaborations between Africa and China, there are criticisms of their collaboration in terms of quality--- the quality is still deficient. It is deficient because of the poor standard of the transfer of developmental skills to Africans.

One could inspire change in China's economic/business relations with Africa; inspire quality development skills' transfer by emphasizing some ethically sound South Asian philosophies. For instance, Solomon and Higgins note that:

> obligations within relationships are reciprocal. A parent has authority over a child, but also an obligation to care for the child. Later in life, the child will have obligations to take care of his or her parents. Someone in authority and a subordinate should each do what is possible to assist the other in fulfilling his or her role. In general, Confucius urges that everyone consider the situation from the other's point of view: 'Do not do to others what you yourself would not want.' Confucius understands it, is essentially relational. We are who we are because we are related to others, as children, parents, siblings, friends, coworkers, and so forth. The nexus of particular relationships we have

with particular others is what makes us who we are (Solomon and Higgins, 2013, p. 356).

It is clear that these far-reaching ethical principles have long being with us (humanity) and can sustain an integrative global ethics undermined by some whimsical political shenanigans. These ethical principles are in line with the formation of personal character (which is not acquired through inheritance or blood line but through good behaviors, practical wisdom, merits, and manners).

For the Chinese, in light of Confucius philosophy, the family should be seen the center and an exemplar of what is most desirable in human community—that is interpersonal harmony, "in which members have various responsibilities with the common aim of fulfilling the needs of all members. Filial piety, respect for one's elders, is consequently a profoundly important Confucius virtue" (Solomon and Higgins, 2013, pp. 354-355). These virtues are what we need in formulating an integrative and engaging ethical business relationship with China, Africa, and the global community. The 5 key terms in Chinese philosophy could serve as connecting points with African philosophy on person and community. These 5 key terms are: *dao*—the Way (the process of living well); *ren*—Humanity-to be human and virtue; *he*—meaning "Harmony"; and *yi*—meaning "Appropriateness"; *li*—meaning "Ritual" (the way things are done, the restoration of social harmony, partnership with others as co-citizens in society or communal engagement). The bottom-line is that the integration of the various positive values of China-African philosophico-cultural worlds. Its ethical dimension demands that African realities should be considered in determining the strategies for African and global development (Rwiza, 2010, p. 74). The beauty of life which resonates with the beauty of our world could play a role in development and ecological crises arising out these economic co-operations between African and China, with much of the negative impact like "the disintegration of African traditional models of family and kinship" (Rwiza, 2010, p. 74). The economic co-operations must yield life-changing transformation for the people rather than being a form of globalization that "reinforced the continent's marginalization, impoverishment, indebtedness and lack of policy of sustainable development" (Rwiza, 2010, p. 70).

In aligning economic co-operations that liberate via integrative global ethics, I see many similarities in philosophical worldviews on person and community between Africa and China. Solomon and Higgins note the central concern in these way: "Whatever their [Chinese] disagreements about the relative importance of nature and society, the Chinese thinkers were in considerable agreement concerning the need for harmony in human life and a larger sense of the "person" than merely the individual" (Solomon and Higgins, 2013, p. 360). This surely has a role to play especially in relation to the China and other countries and other continents. There are of course some critical civilizational and cultural differences between China, Europe, and North America. Meanwhile, the philosophical and cultural relations between Africa and China are tied between their agreeable philosophies and cultural worldviews. On a different note, one has to point out that the comment above does not mean an endorsement that Chinese and African relationship has always been "perfect" for Africa. My analysis above is designed to suggest the fact of these socio-philosophical familiarities between these 2 cultural worlds/civilizations and about their possible mutual economic and socio-political development. Let me point out some areas of limitations in relation to international (global) organizations and global human rights/peace.

Western Philosophico-ethical Tradition: Individuality and Social Contract

I will like to recall our reflections above (*Boethius and Maritain: Person and Individual*) on Maritain's profound presentation on the distinction between person and individual. His distinctive reflection is directly similar to Igbo Nigeria African's notion of person as a becoming being. My task is to articulate African hermeneutical notion of person as well as accord philosophical credit where it is due. European or Western philosophical ethics recognizes the role of the person in relation to being 'subjectivity' or 'individuality'. It seems that at a certain point in the history of thought, subjective individuality became more prominent than the understanding of person (in general economic and socio-philosophical development). In this case, I think of Thomas Hobbes, John Locke, and Jean-Jacques Rousseau. I also ponder on their various notions of the individual in society, social contract, and the role of society to human well-being. According to Solomon and Higgins, Locke and Rousseau describe social contract as necessary agreements between people for their common good in a community because of their social limitations but do not imply the original presence of "state of war", "a war of all against all" (Solomon and Higgins, 2013, p. 305). It is pertinent to note that some of such narratives of 'state of nature' or 'state of war' are fictions and philosophical constructs. However, it is not difficult to understand the possibilities of conflicts in different human conditions. In African cosmology and anthropology, we emerged as people who are naturally good and happy and beautiful. This philosophical understanding is in line with a necessary aspect of Igbo Nigeria Africans' notion of person as the "beauty of life." Igbo Nigeria Africans' view of person and society (community) is one that rejects the idea of human beings as "naturally selfish" (Solomon, p. 305). The 'General Will' is not the primary source of order for naturally bad human beings (p. 305). Human persons are, ontologically speaking, beautiful and good. The pre-eminent role of Igbo Nigeria Africans' hermeneutical notion of person as beauty of life is contrary to the nasty, brutish and short world of conflict and war in the past and contemporary discourses. African hermeneutical ethics/philosophy will conceive and approve a community that "will not only restore something of our natural vitality and utilize our inventiveness but will actually make us into something more than merely 'natural.' Society will make us moral" (Solomon and Higgins, 2013, p. 307). Of course, one can attest to dwindle in the depth of thought that affirms--interpersonal relationship and personhood. In other words, the social contract is not a mere socio-political development, but essentially human because of our 'beauty of life' existential beingness. Society or community is there to lead us to fullness of purposeful being: happier and healthier. In Solomon and Higgins' views, Jean-Jacques Rousseau holds that "our prosocietal ancestors…left one another alone, and even felt pity for others in need" (Solomon and Higgins, 2013, p. 307). I also find Prof. G. O. Ozumba's reflection on the state of nature was applied as if it is universal for Africans as well as Europeans. My position is that the ontological natures of person as the beauty of life as well as a rational being make such consideration of a dangerous state of nature untenable. I am also inclined to follow the direction of Locke and Rousseau.

In search for a happier and healthier and safer world, the Universal Declaration of Human Rights of 1948 was imperative. Unfortunately, I must add here, that the draft of the Universal Declaration of Human Rights (1948) was a project that drew deeply on subjective individuality or liberal individuality, the uniqueness of the individual. The United Nations (UN) had, and still has, a nature of an integrated global organization relatively aimed at protecting a communitarian world, at best, or at worst, a mere collectivistic society. (More reading on related European philosophers similar to African hermeneutical philosophy is on Martin Buber, Emmanuel Levinas, Jacques Maritain, Hans-Georg Gadamer, and Fred Dalmyer). The UN in current light falls short of being a good source for a framework for an integrative global ethics. African scholars and their philosophies were absent (say neglected) in articulating a more integrated ethics on human rights and human dignity (Life, Liberty and the

Pursuit of Happiness). Alan Gewirth has classified some of these human rights into basic well-being (food, shelter, water, etc), non-subtractive well-being (not to be lied to, not to be stolen from, etc), and additive well-being (education, acquisition of work skills, etc) (Anozie, 2016, p. 99). There issues should be part of the motif for now desired and integrative reforms in any inter-relationships, global or international organizations.

Relevant Issues for Integrative Global Ethics

Within the community, there should be the mutuality of rights, persons' obligations and of institutional protections (states, communal institutions). Njoku considers the understanding of community as coming from "the predisposition for care by the African as posting of the self in a free and symbiotic embrace with the other" (Njoku, 2003, p. 66). The African sense of community must embrace a notion of human rights expressed through the mutuality of rights. This notion of human rights provides the basis for socio-economic development and the self-fulfillment of individual persons. The current question is: Could we resolve the contemporary problems of humanity by sticking only to liberal individualism? Or is it not rather time to accommodate other rich philosophical (ethical) traditions, especially those that conceive our humanity from a different, but quite enriching perspective—communitarian, essentially relational and beauty of life intellectual discourse? The basis of future international relationship and socio-economic cooperation between Africa and North America, Middle East, Asia (China), Europe, etc must be based on the much needed intellectual reviewing of the status quo, understanding the depth of what it means to be a person as a relational being. The notion of subjective individuality has in a way come to the zenith of unsustainable growth. We are in an era of reversal of emphases considering the impediments of subjective individuality or liberal individuality/liberal individualism. In this context, critical contributions of Professors Ivan Van Sertima, Yosef Ben Jochannan, Ngugi Wa Thiongo, and John Henrik Clarke are most appropriate. Thiongo specifically calls for the decolonization of the mind, while Clarke condemns the failures to allow the African mind/thought reflect in a world driven my power and control and colonialism. For him, colonialism and slavery changed African(s) frame of mind or consciousness. I hope that an integrative global ethics will be a step to change all this for a better, healthier, happier, safer, and more beautiful world. A step to building a communitarian (collective?) consciousness via integrative ethics of globality—a desideratum!

Conclusion

My goal in this paper has been to emphasize the often neglected ethical views of persons and community of Igbo Nigeria Africans' hermeneutical philosophy, which I consider relevant to a comprehensive global ethics. This opportunity to integrative ethics provides a global approach to addressing human problems in an age of globalization and socio-economic co-operation among peoples, between cultures and civilizations. Of course, I am not suggesting that all civilizations, except Africans', failed to recognize the notion of person as the beauty of life in the sense of interpersonal community in a cosmic beauty. I rather framed my reflections and arguments to buttress the point that communitarian philosophy is common in Asian and African civilizations. I do think that Igbo Nigeria Africans' person as beauty of life truly stands out and ought to be communicated/shared in a world obsessed with global monoculture of capitalism and materialism and individualism. Global capitalism and materialism and individualism, by their nature, obliterate our focus on integral humanism (Beauty of humanity as anchored to a morality of the beautiful existence, quality existence) in what Chinese Confucius considers as person-within-social harmony.

China, as a relatively new business/economic and socio-philosophical ally with Africa (including Igbo Nigeria Africans), could have a better business relationship with Africans because of their common basis of reflection on the nature of person, on cultivating person virtues, and on socio-political harmony. China, in its essential philosophy, also recognises the age long cultural epistemology of Africans that the interests of the person (including the elderly) must be aligned to the interests of communicating truth, common good, and in cosmic harmony. This conclusion does suggest that any other civilization or continent could plug into these basic principles for the good of our common humanity. Our common humanity is not a project that emerged out of a social contract (arising out of a state of nature, of war of all against all) but is intrinsic to the idea of a beautiful person and a good person, a purposeful being —called to live within the framework of an integral moral diet of global ethics.

In global ethics, what should be central is that every individual person or relational being of beauty desires dignity, equity, freedom, justice, peace, tolerance, respect, and happiness or satisfaction (flourishing). These concepts are at the heart of Igbo Nigeria Africans' communitarian ethics of common good but we have to arrive at them through the a careful continual exercise of epistemologies and interpretations of values. We are required to merge these values with contemporary global ethics' demands through a systematic holistic purposive nudging—that is a continual ethics process. As M. J. McVeigh observes, "[W]hat is for human well-being is good and what is not is not good (social ethics, custom-based ethics, society-oriented morality" (McVeigh, 1974, p. 84).

References

Achebe, C. (1983). The Trouble With Nigeria. Enugu: Fourth Dimension Publishing Co. Ltd.

Anozie, S. U. (2016). 'Ethics of Duty Reassessed: Alan Gewirth's Community of Rights Critical Perspective.' In Globality, Unequal Development, and Ethics of Duty. Edited by Mahmoud Masaeli. UK: Cambridge Scholars Publishing.

Anozie, S. U. (2017). 'The Paradox of Non-violent Religions and Violent Cultural Practices.' In The Root Causes of Terrorism. Edited by Mahmoud Masaeli and Rico Sneller. UK: Cambridge Scholars Publishing.

Anyanwu, K. C. and Ruch, E. A. (1981). African Philosophy: An Introduction to The Main Philosophical Trends in Contemporary Africa. Rome: Catholic Book Agency.

Boethius (1953). Tractates Consolation. Trans. H. F. Stewart and E. K. Rand. London: Harvard University Press, 1953.

Bujo, B. (1998).The Ethical Dimension of Community: The African Model and the Dialogue between North and South. Nairobi: Paulines Africa.

Bujo B. (2001). Foundations of an African Ethic: Beyond the Universal Claims of Western Morality. New York: Crossroad.

Coates, J. (1949). The Crisis of The Human Person: Some Personalist Interpretations. London: Longmans, Green and Co.

Cole, H. and Chike A. (1984). Igbo Arts: Community and Cosmos. Los Angeles: Museum of Cultural History.

Dzobo, N. K. (1992). Values in a Changing Society: Man, Ancestor and God. In Kwasi Wiredu and Kwame Gyekye (Eds.). Person and Community: Ghanaian Philosophical Studies. Washington D.C.: The Council for Research in Values and Philosophy.

Ejizu, C. (1986). Ofo Igbo Ritual Symbol. Enugu.

Gikandi, S. (1991). Reading Chinua Achebe: Language and Ideology in Fiction. Portsmouth: Heinemann.

Gyekye, K. (1992). Person and Community in African Thought. In Kwasi Wiredu and Kwame Gyekye (Eds.). Person and Community. Vol. 1.Washington, D. C: The Council for Research in Values and Philosophy.

Hoegberg, D. (2011). Principle and Practice: the Logic of Cultural Violence in Achebe's Things Fall Apart. In M. Keith Booker (Ed.). Critical Insights: Things Fall Apart. Pasadena, California: Salem Press.

Iroegbu, P. (1996). Appropriate Ecclesiology (Through Narrative Theology to an African Church). Owerri: International Universities Press.

Maritain, J. (1965). The Social and Political Philosophy of Jacques Maritain. Joseph W. Evans and Leo R. Ward (Eds). New York: Image Books.

Mbiti, J. S. (1969). African Religions and Philosophy. London: Heinemann Educational Books.

McVeigh, M. J. (1974). God in Africa. Cape Cod, MA: Claude Stark.

Menkiti, I. A. (1984, third edition). Person and Community in African Traditional Thought. In Richard A. Wright (Ed.). African Philosophy: an Introduction. New York: University Press of America.

Njoku, F. O. C. (2004). Development and African Philosophy: A Theoretical Reconstruction of African Socio-Political Economy. New York: iUniverse, Inc.

Odita, E. O. (1973). 'Universal Cults and Intra-diffusion: Igbo Ikenga in Cultural Retrospection.' In African Studies Review (Cambridge University Press), Vol. 16, No. 1 (Apr., 1973), pp. 73-82.

Odozor, P. I. (2003). Moral Theology in An Age of Renewal: A Study of the Catholic Tradition since Vatican II. Notre Dame, Ind.: University of Notre Dame, pp. 101–33.

Onwuanibe, R. C. (1984). 'The Human Person and Immortality in Ibo (African) Metaphysics.' In African Philosophy: An Introduction, Richard A. Wright, (Ed.). New York: University Press of America.

Onyema, A. (1999). The Igbo Culture and the Formation of Conscience. Owerri: Assumpta Press.

Rwiza, R. N. (2010). Urbanization in Africa: An Ethical Challenge. In African Christian Studies (Vol. 26, Number 4, December 2010). Quarterly Journal of the Faculty of Theology. Published by CUEA Press.

Senghor, L. S. (1995). "Negritude: A Humanism of the Twentieth Century (1966)." I am Because We Are: Readings in Black Philosophy. Edited by Fred Lee Hord (Mzee Lasana Okpara) and Jonathan Scott Lee. Amherst: University of Massachusetts Press, 1995.

Solomon, R. C and Higgins E. (2013). The Big Questions: A Short Introduction to Philosophy. Wadworth Publishers, 9th Edition (Cengage Learning).

Chapter 3
The Hermeneutics of Hope in African Igbo Ontology

Stanley Uche Anozie

(Philosophy Department, Boston College, Chestnut Hill, MA, USA, 2022)

Abstract. I will attempt some hermeneutical reflections on three generative themes in African Igbo ontology of hope. These three generative themes are: a) Hope as *Ìhè* (Light as Hope. Light of Hope. A light at the end of the tunnel. Hope as Reality/Essence/Substance) (ontological hope), b) Hope as *Nkuzi* or a part of *Nkuziology* (Life's teaching or social learning, the experience of life forms humanity) (epistemological/pedagogical hope), and c) Hope as *Nchekwube* or *Olileanya* (including Igbo names like *Nchekwubechi, Olileanyachi, Echi-di-ime*---tomorrow has promises, tomorrow is a day of hope or is a day to be hopeful) (anthropological hope). In Professor Pantaleon Iroegbu's trend of African Ontology or Metaphysics as the *Kpim* of philosophy, one is drawn to his African Igbo philosophical concepts. For instance, 'Kpim' is Igbo word for 'the kernel', the substance, the essence of a thing, the reality or the most real of reality; *Hypo-kaimenon* (Greek for underlying entity), etc. I will articulate and advance a hermeneutical equivalent to Iroegbu's *Kpim* (Igbo word for the kernel, the substance, the core of a thing, etc.) to another African Igbo word 'Ihe' (Thingness/Substance/Essence).

Keywords: Hope, *Nkuzi*, *Nchekwube*, African, Igbo, Ontology.

Introduction

In this work, I will attempt some hermeneutical reflections on three generative themes in African Igbo ontology of hope. These three generative themes are: a) Hope as Ihe/*Ìhè* (Light of Hope. A light at the end of the tunnel. Hope as Reality/Essence/Substance) (ontological hope), b) Hope as *Nkuzi* or a part of *Nkuziology* (Life's teaching or social learning, the experience of life forms humanity) (epistemological/pedagogical hope), and c) Hope as *Nchekwube* or *Olileanya* (including Igbo names like *Nchekwubechi, Olileanyachi, Echi-di-ime*---tomorrow has promises, tomorrow is a day of hope or is a day to be hopeful) (anthropological hope).

In Professor Pantaleon Iroegbu's trend of African Igbo Ontology or Metaphysics as the *Kpim* of philosophy, one is drawn to his *Igbo* philosophical concepts[55]. For instance, 'Kpim' is Igbo word for 'the kernel', the substance, the essence of a thing, the reality or the most real of reality; like *Hypo-kaimenon* (Greek for underlying entity),[56] etc. In an attempt to advance the philosophical richness of Professor Iroegbu's contributions to African Igbo Ontology or Metaphysics (or science of being and Being-itself), I will articulate and advance a hermeneutical equivalent to Iroegbu's *Kpim* (Igbo word for the kernel, the substance, the *core* of a thing, etc.) to another African Igbo word *Ihe* (Thingness/Substance/Essence/Entity). *Ihe* has got 2 different connotations depending on the context. These 2 different connotations mutually sustain the understanding of *Ihe* or Being. The *first connotation* is: *Ihe*—means—'Whatness', 'Quiddity', 'Essence' of a thing, the really real or the real thing, or reality itself. For instance, in African Igbo language expression: *Ihe mere ihe oji buru ihe obu*—meaning—'what or that which made a thing what it is' or 'what/that which really makes a thing a thing or whatever it is.' The *second connotation* is: *Ìhè* (Light, Disclosure, the ability to be known, to be transparent)—could be related to 'disclosure' or revealing nature (a liberal interpretation could be like German--*Dasein*—as part of *Sein, Existenz*). *Ìhè* (Igbo for 'light' or 'reveal-ness' or becoming known) is intrinsic to understanding *Ihe* (as being or the kernel of a thing, stuff, being, or Greek *Ousia*). *Ìhè* (light) is directly and epistemically tied to *Ihe* (essence, substance or whatness).

---

[55] Pantaleon Iroegbu, *Metaphysics: The Kpim of Philosophy*, Owerri, International University, Press, 1995, p. 325.
[56] Stanley Uche Anozie, "The Problem of Evil in Plato and Gadamerian Plato", *Revue Roumaine de Philosophie*, 66, 1, 2019, pp. 116-129.

It is only *Ihe* (quiddity, substance, essence or reality) that is strictly associated with *Ìhè* (light, disclosure or transparency). Without *Ìhè* (light, disclosure), the disclosing/transparent nature of *Ihe* (the kernel, substance, essence) will be impossible to comprehend or be encountered. In this inevitable association between *Ihe* (the kernel, substance or being) and *Ìhè* (light or disclosure), I will discuss the significance of *Ìhè* (Light as hope. Light of hope. A light for direction or revelation of being or truth)- as an essential aspect of African Igbo hermeneutics of 'Hope.' The idea of Hope could be communicated through an English expression like the 'light at the end of the tunnel' or 'reality' that truly reveals itself. While 'Hopelessness' depicts darkness, failure, disappointment, etc., I will take a look at some African Igbo expressions in relation to explaining *Ìhè* (light, disclosure, and substance, essence, reality or entity) as important to understanding African Igbo notions of 'Hope':

A) Hope as *IHE/Ìhè*

(i)

African Igbo people often say: *Ihe kwuru ihe akwudebe ya*—meaning—'When a thing stands, then another things stands by it.' (This also means that without a substance, a source, a real thing; then there can be nothing else close to it. *Ihe* (being, substance; *Ìhè*- light, disclosure)—keeps anything in being. It makes a thing possible or capable of being. It is like the word 'substance' (Latin, *Substantia*) or (Greek, *Ousia* or *Hypokaimenon*). Substance is something that is underneath or the underlying entity. As is a common African Igbo wise saying, it is strictly on something that another thing can stand upon. Nothing is superimposed on nothing. On nothing *nothing else* stands. 'Nothing else' is not an underlying entity. One could relate this to my earlier works on African Igbo notion of *Mmadu* (person) as the beauty of life[57], and *The Problem of Evil in Platonism and Gadamerian Plato*.[58] Without substance/quintessence/being there will be no shadow. Shadow is an accident. It is totally supported by substance or being. Accident (not a road mishap) does not exist in itself.[59]

---

[57] Stanley Uche Anozie, *Hans-Georg Gadamer and African Hermeneutic Philosophy*, Chisinau, Generis Publishing, 2020, p. 169.
[58] S. U. Anozie "The Problem of Evil in Plato and Gadamerian Plato", pp. 116-129.
[59] *Ibidem*, pp. 116-117.

(ii)

Another enlightening concept is 'Ihe' in *Ìhè-eke*—meaning—The Light that creates. *Ìhè-Chukwu*—'The light of God'---this could be considered to be the 'action' or 'activity' of Being itself. God (although religiously used does imply the 'Being' or 'Entity' that truly exists in himself, by himself, and for himself. Without this God or Being, nothing else has existence or being. There is also a Christianized utterance like[60] *Ìhè si na-Ìhè* or *Ìhè Nke putara n'Ìhè* (Light of Light. The Un-caused Cause, Causality itself or from Reality itself) (ontological hope).

(iii)

A third consideration of *Ihe* points to something unique in African Igbo Ontology. *Ihe-anyi* or *Ihe-anyi-chukwu*--meaning—'Nothing is impossible to God.' The point of this African Igbo ontological/metaphysical expression is that 'Ihe' is actuality, becoming to being, Being, etc. The actuality or the becoming of the real is also the becoming of hope and hopefulness. The presence of the real reveals, or will eventually reveal, the most real. That which is eventually revealed is the real that becomes, or the becoming-being.

Epistemologically speaking, we know a thing in a limited manner, in potentiality, and truly know in actuality. There is nothing that is fully known in actuality in the physical world (Igbo: *Uwa nkea*). The most real is the most 'true' and the most present. To be present or this 'presence' is understood as that which eliminates the un-truthful, 'hopelessness', despair, helplessness, and builds optimism[61] or hope based on truth. Hope has also been translated in African Igbo language to mean 'Nchekwube'—a kind of optimism for a positive outcome based on fate or destiny, an attitude of positive expectations and understanding of the dynamism of reality, confidence in the unfolding of reality, and in reality's own time. Human beings (*Mmadu ndu*--the beauty of life) are part of this unfolding of reality. Unfolding of reality is the actualization of the fullness of humanity or human becoming (anthropological hope). In the following reflections, I will associate *Ihe* to *Nkuzi* generative theme of African Igbo Ontology of hope.

---

[60] African Igbo language in Igbo Catholic/Christian Creed.
[61] Some Western scholars make a distinction between hope and optimism, especially Michael Himes (of Boston College, Massachusetts, USA). African Igbo Ontology of Hope does not subscribe to such distinctions because of the interconnection between the physical and the spiritual worlds. To have hope is to be optimistic in the determinations of our *Chi* and our individual/particular *chi*. Hope and optimism are not mutually exclusive.

B) Hope as *NKUZI* (Life's teaching or Social learning)

The African Igbo people of Ngwaland[62] (Southeastern Nigeria) have a common saying: *Obu otu ihe uwa nu* or *Obu otu ihe uwa di* –meaning—'That is how reality is or how things are', 'That is how the world is', or 'such is the world/reality.' It is a statement made in relation to acceptance of a situation of things, and hopefulness. 'Hopefulness' comes through truthfulness, true understanding, and forthrightness. Hope arises from Truth or Truthfulness. Hope does not work with falsehood, fantasy, 'make-belief' or something fake. I will relate this to epistemological/pedagogical notion of hope arising from *Nkuzi*—Life's teaching or social learning. Life experiences teach us about reality or truth or give us hope or give us hopefulness in actualized reality. *Nkuzi* does not take place in the false or fake. Life 'crafts' us in the truth, not in the false or fake. Life makes us or cultivates us.[63] I consider this 'cultivation' through *Nkuzi* as part of our actualization of the fullness of being (understanding our *Ihe*/Whatness/Essence or Hope as *Ihe*). African Igbo people express this reality in wise sayings like: *Ndu ka Aku* or *Nduka* (Life is more than wealth) and *Onye ije ka onye isi awomma* (A traveler is better experienced than the untraveled elderly person, or experience [of life] is the best teacher). A teacher is *Onye-nkuzi*.

For me, following the influence of Iroegbu, *Nkuzi* or teaching aligns with the *Ihe* or *Kpim* of education. *Ihe* or *Kpim* "is the quintessence, which is the thingness of a thing and the somethingness of something (Iroegbu, 2002:17)."[64] The African Igbo words *Ihe* and *Kpim* are related to *Nkuzi*ology (teaching) in African Igbo worldview or *Bildung* in German worldview. In Benson Peter Irabor and Okikiola Oludare Olufowobi's essay, "An Exploration of Pantaleon Iroegbu's Pedagogy of Nkuziology for Contemporary Africa," Iroegbu's view is outlined,

> Analytically, *Nkuzi* means to knock, hit, strike aright or to repair, to shape to required proportion. On a piece of iron that is crooked or rugged, one hits with a harmer to straighten it, to make it fine. The same word is used for the verb, to teach, *nkuzi*. In this

---

[62] This could be referred to as "Ndi Ngwa."
[63] S. U. Anozie, *Hans-Georg Gadamer and African Hermeneutic Philosophy*, p. 99.
[64] https://www.academia.edu/43644897/An_Exploration_of_Pantaleon_Iroegbu_s_Pedagogy_of_Nkuziology_for_Contemporary_Africa, accessed: 13 August 2021. See Pantaleon Iroegbu, *Kpim of Theodicy Proving the Existence of God Via Hermeholiontica*, Ibadan, Hope Publications, 2002, p. 17.

transferred, but very real sense, to teach is to knock, straighten or shape the pupil, student or subject aright. This time it is not with harmer[hammer][65] or stone, but with knowledge, instruction, wisdom and good example. [66]

I would like to emphasize here that 'Nkuzi' (*N-kuzi*) does not imply violence. It is all about cultivating a morally balanced person. Like the verb 'kuzi', it means hermeneutically to put to the right path or direction, to align properly, to put in the good state or good character. *Nkuzi* has nothing to do with defiling or dehumanizing the other person/student of life. *Nkuzi* does not take place in an environment of abuse or violation of the dignity of a person. It is a good learning experience or a life-long social learning experience. Time does not weaken the value/quality of the good, and so *Nkuzi* as a life-long social learning experience (the good) does not become undervalued because of age or time or circumstance.

I appreciate the resources and quotations associated with Professor Iroegbu in Irabor and Olufowobi's work. For instance, "Nkuziology therefore, is the balanced upbringing, knocking aright, the teaching of the person to be balanced, good and respectful to order and goodness (Iroegbu, 1995, 264)."[67] The statement above affirms my own understanding of Iroegbu's articulation of *Nkuzi* (teaching) or my advancement of *Nkuzi* by promoting *Hope as Nkuzi* as a generative theme in the hermeneutics of hope in African Igbo Ontology. However, I have chosen to avoid using the term "Nkuziology" because of the linguistic implications of anglicizing or westernizing an African Igbo concept- *Nkuzi*. For me, *Nkuzi* is a thought pattern, a logical approach, a study, a science or a systematic knowledge approach in its own right. *Nkuzi*, as a thought pattern or study, focuses on information for self-development through communication. It is about acquiring the basic skills for a genuine and fulfilling existence. It also includes a reformative or rehabilitative aspect. One could recall here my comments about the *Nkuzi* as the good that does not lose its value based on age, time or circumstance. It is a life-long social learning experience. In fact, it is an

---

[65] I added this correction.
[66]https://www.academia.edu/43644897/An_Exploration_of_Pantaleon_Iroegbu_s_Pedagogy_of_Nkuziology_for_Contemporary_Africa , accessed: 13 August 2021. See Pantaleon Iroegbu, and M. A. Izibili, *Kpim of Democracy Thematic Introduction to Socio-Political Philosophy*, Benin City, Ever-Blessed Publishers, 2004, p. 13.
[67]https://www.academia.edu/43644897/An_Exploration_of_Pantaleon_Iroegbu_s_Pedagogy_of_Nkuziology_for_Contemporary_Africa, accessed on 13 August 2021. See Pantaleon Iroegbu, *Metaphysics: The Kpim of Philosophy*, Owerri, International University Press, 1995, p. 264.

eternal good, an eternal truth. *Nkuzi* (teach/teaching) is about knowledge of the truth, the eternal truth, and the truth of life.[68] *Nkuzi* makes it possible for the manifestation of a life of purpose, a life in accord with one's *Chi*. The manifestation of a life of purpose is same with the 'manifestation' of *Ihe* (Ìhè — light or direction or personal mentor or guardian or *chi onye*). In Irabor and Olufowobi's work, it stated:

> Thus, Iroegbu (2005a:221) avers that knowledge given in teaching has three basic foci: information, formation and reformation. It is information in that it is a communication of ideas and facts that are meant to be used to achieve some goals. It is Formation in that those facts given in information are destined to constitute the mental and personality structure of the recipient. They make him or her behave this way or that, thereby structuring the person's way of life. Teaching also has reformative function in the aspect that it helps to change already formed ways and manners of behaviour. Education thus reconstructs personality. It makes anew; and all things being equal, a better person for oneself and for the society in which one lives and operates.[69]

My goal above is to associate **Hope** to ***Nkuzi*** (from hope to *Nkuzi*) in order to identify this pedagogical aspect of **Hope as *Nkuzi*** (life's teaching or social learning). One should take a good note of the difference between *Hope to* and *Hope as*. For *Hope as Nkuzi*, it means that life teaches every one of us. Life teaches 'life' (how to live) or the art of living. The experiences of life are part of our human becoming or actualization of self (as a part of reality). The challenges or tragedies of life are not ends-in-themselves. They are rather life's teaching moments or means for human experience, true human becoming, en-wisdomization (enwisdomizing experience, to-make-wise experience), transformation in hope, and for the better. The experiences of tragedies help us develop our skills to aspire, to develop hope, or the skills to hopefulness. This hope or hopefulness is the anchor for our becoming or continuity of beingness.

---

[68] There is no desire for that which is false or fake in African Igbo notion of *Nkuzi*. *Nkuzi* is always for the truth, the truth of life. *Nkuzi* is focused on the life of purpose.

[69] https://www.academia.edu/43644897/An_Exploration_of_Pantaleon_Iroegbu_s_Pedagogy_of_Nkuziology_for_Contemporary_Africa, accessed on 13 August 2021. See Pantaleon Iroegbu, "Philosophy of Education: Ethics of Teaching profession" in Pantaleon Iroegbu , A. Echekube, (eds.), *Kpim of Morality: General, Special & Professional*, Ibadan, Heinemann Educational Books, 2005, p. 221.

'To be' is *to exist* with the hope that one's fullness of being is a task that should be accomplished.

In order to conclude this section, I consider the following African Igbo proverbs to be appropriate to Hope as *Nkuzi* or are pertinent to understanding *Nkuzi*. Let me explain these African Igbo proverbs in relation to *Hope (as Nkuzi)*:

a) "The smaller the lizard the greater the hope of becoming a crocodile."[70] This proverb means that one's personal condition of being will determine the quality of aspiration to become great or to excel. Hope lies in the beyond. The beyond is not necessarily that which is temporally distant. It is an interior quality and interior longing).

b) "Hope is a good thing and good things never die." It means that hope is intrinsically associated with being and the good. Hope is the interior longing or aspiration of being. Being-in-fullest is the aspiration of all beings.

c) "With a little seed of imagination you can grow a field of hope." It means that desire or imagination of being brings hope, and to hope/hoping is at the core of being. Every being has the spark or seed of hope. Imagination[71] is the "core" of being itself. It is the essence of being and hoping.

d) "Your greatest hope is your greatest fear." It means that life teaches us through the challenges in the moments of our lives. Our hope is the task of our being. We become our hopes. But what we become is not external or superficial to us. Our hopes are our internal (necessary) aspirations. Our aspirations challenge us in order to actualize ourselves to the fullest. Self-actualization is not to accomplish superfluity or that which is beyond being or human essence, core or *Kpim*.

---

[70] Professor Ikechukwu Anthony Kanu (an APGC research colleague) used this proverb during our July 24th, 2020 international conference on "From Discomfort to Hope" hosted by Alternative Perspectives and Global Concerns (APGC) Research Organization based in Ottawa, Ontario, Canada.

[71] In this case, imagination is not fantasy or the ability to use or combine past 'ideas.' Imagination is the transcendency of being.

KPIM and Ontology: *Nkuzi* (teaching/education) as the 'Kpim' of Life's Teaching or Social Learning

Nkuzi/Education/*Paideia*, like any other human activities, cannot escape the realm of ontology/metaphysics or being. Ontology/Metaphysics, the ultimate reality or innermost essence, is central to any concept of education because it is important that any educational program be based upon fact and reality rather than on fancy, illusion (as sources of despair, helplessness and hopelessness). As earlier pointed out, I am of the view that there is an ontological desire for truth in us. The knowledge/quest/desire of the truth is the same for all rational beings. There is no desire for that which is false or fake in African Igbo notion of *Nkuzi*. *Nkuzi* is always for the truth, the truth of/about life. *Nkuzi* is focused on the life of purpose. The ontological and anthropological aspects of hope are especially important for educators because they are dealing with human beings (as part of reality). *Nkuzi*/Education/*Paideia* and educational process address the epistemological notion of hope (*Hope as Nkuzi*) without overlooking the ontological (the real essence of things) and anthropological (the real services/purposes of things for humanity or human wellbeing) dimensions of hope. At the foundation of African Igbo *Nkuzi*/education or life-long social learning is the understanding of the truth about being/reality or life itself.

I will take a brief look at Chinua Achebe's *Things Fall Apart* to highlight the inherent relationship or dynamism between 'Hope as *Nkuzi*' and 'Hope as *Ìhè*'(include Hope as *Nchekwube* or *Olileanya*) in African Igbo Ontology, and African Igbo language.

Language: Hope as *NKUZI* in Personhood

African Igbo notion of hope could be discerned in the richness of the ontology or metaphysics of beauty. At the core of the concept of beauty or the beautiful is hopefulness, disclosure, light, truth, reality, etc. In African Igbo language 'mma' (*mara mma*—beautiful)[72] is associated with disclosure, truth, reality and hope (to be and to continue to be real). The notion of *Mmadu* (Igbo word for person—as 'the beauty of life') is related to disclosure, truth, reality, and what makes life hopeful. The beautiful makes life hopeful or worth-living. The beautiful is a 'hopeful' pointer to Beauty itself. Beauty makes 'the beautiful' possible. The Greek word for the beautiful is 'kalon'. Beauty could be

---

[72] See my reflection above on African Igbo notion of the person as the beauty of life (mma, mma ndu, madu).

expressed in German as 'schön'--adjective for beautiful, 'die Schönheit'--noun for beauty. For these different languages, the essence (the inner meaning) of the beautiful is expressible or communicable by the respective languages in their own ways. That means there is an inner dimension to language. Our languages express reality or being (language is ontology and ontological). Like Hans-Georg Gadamer the being that is understood is language. Language speaks us. Language or the ability to language comes through *Nkuzi* (teaching, education, cultivating/cultivate, discipline, upbringing, awareness creation, etc.) Hope as *Ìhè* [Ontology] and *Nkuzi* are united in the notion that language (*Okwu* in Igbo)[73] comes through *Nkuzi* (but *Nkuzi* understands/explains life as being/ontology). One truly knows 'being' through, and in, language. Language reveals this being of things.

Language is understood through *Nkuzi*. *Nkuzi* is possible through language. Language (Okwu) and *Nkuzi* are indissociable. *Nkuzi* makes reality become truly present. This present-ness of reality is the realization of hope or what is hoped for. *Nkuzi* makes hope real. *Nkuzi* gives hope. Hope as *Nkuzi* is the realization of self/personhood and reality through experience (not merely experimentation or repetition of a process).

In light of the above, hope as *Nkuzi* discloses understanding and meaning of reality, truth, knowledge and African Igbo notion of 'Hope' (Nchekwube or Olileanya), which emerges through the *Nkuzi* (teaching experience or social learning) of life. Germans will relate this sense of hope as coming through experience or lived-experience (*Erfahrung* or *Erlebenis*). It is also basically 'Bildung' (formation that gives hope, skilled in the hope for self-and-communal-sustainability) in German. In this sense, the purpose of experience is to gain knowledge and understand life/reality. This knowledge or understanding of reality (nature of reality) is also the reward of hope. In *Hans-Georg Gadamer and African Hermeneutic Philosophy*, I explained "Bildung" as "formation or education in the development of human culture and understanding of self. 'Bildung' points to a continual process or movement."[74]

---

[73] *Okwu Igbo* (African Igbo language), *Okwu Bekee* (English or European persons' language), and *Okwu ndi obodo ozo* (a foreign language). *Okwu* is also 'word' or 'logos' or 'being' or 'reality.'
[74] S. U. Anozie, *Hans-Georg Gadamer and African Hermeneutic Philosophy*, p. 99.

Hope and *CHI* (Creative Being) Phenomenon in African Igbo Ontology (ontological and pedagogical hope)

The dynamism between Hope as *Nkuzi*, Hope as *Ìhè* and Hope as *Nchekwube* or *Olileanya* in Achebe's *Things Fall Apart* is hermeneutically enriching. Okonkwo (Achebe's main character) operated within his own structure of hope (nature of being). This structure of hope essentially aligns with African Igbo notion of 'Chi' (God) or 'Chi-onye' or 'chi' (personal guardian). One's *chi* or *Chi* itself determines the 'structure of hope' (nature of being) of the person. This structure of hope is related to 'Ihe' (light or the disclosure of the individual person or group). In order to further explain this personal structure of hope arising from African Igbo names and life-world, I will take a look at Okonkwo's tragedy and hope in *Things Fall Apart*.

In African Igbo societies, Igbo names communicate the message of hope (*Ìhè*, *Nchekwube*, disclosure or light) in the being and names of their bearer. In *Things Fall Apart*, names like *Ikemefuna* (meaning--May my strength not be lost), *Okonkwo* (meaning--A male child born on Nkwo[75] market day). *Nneka* (meaning--Mother is superior or precious), etc. have deeper hermeneutical implications or bear hermeneutical weight in understanding the context and the specific message of truthfulness, reality and hope in the becoming or unfolding of the totality of reality in African Igbo world. Beyond *Things Fall Apart*, names like *Ndukaku* (meaning--Life is more than wealth) resonate with the idea that life gives hope. Life is more than wealth or riches. *Ndudiri* (meaning--As long as there is life, then there is hope or if there is life, then there is hope) affirms this appreciation of life as a hope-filled one. Other African Igbo names like *Ugo-ndu* (meaning--The beauty/splendor on life) draws on the beauty of life emphasized in African Igbo notion of hope and person (as the beauty of life). *Uju-ndu* (meaning--The fullness of life) is also a name that builds on the foundation of hope and hopefulness. *Uju-ndu* is the goal of life of hope. To be happy is to live in *Uju-ndu*. *Uju-ndu* is happiness and it is also hopefulness. *Uche* or *Uchechukwu* (meaning--The Will of God) is another interesting African Igbo name that captures the idea of Hope as *Nkuzi*. Hope is fulfilled through the 'Will of God' (God as *Chi-ka* or the highest of being/fullness of being or pure being). It is only what is hopeful and truthful that gets fully fulfilled in African Igbo worldviews and literature.

The literature of a people gives one a new perspective of understanding their philosophy of life and hope. For instance, the interpretation of some

---

[75] African Igbo worldview recognizes 4 market days: Eke, Orie, Afor, and Nkwo.

African Igbo names, the hermeneutics of the notion of *Chi* --as individual fate in understanding tragedy remains for us an on-going hermeneutical project. In Okonkwo's tragic experience and that of his community, the following African Igbo proverbs were helpful to communicate African Igbo structure of hope or sense of hope as *Nchekwube* or *Olileanya*. The notion of *Chi* is necessarily tied to this hermeneutics of hope and hopefulness. This necessity is emphasized on the point that life itself is a gift. It is a gift that one has to allow to unfold till the end—the revelation of reality (fullness of life and happiness). Here are some African Igbo proverbs with *Chi* (as creative being/force or fate) that resonate with Hope or Hopefulness. For instance,

a) *Chi onye adighi n'izu ma mmadu egbuna ya* (meaning--If one's *Chi* [fate or destiny] is not in agreement, nobody can kill him). This means that 'Chi' (Fate, Creative Force or God) does not conspire against us or undermine our essential nature or self-actualizations. There is hope of success as long as the creative force or fate is on our side.

b) *Omere ma chi ekweghi ndi uta atala ya* (meaning--Whoever that has tried his/her best should not be blamed.) In relation to hope, *Chi* (fate or creative force) guarantees what we hope for and what we strive for. One cannot accomplish more than he/she is destined for. What one accomplishes is part of hope as *Nkuzi* and hope as *Nchekwube* or *Olileanya*. Achebe provides some other proverbs helpful in explaining hope as *Nkuzi* and hope as *Nchekwube* or *Olileanya*.

c) *Dinta muta igba agaghi, eneka amuta ufe akwusighi* (meaning---Men/Hunters have learned to shoot without missing their mark and I [Eneka, the bird] have learned to fly without perching on a twig). That was Eneka/the bird's response when it was asked why it was always on the wing. The hermeneutics of this proverb is on the question of hope and hopefulness. For the bird (Eneka) there is always a solution (hope) to every situation or problem. There is always a way out of every tough or life-threatening situation. Hope is associated with optimism out of a tough or an unpleasant situation. Hope is associated with the ability to adapt or adaptability for excellence. The challenges of life are not fully predictable but human beings can adapt to fulfill their essence or purposeful goals through their structure of hope.

Hope and Tragedy: the Structure of Hope for Achebe's Okonkwo

The African Igbo people use proverbs to express the wisdom of their communities, the traditions that must be handed down or transmitted through direct application in narratives (oral or written). Proverbs help provide the clearness that narratives seek to communicate.

In chapter fourteen of Achebe's *Things Fall Apart* a proverb was used. It says, "[I]f a man said yea his *chi* also affirmed."[76] This proverb illustrates the double aspects of human existence. The double aspects are the divine and the human aspects of existence of hope. For a person to accomplish anything in African Igbo worldviews he/she must live in accord with his/her destiny or fate, and learn from the experience in line with his/her destiny. Destiny or fate is appreciated with hope for the good (even when the seeming bad thing happens or is the outcome). Every incident is hopeful experience as long as it is within the structure of existence of a person or a community, and facilitated by the divine (*Chi okike* or creative being). Some African Igbo people associated this *Chi okike* or *Chi-ka* (He who is the greatest. He is the greatest being that guarantees hope) to *Osebuluwa/Oliseburuwa* (The Being/He who holds the world/universe).[77] Existence involves an unpredictable aspect, which implies that a person has to first accept that he/she is capable of accomplishing a task before one's *Chi* (personal god or guardian) concurs with the same task.

A further discussion of the role of *Chi*[78] in African Igbo worldviews is necessary because of *Chi*'s place in their proverbs and in the events that happen in people's life. A subtle but important distinction to note here is that *Chi* is started with a capital letter to associate it with Igbo religion (as respect to the divine or a higher being or source of being).[79] However, I will retain the use of *chi* (starting with small letter) as is in Achebe's book. They both mean the same thing. For the Igbo, according to Christian Anieke, *Chi* is an important concept in traditional society. It is defined as personal destiny or personalized providence "of the individual which shapes their history and destiny. Some see *Chi* as a divine emanation from...which is responsible for the individual's fate

---

[76] Chinua Achebe, *Things Fall Apart*, Canada, Anchor Canada edition, 2009, p. 131. See Chinua Achebe, *Things Fall Apart*, London, Heinemann, 1958, p. 165.
[77] Professor Ikechukwu Anthony Kanu brought this to my attention. He translated it as 'He who holds the world.'
[78] S. U. Anozie, *Hans-Georg Gadamer and African Hermeneutic Philosophy*, pp. 237-243.
[79] I chose to capitalize '*Chi*' considering its religious connotation in African Igbo thought. The role of *Chi* or fate is essential in Okonkwo's tragedy.

or destiny."[80] The complexity of meanings about the specific role of the *Chi* is still present in the statement made above. But *Chi* involves element of both fate and faith (personal duty blessed by one's *Chi*),[81] in terms of the support one receives from the gods in order to succeed or in hope to succeed in one's individual task. It is in this sense that *Chi's* role could also imply the task of a mediator (a personal guardian[82], a giver of hope or 'destiny helper'—as is currently used in contemporary Christianized African-Igbo narratives).

One's relationship to the Supreme Being (*Chi ka* or *Chi-okike*) is determined by one's relations to his/her *Chi*. Since *Chi* is only an individual relationship, rather than universal, there could be a lucky person (with a good luck *Chi* [*Chioma*] for hope as *Nkuzi* and *Nchekwube/Olileanya*) or even a bad luck person (with bad luck *Chi* [*Chiojoo*] in hope as *Nkuzi*). This reminds us about the place of predestination and freewill in African Igbo traditional world. In relation to the above, there are other proverbs among African Igbo that affirm predestination. For example: *Omere ma chi ekweghi ndi uta atala ya* (He/She that has done his/her best should not blame his/herself if there are failures). It means that we all have our limitations of success. Our hope is always to put in our own and unique best. Another African Igbo proverb says: *Onye kwe ma chi ya ekweghi, o ga-egbu onwe ya?*[83] (It means if one says yes and his/her *Chi* disagrees, should one commit suicide? It also means that one should be positive-minded and hopeful). The second aspect/statement of the proverb above: '*o ga-egbu onwe ya?*' (Should one commit suicide?) aligns with the culture of hope and hopefulness. There is always a possibility that each person's *Chi* (personal god or guardian) could help reverse a tragic situation to become a fortunate or fulfilling or hopeful one.

In Achebe's *Things Fall Apart*, when some of the people of the community referred to Okonkwo as one who is pushing his luck and desperate with the gods, Achebe describes the scene in a proverbial manner, "people said he (Okonkwo) had no respect for the gods of his clan. His enemies said his good fortune had gone to his head. They called him the little bird *nza* (Igbo name for a

---

[80] Christian Anieke, *Problems of Intercultural Communication and Understanding in Achebe's Representation of the Igbo and their Culture*, Enugu, Mbaeze Printing Press, 2008, p. 34. See Pauline Aligwekwe, *Continuity of Traditional Values, The Igbo of Nigeria*, Owerri, 1991, p. 173. See Elizabeth Isichei, *A History of the Igbo People*, London, The Macmillan Press, 1976, p. 75.

[81] Raphael Okechukwu Madu, *African Symbols, Proverbs and Myths: The Hermeneutics of Destiny*, New York, Peter Lang: 1996, p. 183.

[82] S. U. Anozie, *Hans-Georg Gadamer and African Hermeneutic Philosophy*, p. 237.

[83] *Ibidem*, p. 242.

small bird) who so far forgot himself after a heavy meal that he challenged his *chi*."[84] The essence of the *Chi* proverbs in the narrative is to sharpen the image of the hero (Okonkwo) and clearly present the depth of his struggles [with fate.] This same situation is reinforced through other *Chi* proverbs (in chapter fourteen) when Okonkwo returned to his community after his exile of seven years. Achebe's text presents it thus:

> Clearly his personal god or *chi* was not made for great things. A man could not rise beyond the destiny of his *chi*. The saying of the elders was not true-that if a man said yea his *chi* also affirmed. Here was a man whose *chi* said nay despite his own affirmation.[85]

Okonkwo's character clearly surfaces at the stages of his life and within his quest for heroic status. Achebe paints a picture of a man who easily forgets and who hopes that the best has been set for him by destiny. While in exile Okonkwo's accomplishments grew and after his return to Umuofia things seem to improve for him. People felt "that his *chi* [fate or god] might now be making amends for the past disaster"[86] (in chapter twenty). It appears that the gods could change their mind and make things better or hopeful. In normal parlance, only finite human being could "be making amends."[87] I think Okonkwo could not change his own fate by himself alone without the higher approval of his *Chi*. If this is the case, it is in agreement with the line "that his *chi* might now be making amends for the past disaster."[88] (in chapter twenty).[89] I will add that Okonkwo's *Chi* addressed or made amends, and so that implied the culture of hope and hopefulness in his community. I shall now proceed to present the African Igbo notion of *Chi* as a core ontological concept since I have discussed about some '*chi*' proverbs that reflect hope and hopefulness.

---

[84] C. Achebe, *Things Fall Apart*, p. 31. See Chinua Achebe, *Things Fall Apart* London, Heinemann, 1958, p. 26.
[85] *Ibidem*, p. 131.
[86] *Ibidem*, p. 172. See C. Achebe, *Things Fall Apart*, London: Heinemann, 1958, p. 154.
[87] *Ibidem*.
[88] *Ibidem*
[89] This is my reading of that line to express only a wish or a possibility for Okonkwo. Lindfors affirms the complex nature proverbs. There are proverbs that express different views on the same issue. Bernth Lindfors, "The Palm-oil with which Achebe's Words are Eaten", in Francis Abiola Irele (ed.), *Chinua Achebe Things Fall Apart (Authoritative Text, Contexts and Criticism)*, New York, W. W. Norton & Company, 2009, p. 561.

C) Hope as *NCHEKWUBE/OLILEANYA* and African Igbo Notion of *CHI* Implies Hope (Ontological and Anthropological Hope)

In African Igbo lifeworld, *Ihe-bu-ihe* means ultimate entity, main thing, the essential being or ultimate entity. *Ihe-bu-ihe* reflects 'Nchekwube' or 'Olileanya' (looking forward to, 'expecting positive results or outcomes' based on the fact that the most real or the essential being or necessary being makes the real possible). This could be related to Necessary Being and Contingent beings' discussions (ontological and anthropological hope). The Necessary Being (*Chi, Chi-na-eke, Oseburuwa*) makes hope possible for contingent beings. In the Necessary Being is hope fulfilled for contingent beings. Contingent beings are historical beings. *Nchekwube* or *Olileanya* is part of our historical nature as contingent beings. *Nchekwube* or *Olileanya* implies contingency. It is the hope that emerges at the culmination of our historical beingness, within the universal history (that includes the African Igbo historical consciousness).

African Igbo notion of *Chi* is a generative theme for my reflections on *Nchekwube* or *Olileanya* (Hope). Hope is part of African Igbo people's historical consciousness and experience. In Achebe's *Things Fall Apart*, Obierika, Okonkwo's friend, remonstrates that the new culture/civilization and religion has sent Okonkwo to an early grave. This argument suggests that Okonkwo through the narrative did not see any reason to act contrary to the wish of the gods and goddesses of his land. It is rather Okonkwo's fate or destiny or *Chi* that saw him end his life in tragedy. A person's *chi* (personal god or guardian or a mediator of hope) is a basic condition for hope in success. In my view, "[S]uccess or failure in life is measured in Igbo worldviews according to how one lived with one's destiny or…*Chi. Chi* defines an individual's personal destiny and the role of providence."[90]

The set goals or purposes of one's existence are simply what we all 'hope for.' What we hope for is part of the meaning of life or meaning of reality in African Igbo worldview. There is the presence of fate and personal decisions approved by one's *Chi*. One needs the support of his god to succeed in one's task. The *Chi* also acts as a mediator. A 'mediator' brings hope and resolution. Igbo say that: *Ebe onye dara ka chi kwaturu ya*--meaning--Where one falls, is where his/her God pushed him/her down. Another African Igbo proverb states: *Agbisi gba otule, ya amuru ako*--meaning--When the black ant stings the

---

[90] C. Anieke, *Problems of Intercultural Communication and Understanding in Achebe's Representation of the Igbo and their Culture*, p. 34.

buttocks, next time the [buttocks] learns wisdom. (It means that if things have not happened to a person, he/she does not develop wisdom or, simply put, experience is the best teacher).

Following the above, my two hermeneutical conclusions are: first, Okonkwo was faithful to his *Chi* and to the Oracle and, second, Okonkwo's success was from his *Chi* (and so fate, fate lived with hope) and not necessarily from his hard work. His seeming 'personal' tragedy is a tragedy that has befallen Umuofia as a community going through the actual intercultural hopelessness or crisis. Of course it is a communal tragedy experience but it is not one without hope or *Nchekwube/Olileanya*. For African Igbos there is no insurmountable challenge or tragedy as long as one or the community recognized the interconnectedness of all things under the *Chi* (of human history). It is also in this similar sense that dialectics in Western philosophy is essentially a system of hope, of revival, of renewal or renaissance or rebirth. Every worldview is part of the whole view of the world in dialectics of hope (like the process of *Aufhebung*—in German 'to cancel', 'to preserve,' 'to raise up' or 'to sublate'). This is form of contiguity in African Igbo worldview of hope or in hopefulness of actualized reality or existence. We live in ontological hope or hopefulness. For where there is life, there is hope, or, if there is life, then there is hope--*Ndu diri, olileanya di or Ebe ndu di, olileanya di*). To live is to Hope! Existence and Hopefulness are not mutually exclusive in African Igbo lifeworld.

Conclusion

At the influence of Achebe and Iroegbu, as pre-eminent and unassuming African Igbo scholars, I have articulated African Igbo ontology of hope using three generative themes of: a) Hope as **Ìhè** (Light of Hope. The light at the end of the tunnel) (ontological hope), b) Hope as **Nkuzi** (Life's teaching or social learning, the experience of life forms humanity) (epistemological/pedagogical hope), and c) Hope as **Nchekwube** or **Olileanya** (including, *Nchekwubechi, Olileanyachi, Echi-di-ime*--Tomorrow has promises. Tomorrow is a day of hope or a day to be hopeful) (anthropological hope). *Nkuzi* makes reality become truly present. This present-ness of reality is the realization of hope or what is hoped for. *Nkuzi* makes hope real. *Nkuzi* gives hope. Hope as *Nkuzi* is the realization of self/personhood and reality through experience (not merely through experimentation). This experience comes from the 'craft' or 'formation' or 'molding' or 'upbringing' that goes with *Nkuzi*. *Nkuzi* is not an abuse or should not be intended to defile/dehumanize the other person (student). Our existential humanity is part of the unfolding of the totality of reality (Hope as *Ihe/Ìhè* --- reality or light that reveals reality). Unfolding of reality is the actualization of the fullness of humanity or the fullness of human becoming (anthropological hope). These 3 generative themes on hope are intrinsically interconnected in African Igbo Ontology or worldviews.

Reference List

Achebe, Chinua, *Things Fall Apart*, Canada, Anchor Canada edition, 2009.

Anieke, Christian, Problems of Intercultural Communication and Understanding in Achebe's Representation of the Igbo and their Culture, Enugu, Mbaeze Printing Press, 2008.

Anozie, Stanley Uche, *Hans-Georg Gadamer and African Hermeneutic Philosophy*, Chisinau, Generis Publishing, 2020.

---------"The Problem of Evil in Plato and Gadamerian Plato", *Revue Roumaine de Philosophie*, 66, 1, 2019, pp. 116-129.

Iroegbu, Pantaleon, *Metaphysics: The Kpim of Philosophy*, Owerri, International University Press, 1995.

---------*Kpim of Theodicy Proving the Existence of God Via Hermeholiontica*, Ibadan, Hope Publications, 2002.

Iroegbu, Pantaleon; Izibili, M.A, *Kpim of Democracy Thematic Introduction to Socio-Political Philosophy*, Benin City, Ever-Blessed Publishers, 2004.

Iroegbu, Pantaleon, "Philosophy of Education: Ethics of Teaching profession", in Pantaleon Iroegbu; A. Echekube, (eds.), *Kpim of Morality: General, Special & Professional* Ibadan, Heinemann Educational Books, 2005, p. 221

Lindfors, Bernth, "The Palm-oil with which Achebe's Words are Eaten", in Francis Abiola Irele (ed.), *Chinua Achebe Things Fall Apart (Authoritative Text, Contexts and Criticism)*, New York, W. W. Norton & Company, 2009, pp. 560-561.

Madu, Raphael Okechukwu, *African Symbols, Proverbs and Myths: The Hermeneutics of Destiny*, New York, Peter Lang: 1996.

Part II:
African Hermeneutics of Culture and Spirituality/Esotericism

Chapter 4
The Paradox of Non-Violent Religions and Violent Cultural Practices: Igbo Nigeria Africans

Stanley Uche Anozie

(Peterborough, Ontario, Canada, 2017)

Abstract. In Igbo practice of African Tradition Religions, there is a paradox of violent cultural practices found at the background of "I-We" or Ubuntu religio-cultural principles. The individual citizens of the community are under domination and fear/terror coming from groups like Okonko, Ekete-nsi, Okoroshi/Owu initiates.

The un-initiated innocent citizens become victims of systematic violent activities or a form of institutional or structural terrorism (victims of recognized socio-cultural institutions). It is the primary duty of government and those in charge of our traditional institutions (religious and cultural) to guarantee the rule of law, protect human rights, and provide security. As a community, we could still review some of cultural groups/institutions and their practices that may support violence so as to discourage every negative influence on our youth.

Keywords: Structural terrorism, initiated, traditional religions, ubuntu (care and respect), I-Thou, I-We, paradox, contradictions, violence, Igbo people

Introduction

This paper takes a descriptive and interpretive approach to what is recognized as African Traditional Religions. African Traditional religions are not uniformly practiced. Africans do not worship God, the gods/goddesses, and ancestors for mystical and spiritual purposes. As Africans, our acts of worship "are pragmatic and utilitarian" (Mbiti, 1969, p. 4). The notion of religion in Igbo

(Africans) tradition involves manipulation for human well-being (Ebeogu, 1983p. 74).

My critical enquiry of African Traditional Religions presents the complex non-violent religious practices of Igbo people of Southeastern Nigeria. African Traditional Religions accept that everyone is respected and believed to share in the common brother or sister-hood. This is the basis of the principle of "I am because We are" (I-We [I-Thou] relationship), or the principle of *Ubuntu* (ethic of brotherhood and respect). At the same time, unfortunately, there is a paradox of violent cultural practices found at the background of "I-We," or *Ubuntu,* religio-cultural principles.

Could such paradoxical cultural practices by the youth (platonic guardians in violent activities) be classified as a form of structural terrorism in a democratic world? How do we explain this paradox in regard to the emergence of new facts about contemporary terrorism?

The Religious and Socio-Cultural Principle of "I am because We are" (Ubuntu)

Ubuntu is an African Bantu word. South African, Desmond Tutu, describes *ubuntu* as the essence or quiddity of our being human. We share in a common humanity. "I am because we are," bound up in each other. *Ubuntu* involves hospitality, generosity, availability, and affirmation of the other. In principle, what dehumanizes the other, dehumanizes us.

Ubuntu is similar to what the Igbo understand as "Umunna" (another Igbo word for I-We community).But anyone outside this Umunna (Community) could experience possible violence from/by a group for its selfish purposes. Some cultural practices could become violent with time. The limited application of a rather "universal" and "perfect" *ubuntu,* or "I-We" principle, has led to violent, fearful, and terrorist acts. But then, principles are naturally distinct from the implementation or practice of principles.

In order to portray how some of these principles apply in daily lives, African scholars developed a notion of person, in which traditional African elements, as well as the idea of an individual with human rights, are respected. Following development of this notion, concepts like: individual, human rights, mutuality, and interpersonal community, need an African philosophy of the person which centers on "I am because we are, and since we are, therefore I am"

(Mbiti, 1969, p. 113). African society puts more emphasis on the community than on the individual person or personhood (Senghor, 1964, pp. 93-94).

Personhood implies being in human community and it is rooted "in an ongoing human community" (Menkiti, 1984, pp. 171-172). The community takes precedence over the individual without necessarily obliterating the person. In the community the individual person genuinely thrives. Benezet Bujo, argues that the "I-We" person and community philosophical thought, "within the African context, makes it clear that the individual is an incomplete being who is basically dependent on the community" (1998, p. 148).The concern is that the communitarian notion of person may limit or undermine the inviolable rights and dignity of the person as an individual (Gyekye, 1992, p.102; Njoku, 2004, pp. 154-155). Let us take a look at Igbo (African) consideration of person.

Igbo African Philosophical Thought on Person and the "I-We"

a) *Person as the Beauty of Life*

According to the Igbo of Southeastern Nigeria (Africa), "human being" and "person" are used interchangeably. Human being and person are the same. So it is for most African communities and nations. The Igbo (Ibo) articulate person as "Mmadu," which comes from the combination of "Mma" (Beauty), and "Ndu" (Life); that is, "The Beauty of Life." Both will give this literary concept of person as the beauty of life or an expression of the totality of beauty of all things. A metaphysical analysis of this concept of person hinges on person as having a transcendental connection to "Beauty," which for philosophers like Aristotle, Thomas of Aquinas, and Kant, is an essential transcendental quality of being (One, Truth, Good, Beauty). Thomas of Aquinas sees it in terms of perfection (beauty goes with perfection). Njoku notes that persons "are the beauty of earthly life, and as a home beauty" (Njoku, 2004, p. 163).

The association of person and beauty is philosophically and mutually enriching. This is because only beauty, per se, can truly reveal itself. If person is described within this context, then "person as beauty of life" does give a sense of manifestation, presence, and openness. This, in a way, relates to the Heideggerian notion of Da-sein as the being that stands out, discloses, or reveals itself. It is that "whose essential structures are centered in disclosedness" (Heidegger, 1996, p. 18; p. 20; p. 231). This notion attributed to the meaning of *person* is common for Africans.

The African notion of person connects to the metaphysical. Person has the spiritual (transcendental) and the physical (material or bodily) aspects. This fact makes it difficult to solely discuss person from a materialist perspective (which sees person as matter), while also explaining soul as a special form of matter. African philosophical thought conceives of person as an ensemble of spirit, soul and body. Thus, person is not only matter, but a totality of spiritual and material aspects. Richard C. Onwuanibe, further explains: "The Ibo [Igbo] notions of soul (mkpuru obi) and spirit (mmuo), as essential aspects of man, bear out the transcendence of the human person from the metaphysical point of view" (1984, p. 185). African philosophical thought sees a person, no matter what his/her circumstances in life, as a person with transcendence (spirit, the beyond), potentiality, dignity and relational nature.

b) *Person as Relational (I am because we are)*

African person philosophy paradigm centres on "I am because we are, and since we are therefore I am" (Mbiti, 1969, p. 113). This philosophical paradigm reflects the essential principle that underlines what person is and what community means for the African. Both reflect the notions of being, the self-conscious and unique individual, as well as the relation-bound person in terms of the community of persons. The analysis of such a philosophical paradigm does not depend on the postulation of independent rational beings, but on an independent being that is as well dependent because of his/her intrinsic relational nature. One does not lose his/her individuality by becoming a person living in human community. The effects of an over-bearing precedence of community, over the individual person, are often obvious and cause reactionary quests for individualist alternatives. Benezet Bujo, however, in defense of "I-We" person, and community philosophical thought, explains that: "because there is interdependence between the community and the individual, the community must not subordinate what is particular, but should promote and support it" (Bujo,1998, p. 148). This concept of the "I-We" is based on dialogue and reciprocity. Senghor clarifies that some ethnologists acknowledge the unity, and the harmony that are "based both on the community and on the person" (Senghor, 1995, p. 50; Gyekye, 1992, p. 101). The relevance and possibility of a true "I-We" person, is one based on the classical philosophical argument in the Igbo African concept of person, in terms of the I-Thou relation, as a dialogical and necessary relation. The genuine "We," like the "I-Thou," involves also an essential relation of persons, but the "I-It" relation, is one of manipulation, exploitation, use, domination, and fear. In other words, the "I-Thou" relation, not the "I-It", leads to a genuine African I-We, or sometimes rendered as "essential We" (Dzobo, 1992, p. 229). The "essential We," or a genuine "I-We" community, means there has to be an authentic recognition of the other as a Thou or person with dignity and potential. Within the community, the individual relates with others in the context of the common good required for a genuine "I-We" community (healthy, non-oppressive, non-violent community).

Having carefully presented African non-violent notion of person and community, let me now develop the issue of paradox in violent cultural practices among the Igbo.

The Paradox: Violent Cultural Practices

An ethnic group or people may see as normal, the conflicting activities or contradictions that form the essential part of their existence (Gikandi, 1991 p. 38). This includes the conscious acceptance of both non-violent religious principles and conflicting violent cultural practices.

Violence involves the use of force to accomplish a purpose. Violence could be individual or collective. David G. Bromley and J. Gordon Melton (2002) affirm that collective violent actions include war, revolution, repression, terrorism, etc. In these cases, violence is relational and processual. Collective violent acts could be committed by individuals, but that does not mean that they are mere individual violent acts. They are rather committed in the name of the movement or a control agent. These violent actions, as collective violence, are done for some organizational purpose. Collective violence does not mean that there has to be a consensus (Bromley,& Melton, 2002, pp. 1-10). This notion of collective violence is at the basis of my thesis. My analysis addresses the argument that there are only individual actions committed in the frenzy of youthful excitement and not an organized action for an organizational interest. Another point is: we are discussing violent cultural practices and not individual violent actions. Culture includes values, attitudes, and assumptions of a group of people in a given period. What is cultural violence? David Hoegberg (2011) says that cultural violence:

> refers to violence that is encouraged by the beliefs and traditions of a given culture and practiced upon its own members. "Cultural violence" used in this sense would include ritual sacrifices,

punishments for crimes, and other kinds of communally sanctioned violence. Often, the communal sanction given to acts of violence springs from unexamined assumptions and contradictions within the culture and shared by a majority of its members. (p. 145)

A look at some examples of "communally sanctioned" (Hoegberg, 2001, p. 145) violent cultural practices among the Igbo is now necessary.

Religio-Cultural Rituals

Some of the violent cultural practices in Igbo culture include the rites of burial of kings, and of community warriors. These rites require the killing of people for the burial of dead kings or warriors. Through the violent activities of traditional masquerade groups or "secret societies" recognized in the community, human heads are used as a part of cult worship. The groups usually swear to secrecy. The groups are also used to serve the interests of the elders, as the "platonic guardians" of the community, with little respect for the rights of the individual through dialogue. The interests of the traditional institution or community of elders instills a domination, fear, and terror over the individual citizens of the community (Wiredu, 1997, p. 40).

Solomon O. Iyasere (2009) explains a form of violent activities that could be supported by the demands of African religions and societies. As he notes, "the peace of the tribe as a whole takes precedence over personal considerations. The decrees of the gods are always carried out with dispatch, even if it means a ruthless violation of human impulses" (2009, pp. 372-373). The question that comes to mind is what exactly is the "peace of the tribe"? Could the wishes of the elders or a select group be the only basis for determining the way to "the peace of the tribe"? Such violent religio-cultural activities, believed to be sanctioned by the gods of the land and elders, could be classified as terrorism in a democratic world, since secret youth groups use domination, terror, or fear to accomplish some socio-cultural-political advantages for themselves. The un-initiated innocent citizens become victims of systematic violent activities or a form of structural terrorism.

Let me briefly highlight the violent activities of some Igbo youth groups during cultural festivals.

The Ekete-nsi Festival

This is an aspect of the harvest festivities, called New Yam festival, that takes place in Igboland, especially in Bende communities in Abia State, Southeastern Nigeria. According to oral tradition, during the Ekete-nsi festival the initiated youth members participate in the Imere-ogwu (invocation of potency or medicinal reinforcement). It involves invocation of some magical powers. There is also Abba (white substance) used to attack people by feeding them with an overdose. It could be considered as a drug but one has to remember that we are describing a secret event and material used. Abba could also be described as food for the secret group members during the festival season. The young people (while in a kind of trance) seek to have a sufficient supply of Abba (magic potency, spirit food, etc.) from the spirit world of the ancestors. Abba could kill when it is too much in an individual. Membership to the Ekete-nsi group is not forced. Young people join when they are about fifteen years old. They are initiated through the Ituanya (initiation) ceremony.

The Ituanya - initiation ceremony - requires Okuko (fowl) and Mmaya (palm wine). These are used for the initiation rite (The word "Ituanya" is literally translated as "eyes washing"; Igbo translation - Isa Anya or Itu Anya. Kwasi Wiredu (1997), a Ghanaian philosopher, similarly reflects on "eyes washing," which he better describes as "medicinally reinforced eyes" (p. 38). He says:

> [C]ertainly, 'spirits' are regarded as being out of the ordinary, but they are not felt to be out of this world. Moreover - so the belief goes - they can actually be seen and communicated with by those who have medicinally reinforced eyes and appropriate resources of communications. (p. 38).

Ituanya includes a form of purification done in the market place, in the forest, and in wrestling contests with spirits (most likely bad or dangerous spirits) to acquire power. Wiredu further makes reference to the power of "spirits" (1997). He observes:

> The "spirits" are credited with the ability to help or harm human beings in ways that surpass the causes and effects familiar in everyday life. For this reason people are careful to try to establish good relations with the more susceptible ones, and this often involves "rituals" replete with supplications sweetened with flattery. (1997, p. 36).

It is only those who have "won" in the wrestling contests with the spirits who get to join the Ekete-nsi group. These encounters are not within the levels of scientific proofs. But it is akin to military training and graduation to the using of weapons or operating equipment.

There is the aspect of "Ifo-ogwu" (literally translated as procurement of herbs or magical powers per the initiation). As the tradition holds, when one of the newly initiated is in trouble (under attack in the Spirit world), the bare-naked ladies' group helps to release the young male from the often deadly attack. The group can relieve the individual of the "Abba" (white substance) or him to get better.

"Ima-aka" (contest), is an aspect of the Ekete-nsi festival. It involves violent attack and counter-attack contests with medicinal powers etc. The first aspect of the fight mentioned earlier is between men and spirits, while the Ima-aka (discussed here) is between men and men (or the youth group). Elders, parents, and guardians could stop these violent confrontations/wrestling competitions. I relate the contests to Chinua Achebe's (1958) *Things Fall Apart* wrestling match that usually takes place after the harvest season, between communities from Umuofia to Mbaino (these are Achebe's fictional communities; the communities represent true Igbo communities). At this time the people have less work to do and more time to entertain themselves. In other communities in Igboland and there are other festivals.

Owu Festival

Another socio-cultural festival that involves cultural violence is the "Owu" festival in Ogbaku, Owerri, Imo State, in Southeastern Nigeria. It is a yearly festival that marks the end of the farming season (around June when the raining season has taken its full course). The festival includes dancing by the male adults of the community. Women are not allowed to participate in the dance. When a woman participates, she is punished. This chauvinistic cultural practice is an opportunity some young men use to abuse women and other young persons who are not qualified to belong to the group.

The "Ito-nkwa" is an important part of the festival. It is done before the "Owu," and in the night. It is attended only by the male adults of the community. It ushers in the "Owu" festival after sixteen market days. There is a general belief that no man or woman should be seen fighting, stealing, etc., after the Ito-nkwa.

People who are found guilty of such offences are severely punished by the youth group (as Platonic guardians). The masquerade group is used for social control and compelling individuals in the society to comply with socio-cultural and religious traditions of the community (Mkhize, 2010, p. 30).

Let me now use Achebe's (1958) classic Igbo narrative to highlight paradoxes between non-violent religious principles and violent cultural practices.

The Paradox: Achebe's *Things Fall Apart* (1958) and the hermeneutics of the Oracle

Why Achebe's Novel? Achebe's *Things Fall Apart* is one of the most accessible and widely read books about the culture, festivals, religions, thoughts, language, ethno-philosophy, etc., of the Igbo people. It recently celebrated fifty years of its first publication, with about ten million copies sold. It was translated into 50 languages, and is one of the most widely read African literatures. Francis Abiola Irele (1978) considers this historical aspect of Achebe's work as ideal for understanding Igbo culture, thought and religions, including Igbo relationship to deities. Let me offer a brief comment about Igbo deities and then proceed with the relevance of *Things Fall Apart* to this paper.

A Brief Comment on Igbo Deities and Achebe's Things Fall Apart

Amadioha (Igbo literal meaning free will of the people) is the Alusi (god) of thunder and lightning of the Igbo of Nigeria. He is amongst the most popular of Igbo deities. Amadioha is worshipped on Afor day (one of the four-day market days: Eke, Orie, Afor and Nkwo). The calendar year begins in February (Onwa mbu, the 3rd week of February) and ends in January to early February (Onwa uzo alusi) (Angulu, 1981). There are small gods and goddesses in Igbo communities. The gods and goddesses give oracles through their priest or priestess as an essential part of Igbo religious and cultural practices.

Igbo people are very religious but their religious practices involve some puzzles with clear utilitarian reasons. Wiredu agrees that "it is a commonplace of African studies that the African attitude to the spirits, often hyperbolically called 'lesser gods,' is purely utilitarian. Ritualized praise is rendered unto them only because of expected benefits" (1997, p. 39). In relation to 'lesser gods' and 'gods', Wole Soyinka, an African Nobel laureate (at the University of Ghana in 1975), was said to have described Yoruba (another tribe in Nigeria) "gods" as creatures of the Yoruba people. That is, the Yoruba people "create" their own gods (like the god of power or electricity or prosperity) and "[on] occasion kill them" (Wiredu, 1997, p. 39). Africans are described as naturally religious because the worship of God/gods/spirits manifests itself in every aspect of our life. People are unconsciously traditional and religious (Mbiti, 1969, p. 275). In times of natural disasters, famines, internecine warfare, invasions, etc., people resort to religious activities to placate God, or the gods of the land, to find favours. Afam Ebeogu (1983), an Igbo, affirms "paradoxically, the Igbo folk think that the individual can somehow manipulate this personal enigmatic force called chi, and that one's chi is always included to consent to one's wishes" (p. 74). Now to put this project in perspective we consider Achebe's *Things Fall Apart* (1958).

Achebe's *Things Fall Apart* (1958) is a classic book about the life of the Igbo ethnic group and their encounter with Europeans and Western Christian missionaries. It is a fictional novel that corresponds to Igbo reality. Achebe's main aim is to provide a true and correct narrative of his people: the Igbo tribe and their religious practices. Okonkwo, the hero of Umuofia (Achebe's main character), was asked by the community to keep in his care, Ikemefuna, a boy taken as reparation for the killing of a lady from Umuofia. Ikemefuna lived for three years in the household of Okonkwo, so that he almost became a member of the family. Ikemefuna became the best friend of Okonkwo's son, Nwoye. He called Okonkwo his father, having adapted to his new family and community. After three years, the community oracle demanded that Ikemefuna be sacrificed (ritual killing). As it turned out, it was Okonkwo (his adopted father) who killed Ikemefuna when he ran to him for protection. We will explore some examples in Achebe's book.

a) *Violence of Ritual killing*

Ritual killing is part of the Igbo cultural life. It could be religiously sanctioned by the oracles, but often there are alternative sacrifices as recommended by the oracle's chief priest or priestess. Ikemefuna was doomed to be killed for the good of the community. On my view, the boy's ritual killing indicates cultural ethos of the Igbo. The paradox is noticed in Ogbuefi Ezeudu's (a community elder) words to Okonkwo: "[Y]es, Umuofia has decided to kill him [Ikemefuna]. The Oracle of the Hills and the Cave has pronounced it" (Achebe, 2009, p. 57). But did Okonkwo go against the demands of the oracle?

Some cultural scholars and philosophers hold that there is nothing to indicate that Okonkwo violated the demands of the oracle. Okonkwo himself justifies his position: "the Earth cannot punish me for obeying her messenger" (Achebe, 2009, p. 67). In line with this, Alan R. Friesen (2011) interprets: "[Okonkwo was never ordered] to stay out of it, and so cannot be faulted for disobeying an elder by landing the fatal blow [that killed Ikemefuna]" (p. 286). Doing otherwise would have been clearly against the will of the oracle. Wiredu (1997) affirms the likelihood that the gods lack of moral credentials (heard through oracles); the gods could ask for what is ethically questionable or violent. He notes: "the 'gods,'" not unlike the Greek varieties of old, are not of a uniform moral standing: some are good, some bad, others nondescript" (1997, pp. 39-40). For Jude Chudi Okpala (2002), there is precise morality among the gods. In the case of Ikemefuna, he says, "Okonkwo broke the law of the gods…[when]…he killed Ikemefuna"(p. 562). In light of this discourse, the paradox is present because of the enabling forces of violence among the Igbo despite the demands of cordial religious principles in traditional religious rituals. The frequency of cultural violence through human rituals is puzzling. Hoegberg affirms, although the majority of the Igbo people in Achebe's novel have a less violent attitude than Okonkwo, there are "widespread cultural forces that foster violence" (2011, p. 145).

b) *Violence: The Oracle and Peace Week*

Achebe recalls that violence in Igbo culture has gradually receded. When Okonkwo broke the Peace Week ordinance, a village elder, Ogbuefi Ezeudu, says to Okonkwo, "in the past a man who broke the peace was dragged on the ground through the village until he died" (Achebe, 1958 p. 31). These violent practices were stopped because they spoiled the peace which they were meant to preserve. The issue is that between good principle and practices, the event of violence is a sign of disparity between religious principle and cultural practices. Hoegberg affirms this positive non-violent cultural change in *Things Fall Apart*. He observes:

> At a certain point, it occurred to enough people that it made no sense to enforce a rule of non-violence with violence. What are the conditions of possibility for such a cultural change? First, majority

of people must have the freedom and the desire to analyze their traditions for moral and logical consistency. Second, they must see the general principles involved as more valuable than specific rituals or traditions. (2011, p. 146)

Patrick C. Nnoromele (2011) avers that when Okonkwo violated the Peace Week by beating his youngest wife, he accepted "to make offerings as demanded by the custom of Umuofia. In fact, he offered an additional pot of palm-wine" (Achebe, 1996, p. 22). There are alternative ways of placating the gods and goddesses of the land. In like manner, I add, most cultural activities that have violent consequences do have alternative ways of resolving them. That means that resorting to violence is unnecessary. The way of violence multiplies violence.

c) *Cultural Martial Ethos*

In Achebe's (1958) world there is a culture that admires a martial ethos, a form of bravery. It, however, involves a disposition like that of a soldier in the line of duty. A soldier who knows that he/she is in war should be ready for the day's duty. This is the kind of attitude that is typical of Igbo society. People are business minded and ready to show bravery. This situation often gives way to violence, especially towards the not-so-brave people in the community. The mighty and the powerful dominate every aspect of the life of a traditional Igbo community.

A martial ethos comes with the dialectics of a cultural society that readily distinguishes the brave and the coward, the advantaged and the disadvantaged, the able and the challenged. It is a kind of eugenic approach where the robust and powerful are categorized, excessively praised and their qualities promoted, while the not-so-powerful are treated as cowards, weaklings, and, sometimes, outright classified as being lazy. Richard Begam (2011) argues, "Okonkwo is, in other words, identified with his community to the extent that it esteems the martial ethos he embodies…his village certainly does more than make war" (p. 209). Irele (2009) adds that it is within such an influencing society that Okonkwo developed his character. He continues, "Achebe casts him in what is clearly a heroic mould, as befits his warrior status" (p. xiii). Igbo culture demands the display of heroic acts. Most African writers and scholars agree with this line of argument, that a martial ethos or character is part of the core values of the Igbo.

d) *The War-mongering Attitude*

Igbo cultural tradition has many instances of internecine or tribal wars between communities, especially over land disputes, retributive violence, etc. Tribal disputes could also erupt because of community dominance over other communities, and because of marriage crisis. One village could attack another because of the violent treatment of a woman from another community. Such tribal wars are most often justified through religious rituals and oracle consultations. Those who have achieved significant status in the community are classed based on public display of aggressiveness, prowess, and war trophies (display of conquered people and their heads for rituals) during war. With regard to these war trophies that encourage violence, Nnoromele (2011) notes that "[T]he ultimatum of war that he(Okonkwo) delivered to the enemy of Umuofia yielded immediate results" (p. 42).

War-mongering attitudes are ways of urging violent aggression and involve reminiscing on the bounties of war, or war-ransom. Alan R. Friesen (2011) agrees with this interpretation in what he calls "the war-ransom" (p. 285) that could be prevalent in internecine wars between communities in Igboland. These war-mongering-enabling cultural practices are present in Igbo linguistic expression and peculiar proverbs. Ogede (2007) notes:

> By this proverb, the novel is intent upon sustaining Okonkwo's personality, his warmongering instinct, which later becomes somewhat dormant, and then suddenly rises again when he cuts down Ikemefuna, his foster child. It is the same emotion that spurs him on to murder the Court Messenger and then terminally to accomplish his own self-annihilation. (p. 30).

e) *Cultural Personage: The struggle for recognition and the cultural world of survivalism*

Okonkwo has an ideal Igbo cultural personage. It is a cultural personage that struggles for recognition. A cultural personage struggling for recognition is a conspicuous theme developed in Okonkwo's story. It seems to be a universal human predicament which could be said to be beyond an individual, culture, or people. Igbo cultural practices sometimes overemphasize personage and the image of self. It is a culture that is obsessed with cult-image personality.

In many perspectives, one gets the impression that Okonkwo is ideal for a community's hero personality. Although Achebe (1958) recognizes of the contradictions in Okonkwo, he does not deny the fact that Okonkwo was after his selfish person ideal. Irele (1978) observes that we easily notice that Okonkwo adopted an exaggerated sense of his manly ideal. The anti-climax of this self ideal was when he returned to Umuofia, but not to a hero's welcome. He eventually lost everything, including his social standing, and it dawned on him that his final downfall was inevitable. He was a victim of his own cultural-ideal-person-image obsession. It could be interpreted in what I describe as a cultural trait for survival (survivalist culture).

Survivalist cultural practices nurture violence and confrontational qualities in the young, especially when they have to fight their way through obstacles. To survive, means, or even demands, a form of struggle which is often violent when it meets another violent force or opposition. This is how a survivalist attitude becomes a common lifestyle in a society. We are what our society makes us. There is a mutual reciprocity between society and the individual. Irele (1978) acknowledges that in many aspects Okonkwo is a product of his society:

> in so far as the society has made the man by proposing to him certain values and lines of conduct. On the other hand, the man's personal disposition, his reaction to these social determinations stemming from his subjective perception of them, prepares his individual fate. (pp. 10-11).

Irele further addresses this survivalist culture when he notes that Okonkwo is "a man who has grown up in a community which, because of its passionate desire for survival, places its faith above all in the individual quality of 'manliness'" (p. 11). The survivalist cultural attitude is perceived in the show of "manliness," which is associated with a violent/fierce approach to things in life. It could manifest at some point as perversion, especially when one is desperate to survive, be heroic, and be recognized. Irele argues that "Okonkwo's way of conforming, besides being an inverted sort of nonconformity, is a perversion. The meaning he attaches to manliness amounts to fierceness, violence" (p. 12). The possession of power sometimes leads to the show of violence and dominance. In a society of unequal opportunities, those who possess power impose it against the will of others. Irele concludes, "[T]he cult of 'manliness' that Okonkwo espouses reflects a collective passion for survival" (2009, p. xiv).

f) *Violence for Purification*

After the accidental killing of Ogbuefi Ezeudu's son, the destruction of Okonkwo's house is indicative of the mind of the gods. The hermeneutics of such destruction is socio-cultural and religious purification. Irele explains that the destruction of Okonkwo's compound by the people (youth group, adults) following his exile

> "provides... [the] insight into the mores of the land: 'They had no hatred in their hearts against Okonkwo. His greatest friend Obierika was among them. They were merely cleansing the land which Okonkwo had polluted with the blood of a clansman." (Irele, 2009, p. xiv; Achebe (2009, p. 125).

It seems that African traditional communities existed without alternative ways of resolving problems except through violence. But I doubt if that is a satisfactory line of thought. Considering an earlier argument, when Okonkwo broke the Peace Week ordinance by beating his youngest wife at that time, he had to make sacrifices to appease the goddess of the land. Achebe (1958) did admit the wind of change against violence at that time in Umuofia. He suggests (in the words of character Egbuefi Ezeudu) that there was already too much violence in the land, which caused lack of peace. In the apparent absence of other options for appeasing the goddess of the land, Okonkwo (after accidentally killing Ezeudu's son) is left with one option: to flee from his community after his compound is destroyed (p. 88). Yet these violent house destructions were carried out innocently by the community. The situation makes it seem there is a cultural demand among the Igbo that life must be a mixture of fame and shame, glory and gore, greatness and grave destructiveness, heroes and villain. A time to build and a time to destroy!

I shall now relate the above narrative of paradox of violent cultural practices to facts about contemporary terrorism.

Contemporary Understanding of Terrorism

I have previously described terrorism as:

> the use of violent acts as means of creating fear (terror). It could be perpetrated for a religious, cultural, political, or ideological reason. It involves deliberately targeting innocent citizens or non-

combatants or civilians.... Some individual terrorists are motivated by a desire for social solidarity with other members of their organization and not necessarily by a political agenda.... Terrorism is a politically and emotionally charged concept. It is a loaded or controversial term. (Anozie, 2012, p. 216).

The cases of militancy and terrorism, in the Niger Delta, have been considered by some as a legitimate cause for greater good. The perpetrators of these violent acts are sometimes referred to as militants, freedom fighters, human right activists, revolutionaries, etc. These descriptions have also been extended to narratives of terrorism by Boko Haram in Northeastern Nigeria, especially in the Hausa language translation of Boko Haram as "Western education is forbidden"--implying Boko Haram is a freedom fighter war against Western education and against a form of Western imperialism. Boko Haram is a war effort to affirm the supremacy of Islamic culture and civilization (Audu, 2012, pp. 184-194). For this paper, I reaffirm that "whether perpetrated by militia groups or government, the common feature is the use of violence against civilians for the purpose of gaining publicity as a means of accomplishing a cause" (Anozie, p. 216).

Now let me briefly focus on structural terrorism or institutional terrorism because it is the likely form of terrorism taking place in Southeastern Nigeria (Igboland).

Cultural Institutions' Influence on Structural Terrorism in Southeastern Nigeria

According to Human Rights Watch report "from the early 1990s a cycle of protest and repression had led to the militarization of large parts of the delta, notably in Ogoniland, a small area of Rivers State"(Human Rights,2002, p. 2).

A Human Rights Watch report attested that, in 2005: "[T]he violence is aggravated by the widespread availability of small arms" (Human Rights, 2006, p. 118). Following the continued circulation of illegal weapons in the region, the confrontations between government agencies and the militant youth of both the Niger Delta and Northeastern Nigeria have affected the lives of millions of Nigerians. Nigeria as a country had many bomb blasts on the day before the April 2011 election, and many more from 2011 to 2015. Over 15,000 people have been killed, and millions displaced. This, in my view, is as a consequence of the indirect influence of traditional institutions' support for violent cultural practices and its adaptation to an aggressive-global-terrorist approach.

Recent elections' killings, destructions, and intimidations, are indications of the surge of violence as evidence of a socio-political crisis involving unemployed young Nigerians (youth).These violent and terrorist activities also point to the consequences of un-controlled or un-checked violent institutional practices, as well as the global terrorist influence in youth groups like MEND, OPC (reacting to violent actions across the country, but mostly in Yorubaland), and Boko Haram (Muslim fundamentalists using violence to seek Sharia laws in the Northern states of Nigeria). The inability of the government to tackle terrorism caused by the groups (MEND or OPC or Boko Haram) has evoked similar terrorist acts in other groups (a form of copy-cat experience carried out by cultural institutions like youth groups). MEND[i] has promised more terrorist activities if Boko Haram continues it acts of terrorism on the Christian population living in the Northern part of Nigeria. They further accused Boko Haram of being supported by Northern traditional elders and leaders who reject the era of a southern Christian president in Nigeria (now former President Goodluck Jonathan). Terrorism in Southeastern Nigeria has taken the form of citizen-terrorism or cultural group-based terrorism through kidnapping, political thuggery, and assassinations. This was true especially before and after the 2015 presidential, state-governor, federal and state-assemblies, and other government elections. The teaming unemployed youth are recruited as agents of these violent activities. Each group, in a bid to defend its section of the country, despises the rule of law and threatens war and violence if its interests are not met.[ii]

African traditional communities have history of cases involving violence in the socio-cultural aspects of the community, especially with the use of violent youth and secret groups (Ekete-nsi, Owu groups) by the some of the elders to accomplish some political or economic interests. One could consider the politicians sponsoring these bad elements as political elders in the communities. Meanwhile, on some occasions, the socio-cultural violent practices have precipitated legitimate development in the local communities or some justifications, e.g., violence as a means to providing a limited peace and order in the community. Violent cultural practices or terrorist acts are not independent activities of a culture. Man, through history, has lived with the use of violent domination, intimidation, and fear against opponents and others outside their close selected groups.

The discourse hermeneutically reflects on the violent cultural life-world of the Igbo. If violence lacks a systematic approach, then it is difficult to be precise in its classification, but it does not deny the approximations that violence is violence. According to Theophilus Okere (1983), we have the inclination to give meaning and interpret issues (pp. 32-54). We are bound in time, context, culture, history, and tradition. The socio-historical circumstances provide framework to understand the paradoxes of our life.

I have descriptively/interpretively and critically analyzed the puzzling situations in the practices of African traditional religions and socio-cultures, focusing on the Igbo. I have made clear distinctions between the non-violent religious principles in the Igbo life-world and the unfortunate violent cultural practices. The paradoxes present in the religious principles of "I am because we are" (I-We), or the "ubuntu," the African notion of person as the beauty of life, and the violent cultural practices of the people, are intriguing. These humane and rights-guaranteeing principles live side by side with ritual killings, internecine conflict, aggressive struggles for recognition, and survivalist violence. Such violence feeds the desperation for terrorist acts. The Southeastern region of Nigeria is now sitting on a keg of explosives and aggressive militancy as a result of unequal opportunity and socio-cultural crises in the communities. A martial ethos and war-mongering attitudes are influencing new interests in terrorist acts against government and traditional institutions. Examples from real cultural violent practices during New Yam festivals and Achebe's *Things Fall Apart* illustrate a history of violence in the cultural practices of the Igbo. It means violence has a history of influence and is one that truly raises legitimate concerns about a cultural paradox in Igbo life-world, a life-world that demands sustaining non-violent Igbo religio-cultural principles.

Conclusion

Despite these violent cultural practices, it is not sustainable to argue that the entirety of Igbo culture is intrinsically violent. The influence of violent cultural practices on contemporary terrorism is subtle but significant. According to Hoegberg (2011), "violence is not an inherent feature of Igbo society or a necessary consequence of its religious beliefs" (p. 147). As I have substantiated, non-violent religious practices go with significant violent cultural practices among the Igbo. The other issue is that the paradox persists because the traditional people "feel no contradiction in holding a mixture of belief and practice from two or more traditions in Africa" (Mbiti, 1969, p. 275). It is a culture that is "full of contradictions" (Nnoromele, 2011, p. 274). The youth groups as members of organized traditional institutions are readily used as the "platonic guardians" of the community with little respect for the rights of other individuals through dialogue. The individual citizens of the community are under domination and fear/terror coming from groups like Okonko, Ekete-nsi, Okoroshi/Owu initiates. Activities of this kind could be classified as terrorism in a democratic world since they use acts of terror or fear to accomplish socio-cultural-political advantage. The un-initiated innocent citizens become victims of systematic violent activities or a form of institutional or structural terrorism (victims of recognized socio-cultural institutions). It is the primary duty of government and those in charge of our traditional institutions (religious and cultural) to guarantee the rule of law, protect human rights, and provide security. As a community, we could still review some of cultural groups/institutions and their practices that may support violence, so as to discourage every negative influence on our youth.

References List

- Achebe, C. (1958). *Things fall apart*. London: Heinemann.
- Achebe, C. (1959). *Things fall apart*. NY: Fawcett Crest.
- Achebe, C. (1962). *Things fall apart*. London: Heinemann.
- Achebe, C. (1996). *Things fall apart*. Portsmouth: Heinemann.
- Achebe, C. (2009). *Things fall apart*. USA: Anchor Canada.
- Achebe, C. (1983). *The trouble with Nigeria*. Enugu: Fourth Dimension Publishing Co. Ltd.
- Agbola, T. & Alabi, M.(2003). Political economy of petroleum resources development, environmental injustice and selective victimization: A case study of the Niger Delta Region of Nigeria. In J. Agyeman, R. D. Bullard & B. Evan [Eds.], *Just sustainabilities: Development in an unequal world*. London: Earthscan Publications Ltd.
- Alagoa, E. J., Anozie, F. N.,& Nzewunwa, N. (Eds.). (1988). *The early history of the Niger Delta*. Hamburg: Helmut Buske Verlag.
- Anozie, S. U. (2009). *Authentic integration process in Canada and the contemporary African concept of the human person: Martin Buber's I-Thou social philosophy* (Unpublished master's thesis). Dominican University College, Ottawa.
- Anozie, S. U. (2012). Human rights and terrorism: The Niger Delta oil war. In M. Masaeli (Ed.), *Morality and terrorism: An interfaith perspective*. Orange County, California: Nortia Press.
- Audu, S. D. (2012). The almajiri institution, boko haram, and terrorism in Northern Nigeria. In M. Masaeli (Ed.), *Morality and terrorism: An interfaith perspective*. Orange County, California: Nortia Press.
- Begam, R. (2011). Achebe's sense of an ending: History and tragedy in things fall apart. In M. K. Booker (Ed.), *Critical insights:* Things fall apart. Pasadena, California: Salem Press.
- Bromley, D. G., &Melton, J. G. (2002). Violence and religion in perspective. In D. G. Bromley, & J. G. Melton (Eds.), *Cults, religion, and violence*. Cambridge: Cambridge University Press.
- Bujo, B. (1998). *The ethical dimension of community: The African model and the dialogue between north and south*. Nairobi: Pauline's Publication Africa.
- Chukwudum, M. A. (1983). *Nigeria: The country in a hurry*. Lagos: John West Publication Ltd.
- Dzobo, N. K. (1992). Values in a changing society: Man, ancestor and God. In K. Wiredu,& K. Gyekye (Eds.), *Person and community: Ghanaian philosophical studies*. Washington D.C.: The Council for Research in Values and Philosophy.
- Friesen, A. R. (2011). Okonkwo's suicide as an affirmative act: Do things really fall apart? In M. K. Booker (Ed.), *Critical insights:* Things fall apart. Pasadena, California: Salem Press.
- Gikandi, S. (1991). *Reading Chinua Achebe: Language and ideology in fiction*. Portsmouth: Heinemann.
- Gyekye, K. (1992). Person and community in African thought. In K. Wiredu,& K.Gyekye(Eds.), *Person and community*:(Vol. 1).Washington, D. C: The Council for Research in Values and Philosophy.
- Hoegberg, D. (2011). Principle and practice: The logic of cultural violence in Achebe's things fall apart. In M. K. Booker (Ed.), *Critical insights:* Things fall apart. Pasadena, California: Salem Press.
- Hoffman, B. (2006). *Inside terrorism*. New York: Columbia University Press.

- Ilo, S. C. (2009, March 16). *Campaigning for eco-justice in Nigeria's oil producing Niger Delta: How local NGOs internationalized the environmental crisis in Nigeria*. Paper Presented at the 12th International Conference of the International Society for Third Sector Research, Israeli Center for Third Sector Research, Ben Gurion University, Negev, Dead Sea, Israel.
- Irele, F. A. (1978). The tragic conflict in the novels of Chinua Achebe. In C. L. Innes, & B. Lindfors (Eds.), *Critical perspectives on Chinua Achebe*. Washington DC: Three Continents Press.
- Irele, F. A. (2009). Introduction. In F. A. Irele. (Ed.), Things fall apart *Chinua Achebe: A Norton critical edition*. NY: W. W. Norton and Co, Inc.
- Iyasere, S. O. (2009). Narrative techniques in things fall apart. In F. A. Irele (Ed.), Things fall apart *Chinua Achebe: A Norton critical edition*. NY: W. W. Norton and Co, Inc.
- Mbiti, J. S. (1969). *African religions and philosophy*. London: Heinemann Educational Books.
- Menkiti, I. A. (1984). Person and community in African traditional thought (3rded.). In R. A. Wright (Ed.), *African philosophy: An introduction*. New York: University Press of America.
- Mkhize, D. N. (2010). The portrayal of Igbo culture in Zulu. In H. Bloom. (Ed.), *Chinua Achebe's* things fall apart. NY: Infobase Publishers.
- Njoku, F. O. C. (2004). *Development and African philosophy: Atheoretical reconstruction of African socio-political education*. New York: iUniverse, Inc.
- Nnoromele, P. C. (2011). The plight of a hero in Achebe's things fall apart. In M. K. Booker. (Ed.), *Critical insights:* Things fall apart. Pasadena, California: Salem Press.
- Nyerere, J. (1968). *Ujamaa: essays on socialism*. Nairobi: Oxford University Press.
- Ogede,O. (2007). *Achebe's Things Fall Apart: Areader's guide*. London: Continuum International Publishing Group.
- Oguejiofor, O. J. (Ed.). (2003). *Philosophy, democracy and responsible governance in Africa*. Munster: Lit Verlag.
- Okere, T. (1983). *African philosophy: Ahistorico-hermeneutical investigation of the conditions of its possibility*. New York: University Press of America.
- Okolo, C. B. (1994). *Squandermania mentality: Reflections on Nigeria culture*. Enugu: University Trust Publishers.
- Okpewho, I. (Ed.) (2003). *Chinua Achebe's* things fall apart: *Acasebook.* London: Oxford University Press.
- Okpala, J. C. (2002, Spring). Igbo metaphysics in Chinua Achebe'sthings fall apart. *Callaloo,* 25(2),559-66.
- Onwuanibe, R. C. (1984). The human person and immortality in Ibo (African) metaphysics. In R. A. Wright (Ed.), *African philosophy: An introduction*. New York: University Press of America.
- Senghor, L. S. (1995). Negritude: A humanism of the twentieth century (1966). In F. L. Hord (Mzee Lasana Okpara),& J. S. Lee (Eds.), *I am because we are: Readings in black philosophy*. Amherst: University of Massachusetts Press.
- Seto, T. P. (2002, June). The morality of terrorism. *Loyola of Los Angeles Law Review*, 35, 1227.
- Human Rights Watch. (2002, October). *The Niger Delta: No democratic dividend,* 14(7).
- Human Rights Watch.. (1999). *The price of oil: Corporate responsibility and human rights violations in Nigeria's oil producing communities*. USA.

- Wiredu, K. (1997). African religions from a philosophical point of view. In P. L. Quinn,& C. Taliaferro (Eds.), *A companion to philosophy of religion.* Oxford: Blackwell Publishing Ltd.

Chapter 5
The Nigerian Government War Against Boko Haram/Terrorism (an Ellulian Communicative Perspective)

Stanley Uche Anozie

(Philosophy Department, William Paterson University, Wayne, New Jersey, USA, 2017)

Introduction

This chapter focuses on how to prosecute the Nigerian government war against terrorism as a necessity and the demand to communicate humanly even when the inevitable destructions of war are overwhelming. How are the war information managed and how is the agency of propaganda applied in the governance of the Nigerian people, especially with the recent war against Boko Haram? How does Jacques Ellul's communicative perspective provide the critical consideration for communicating humanly and with dignity while pursuing the war effort? The central idea is on the indignity of using the power of communication as propaganda tool to counter terrorism or in war against insurgency. This approach in communication has raised concerns and caused reactions from scholars and the international community. The central issue here is that generally propaganda is subtly applied by government with a "politically motivated strategy for controlling a population."[91] In some instances, propaganda is used against the people to "weaken their interest in society."[92]

The bottom line for this work, in other words, is a discourse on the ethics of responsibility in the light of Ellul—which is described as the permissible approach to violence (as a necessity) that recognises at the same time the role of prudence and care while in countering violence. Randal Marlin describes it as "the necessity of using violence to prevent the potential violence of others from being actualized against innocent people."[93] Could the war against terrorism or insurgency in Nigeria be successfully carried out with a sense of dignity and without distortions of facts?

Nigerian Government

The Fourth Republic began with the election of Retired General Olusegun Obasanjo of the People Democratic Party (PDP) as president. His leadership lasted from 1999 to 2007. PDP was again elected to into office with Alhaji Musa Yar'adua becoming the president and Dr. Goodluck Jonathan the vice-president. The death of Yar'adua on the 5th of May, 2010 saw the emergence of Jonathan as the new PDP president of Nigeria.

President Jonathan started from 6th of May, 2010 as the fourteenth Head of State. On the 18th of April, 2011 he defeated Retired Major-General Muhammadu Buhari of Congress for Progressives Change (CPC) party (with 59 percent of the votes). Jonathan opened a Facebook account on 29th of June, 2010 in order to communicatively and interactively reach-out to young Nigerians in a technological era. He also wanted to involve the young people in issues of national importance. These issues include employment opportunities, militancy in the Niger Delta, and the emerging crisis of insurgency—Boko Haram group (by 2009 Boko Haram was not considered a terrorist organization by the Nigerian government.)[94]

---

[91] Randal Marlin, *Propaganda and the Ethics of Persuasion* (Peterborough: Broadview Press Ltd, 2003), p. 34.
[92] Randal Marlin, Propaganda and the Ethics of Persuasion (Peterborough: Broadview Press Ltd, 2003), p. 34.
[93] Randal Marlin, Propaganda and the Ethics of Persuasion (Peterborough: Broadview Press Ltd, 2003), p. 155.
[94] Sunday Didam Audu, "The Almajiri Institution, Boko Haram, and Terrorism in Northern Nigeria, "in *Morality and Terrorism: an interfaith perspective,* edited by Mahmoud Masaeli (Orange County, California: Nortia Press, 2012), pp. 190-191.

The Nigerian government has been waging war against the Niger Delta militants who disrupted oil exploration and attacked expatriates of oil corporations. On 1st of October, 2010, during the Independence Day Celebration at Eagles Square, Abuja, the citizens in attendance were attacked with multiple bomb blasts.[95] It was not long, in 2010, Boko Haram's destructive activities began to be considered as terrorist activities. The response of the Nigerian government to these attacks, insurgencies and terrorisms was followed with psychologically persuasive or motivated approaches to influence the Nigerian masses to respond against terrorism and support how government deals with the situations. It became difficult to distinguish between facts and fictions, truths and half-truths, and misleading information regarding the war effort against terrorism taken up by government.

In our age where there is almost information overload, use of trickery, and misleading information to influence people, following the contributions of Jacques Ellul on Propaganda and Communication and Terrorism, one has to constructively and critically question government's role in the use of propaganda machinery to manipulate her citizenry. The Nigerian government's war against Boko Haram terrorists' group smacks of propaganda and inhuman communication of the casualties of the war. Government agencies use this information to arouse "shock and awe," and show graphic or uncensored pictures of the ugly sides of war. In an ethically sensitive world, we live in a time when Ellul demands "communicating humanly in the age of technology,"[96] especially when technology makes propaganda so effective by reaching a very good number of people in a limited time and in a relatively good supersonic speed. As Ellul suggests, "[E]lectronics can greatly alter the picture and take away any message. Television puts us in a world of falsehood, trickery, and deception."[97]

Boko Haram: the Motif!

According to Dr. Godwin Jeff Doki, Senior Lecturer at the Department of English, University of Jos, Boko Haram "seeks primarily to establish a strict

---

[95] Stanley Uche Anozie, "Human Rights and Terrorism: The Niger Delta Oil War," in *Morality and Terrorism: an interfaith perspective*, edited by Mahmoud Masaeli (Orange County, California: Nortia Press, 2012), pp.206-222.
[96] The enlightening topic of 2014 Jacques Ellul's International Conference held in Ottawa (Carleton University and Dominican University College, Ottawa), July, 2014.
[97] Jacques Ellul, The Technological Bluff, (Grand Rapids, Michigan: William B. Eerdmans Publishing co., 1990), p. 336.

Islamic law in most of the semi-desert areas of West and Central Africa with spiritual headquarters in Maiduguri. Its leader, Mohamed Yusuf, was captured and killed some time ago but the group has become more powerful and vicious under the leadership of its new leader Abubakar Shekau."[98] After the extra-judicial killing of this young man, the heavens were let loose by this group of young Muslims. I think the situation resonates with the case of Ken Saro-Wiwa who was killed during the campaign against human rights abuse and environmental degradation in the Niger Delta of Nigeria. Saro-Wiwa's death, or rather how he was tried and condemned to death, emboldened the Niger Delta militants to an all-out war against the Nigerian government.[99] Like the Niger Delta militants, of course, the transition to the current 'almost irresistible force of militant jihadists' called Boko Haram was a gradual process.[100]

The gradual process and development of this Boko Haram force of resistant against Nigerian soldiers for killing their leader is stunning as well as alarming. Many scholars have provided different purposes for the establishment of Boko Haram. It is now an insurgency group that shapes its purpose with the needs of time in relation to whatever they understand as "the teaching of Islam."[101] Some commentators hold that Boko Haram simply means *"Western education* is banned or forbidden" in Hausa (One of the main languages of Nigeria, and a predominant language in Northern Nigeria.)[102] According to Sunday Didam Audu, "Boko" is Hausa for "Western Education,"[103] while

---

[98] Vanguard (Nigerian Newspaper) Monday, 9th June 2014. See Sunday Didam Audu, "The Almajiri Institution, Boko Haram, and Terrorism in Northern Nigeria, "in Morality and Terrorism: an interfaith perspective, edited by Mahmoud Masaeli (Orange County, California: Nortia Press, 2012), p.192.

[99] I discussed this issue on the execution of Saro-Wiwa and 8 human rights campaigners by the Nigerian military junta of General Sani Abacha. "They were treated like terrorists and were executed like terrorists." (Anozie, ibid., p. 219.) See Stanley Uche Anozie, "Human Rights and Terrorism: The Niger Delta Oil War," in Morality and Terrorism: an interfaith perspective, edited by Mahmoud Masaeli (Orange County, California: Nortia Press, 2012), p.209.

[100] Sunday Didam Audu, "The Almajiri Institution, Boko Haram, and Terrorism in Northern Nigeria, "in Morality and Terrorism: an interfaith perspective, edited by Mahmoud Masaeli (Orange County, California: Nortia Press, 2012), p. 191.

[101] Sunday Didam Audu, "The Almajiri Institution, Boko Haram, and Terrorism in Northern Nigeria, "in Morality and Terrorism: an interfaith perspective, edited by Mahmoud Masaeli (Orange County, California: Nortia Press, 2012), p. 192.

[102] Sunday Didam Audu, "The Almajiri Institution, Boko Haram, and Terrorism in Northern Nigeria, "in Morality and Terrorism: an interfaith perspective, edited by Mahmoud Masaeli (Orange County, California: Nortia Press, 2012), p. 185.

[103] Sunday Didam Audu, "The Almajiri Institution, Boko Haram, and Terrorism in Northern Nigeria, "in Morality and Terrorism: an interfaith perspective, edited by Mahmoud Masaeli (Orange County, California: Nortia Press, 2012), p. 191.

"Haram" simply means "forbidden." "Halal" means "not forbidden" in Hausa language.

A Northern Nigeria scholar, Mallam Sanni Umaru, affirms that for the Islamist Jihadist in Nigeria, Boko Haram actually means *"Western Civilization is forbidden,"* not merely *Western education* is forbidden. Boko Haram adherents believe in the supremacy of Islamic culture and civilization over any other form of civilization. We consider that view as noteworthy because as Seyyed Hossein Nasr confirms, "Islam is both a religion and a civilization, a historical reality...It is also a spiritual and metahistorical reality that has transformed the inner and outer life of numerous human beings in very different temporal and spatial circumstances...and historically Islam has played a significant role in the development of certain aspects of other civilizations, especially Western civilization."[104] Freedom C. Onuoha also addresses this point in his work.[105] Boko Haram, as an Islamic youth group, studying Koran in Maiduguri is an important aspect of the narrative that one has to remember.[106] Boko Haram is proper to be identified as people committed to the preaching of the Mohammed and opposed to any form of Westernization and secularism.[107] In a way, it could be confusing to consider the Prophet's teaching as exactly what the Boko Haram Islamists' youth group take it to be. However, like any religion, there are various different versions or interpretations of its core message. The current trend identified in Boko Haram is not the last of the ongoing interpretation of its motif!

Ellul and Propaganda

According to Marlin, propaganda is defined as, "[T]he organized attempt through communication to affect belief or action or inculcate attitudes in a large audience in ways that circumvent or suppress an individual's adequately

---

[104] Seyyed Hossein Nasr, *Islam: Religion, History, and Civilization* (New York: HarperCollins Publishers, Inc., 2003), p. xi.
[105] Freedom C. Onuoha, The Islamist Challenge: Nigeria's Boko Crisis Explained; African Security Review, 19:2, 2010, pp. 54-67.
[106] Binneh Minteh and Ashlie Perry, Terrorism in West Africa-Boko Haram's Evolution, Strategy and Affiliations, presented at the Mid-West Political Science Association's 71st Annual Conference Palmer House Hotel, Chicago Illinois, April 2013. See Al-Jazeera, 2010.
[107] Sunday Didam Audu, "The Almajiri Institution, Boko Haram, and Terrorism in Northern Nigeria, "in Morality and Terrorism: an interfaith perspective, edited by Mahmoud Masaeli (Orange County, California: Nortia Press, 2012), p. 185.

informed, rational, reflective judgment."[108] This definition above corresponds to Ellul's articulation of propaganda as a "means of gaining power by the psychological manipulation of groups or masses, or of using this power with the support of the masses."[109] This properly describes what is going on with the people in charge of the media and publicity and public policy issues for the current Nigerian government. There is the conscious effort to manipulate and control-manage the direction of opinions of the Nigerian people.

Propaganda is not all about manipulation and control of opinions, lies and "tall stories." It could be half-truth, limited truth, and truth-out-of-context. Even accuracy of information could be used as part of propaganda in order to change people's opinion. Propaganda is not all about changing opinion. Changing opinion is only an aim. Propaganda is aimed at "intensify[ing] existing trends, to sharpen and focus them… to lead men to action…to prevent them from interfering."[110] Ellul explains that propaganda is "too oppressive and [used] to persuade man to submit with good grace."[111] It goes with mass media that is brought "under single control"[112] in order to prevent any multiple and confusing source of communication. For one to really control the agency of communication, every other channel of 'divisive' communication must be under check. The information provided to the people is vetted for 'well-directed' consistency.[113] This well-directed consistency and control are aimed at the populace. Without the populace the purpose of propaganda is not complete or comprehensive. Ellul adds, "no propaganda can exist unless a mass can be reached and set into motion."[114]

The masses in Ellul analysis consist of the poor or, the 'wretch of the earth,' as Frantz Fanon will say. But these poor people are not easy to be controlled or manipulated. In other words, one's socio-economic status

---

[108] Randal Marlin, Propaganda and the Ethics of Persuasion (Peterborough: Broadview Press Ltd, 2003), p. 22.
[109] Jacques Ellul, "propaganda," *Larousse, La Grande Encyclopedie* (1975), 9888. See also Randal Marlin, *Propaganda and the Ethics of Persuasion* (Peterborough: Broadview Press Ltd, 2003), p. 19.
[110] Jacques Ellul, *Propaganda: the formation of men's attitude*, (See Preface by Konrad Kellen), (New York: Vintage, 1973), p. vi.
[111] Jacques Ellul, Propaganda: the formation of men's attitude, (See Preface by Konrad Kellen), (New York: Vintage, 1973), p. xviii.
[112] Jacques Ellul, Propaganda: the formation of men's attitude, trans. by Konrad Kellen and Jean Lerner, (New York: Vintage, 1973), p. 102.
[113] Randal Marlin, Propaganda and the Ethics of Persuasion (Peterborough: Broadview Press Ltd, 2003), p. 22. Marlin describes it as well-intentioned propaganda.
[114] Jacques Ellul, Propaganda: the formation of men's attitude, trans. by Konrad Kellen and Jean Lerner, (New York: Vintage, 1973), p. 104.

determines one's accessibility or availability to effective propaganda. Ellul explains that "[M]odern integration propaganda cannot affect individuals who live on the fringes of our civilization or who have too low a living standard."[115] There is that paradox which rather points to the accessibility of the rich and relatively independent to the influence of propaganda.

This interesting paradox confirms the level of influence of propaganda. As Ellul notes about developed/developing countries and effective propaganda, "the ascent to that level is gradual, the rising living standard in the West, as well as in the East and in *Africa* makes the coming generations much more susceptible to propaganda."[116] It is through propaganda that "facts become known and attention to certain questions is aroused."[117]

Propaganda and Credible Information

Ellul notes, propaganda is an essential aspect of communication and modern humanity's world. New technology has made people be so obsessed with the so called facts. Ellul thinks that the modern man worships "facts" as the end all and be all of reality.

Propaganda is the second critical concept used by Ellul. According to Kluver, in light of Ellul's comment on propaganda as *an inescapable necessity*, "those responsible for public discussions of issues such as the media systems and the government, now use the techniques [118]of propaganda to override rational discourse and critical thinking."[119] In this way, propaganda has the meaning as a negative technique of control and influence so as to prevent the capacity to constructive thinking. However, for Ellul, propaganda is more than a negative technique for the manipulation of other people. In fact, in Ellul's perspective, propaganda carries a neutral character. It could be used for good or for evil. It becomes what our motives are or our desires are. The negative use of propaganda is very inimical to the value of facts and truth. Ellul further explains

---

[115] Jacques Ellul, Propaganda: the formation of men's attitude, trans. by Konrad Kellen and Jean Lerner, (New York: Vintage, 1973), p. 105.
[116] Jacques Ellul, Propaganda: the formation of men's attitude, trans. by Konrad Kellen and Jean Lerner, (New York: Vintage, 1973), p. 106.
[117] Jacques Ellul, Propaganda: the formation of men's attitude, trans. by Konrad Kellen, (New York: Vintage, 1973), p. 113.
[118] http://ellul.org/ELLUL%20FORUM%20ARTICLES/ISSUE37.pdf. See the Jacques Ellul, "The Ethics of Propaganda," in Communication, 6 (1981): 159-175. Translated from the French by D. Raymond Tourville.
[119] Kluver, ibid., p.100.

that this form of propaganda aim at the destruction of "truth and freedom...no matter what the good intentions or the good will may be of those who manipulate it."[120] In the end, the manipulation of information is accomplished through what *appears as facts* and credible. Whether propaganda is used for negative or positive reason, being credible and believable must be one of the conditions of its effectiveness. However, any propaganda, no matter how credible and effective it is, ceases when it stops.[121]

For propaganda to be effective, it also has to include important or significant information. Non important issues are not suitable for serious propaganda. Ellul notes that "propaganda to politically ignorant groups can be made only if preceded by extensive, profound, and serious information work."[122] The information used in manipulating or eliciting an expected response from the people must not necessarily be false, but usually something credible. When the information is not-believable or non-credible, it affects the quality of propaganda or the result of its influence on people. The "information provides the basis for propaganda but [also] gives propaganda the means to operate."[123] Propaganda feeds on data of communication and images that evoke a predetermined response from people. Propaganda is effective when the goal is to control the other. According to Leonard Doob, it is "the attempt to affect the personalities and to control the behavior of individuals towards desired ends."[124] These desired ends must be acceptable with credible quality or nature.

Now having earlier established the fact of the credible nature of the facts used in propaganda, it is important to look at the form of society that are often the victim of propaganda. Not everyone is a subject or victim of effective propaganda. Some have more proclivities to become easy targets or victims of propaganda than others. The seeming disinterested or passive crowd is usually among those easily swayed by the intrigues of propaganda. The educated members of society could also become victims of propaganda; however, the most vulnerable is the public (poor masses or the easily-believing crowd). The

---

[120] Jacques Ellul, Propaganda: the formation of men's attitude, trans. by Konrad Kellen and Jean Lerner, (New York: Vintage, 1973), p. 257.
[121] Ellul, *Propaganda*, p. 296. There are recent reports about some young people in the North stoning the entourage of President Jonathan during his election campaign stop.
[122] Jacques Ellul, Propaganda: the formation of men's attitude, trans. by Konrad Kellen, (New York: Vintage, 1973), p. 113.
[123] Jacques Ellul, Propaganda: the formation of men's attitude, trans. by Konrad Kellen, (New York: Vintage, 1973), p. 114.
[124] Timothy Richard Glander, *Origins of Mass Communications Research During the American Cold War* (Language Arts and Discipline, 2000), p. 22.

public, Ellul affirms, "is just an object... that one can manipulate, influence, and use."[125] In the above, propaganda is not necessarily seen as bad but a technique that could be used to present a different social need and create the relevant awareness about issue of national importance.[126] It is in this sense of recognizing the good effect desired in using propaganda that our paper calls for true consideration of communicating humanly (even under the pressure of exacerbating and destructive war against terror.)

Ellul holds that "one cannot determine with any degree of accuracy how many people are being reached by a propaganda campaign."[127] The effect of propaganda is continual and advances among the various spheres of the community. Public opinions, perceptions of 'facts,' etc are all factors in understanding how effective propaganda has become. At times people who are under the influence of effective propaganda live in denial of this influence, especially when the facts used in distortions are believable. But when people challenge the sources of information/propaganda or the scheme of the propagandists, then a level of validation or credibleness is at stake.

The effectiveness of propaganda could lead to a challenge of government's sources of information, as is with the strong emergency of Boko Haram, despite the assumptions that the military are in control of the situation. When this happens, when facts are no longer credible then propaganda has become ineffective or inefficient.

Boko Haram and the Nigerian Government: Propaganda and the Crisis of Information/Communication Management

In the section above, we discussed the issue of credibleness of facts used in propaganda and we also talked about the people who are easily swayed or easily take what we prefer to describe, for lack of a better term, *"customised or self-confirmed truth"* as used in propaganda. We are not dealing with issues that are probable, but rather issues that are believable or credible. In Ellul's comment on indoctrination, which is a form of propaganda, he says, "as soon as the individual has been indoctrinated with the "truth," he will act as he is expected

---

[125] Jacques Ellul, Propaganda: the formation of men's attitude, trans. by Konrad Kellen, (New York: Vintage, 1973), p. 118.

[126] Jacques Ellul, Propaganda: the formation of men's attitude, trans. by Konrad Kellen, (New York: Vintage, 1973), p. xviii.

[127] Ellul, Propaganda, p. 262. See also Harold D. Lasswell and Dorothy Blumenstock, World Revolutionary Propaganda (New York: Alfred A. Knopf, 1939, Chapter 11).

to act, from the "spontaneity" of his conscience. This was the principle aim of propaganda in Hitler's army."[128] Ellul observes that "without this need for propaganda experienced by practically every citizen of the technological age, propaganda could not spread…there is a citizen who craves propaganda from the bottom of his being and a propagandist who responds to this craving."[129] He adds, "[I]t is a strictly sociological phenomenon, in the sense that it has its roots and reasons in the need of the group that will sustain it."[130] (both groups consciously, and some unconsciously, work together for propaganda to be effective.)

a) Media Empire and Defense of Powerful Interest: Communicating Humanly in Nigeria

There is, as is common knowledge, the oligopoly and monopoly of our media houses.[131] It is not so difficult at times to know whose interest is served. We live in a time when powerful individuals own Media Empire and so determine the quality of information communicated to the public. In this way, they control information and use propagandist approach in twisting information to benefit their owners.

Certainly, in many countries, some media houses serve the interests of powerful individuals and sympathetic governments. The recent incidents in Nigeria in terms of National Newspapers and Public Television houses serving the interests of the ruling government open our minds to the power of government in the developing democracies to influence their people through media outlets. Ellul observes, "[T]o make the organization of propaganda possible, the media must be concentrated, the number of news agencies reduced, the press brought under single control"[132]—psychological control.

Let us look at the use of 'technique' to explain the nature of this psychological influence.

---

[128] Jacques Ellul, Propaganda: the formation of men's attitude, trans. by Konrad Kellen and Jean Lerner, (New York: Vintage, 1973), p. 120.

[129] Jacques Ellul, Propaganda: the formation of men's attitude, trans. by Konrad Kellen and Jean Lerner, (New York: Vintage, 1973), p. 121.

[130] Jacques Ellul, Propaganda: the formation of men's attitude, trans. by Konrad Kellen and Jean Lerner, (New York: Vintage, 1973), p. 121.

[131] One has to recall the monopoly influence that Times Newspaper, Wall Street Journal, etc they have in the world and in general American news media.

[132] Ellul, Propaganda, p. 103.

La Technique—is not exactly English "technique" or technology. *La technique* is about the mode of consciousness inherent in over-dependence on technical means. It means "a self-directing and self-augmenting social process." Kluver adds, "Ellul does not argue against technique or technology itself, but rather the human mindset that replaces critical moral discourse with technological means and values."[133]

Many people have the understanding that technology has changed the world and almost everything about the world. In that sense, people are easily influenced through the power of technology in terms of information dissemination and manipulation and influence of perceptions. It is only a very limited part of our world—even this limited part is shrinking each day—is free of this powerful influence through mass communication and information technology. Ellul notes, "the technical phenomenon is the main preoccupation of our time; in every field men seek to find the most efficient method." [134] The question is that in an age of quite an expanding "information society"[135] the approach of propaganda is more complicated and holistic than it was when information technology was not so developed. Propaganda, some years ago, will mean, "comprising primary rhetorical and media techniques."[136]

Considering the prevalence of the use of propaganda through the media, from an Ellulian perspective, Kluver observes that the mass media (radios, movies, newspapers or newsprints) has become the "means by which collective life is lived and the collective consciousness is shaped. Moreover, the centralized nature of the mass media means that rather than encouraging thought, the media instead have been a crippling force of social control."[137] The end of propaganda is not making people understand but to psychologically compel them into "compliance."[138] The propagandist is not interested in people accepting his/her views. He or she is interesting in ramming the people into following the 'fixed' trend or 'determined' route of expectations. So there is nothing about it other than people's response, not their agreement. Ellul adds, "[T]o the extent that propaganda rests on a contempt for man viewed as an object to shape and not as a person to respect, this signifies that the cause defended by propaganda implies a de-gradation of man, the impossibility of his

---

[133] Kluver, p. 99.
[134] Ellul, Technological Society, 1954/1964, p. 21.
[135] Kluver, p. 99.
[136] Kluver, p. 100.
[137] Kluver, p. 101, relate this to Ellul, 1954/64
[138] Kluver, p. 101.

acceding to his majority, to his personal responsibility, and that propaganda is evidently a negation of a freedom."[139] In other words, people lose the ability to individual decide or make judgements or be more creative in dealing with information.[140] Now we take a look at how this information and communication technology is being used by the Nigerian government to control the masses in relation to war against terrorism.

b) Propaganda Forces: Media Control in Nigeria

How do we communicate now and how have we used information technology in influencing other people's thought and views? How has spin factor been used in leadership/governance in Nigeria? What is the role of the private media establishments and federal institutions (Nigerian Television Authority (NTA), Nigerian Television of Authority International (NTA international), African Independent Television (AIT, private media),[141] etc) buy into the "psychological framework" that the government wants (technological society). Propaganda as we recall is about justification of self rather than explanation of the situation or reality. Public institutions at the charge or care of the federal government have now become tools of propaganda in the hands of serving leaders. This situation could be seen in the use of the federal military and police to intimidate the Opposition parties during elections or to use them to support exclusively the interests of the ruling party. The military and police

---

[139] http://ellul.org/ELLUL%20FORUM%20ARTICLES/ISSUE37.pdf (Accessed December 9, 2014). See the Jacques Ellul, "The Ethics of Propaganda," in Communication, 6 (1981): 159-175. Translated from the French by D. Raymond Tourville.

[140] Kluver, p. 103. Kluver also notes that propaganda sends a totalizing effect on the masses by disallowing "true competitive discourse." (p. 104).

[141] AIT is owned by High Chief Raymond Dokpesi (Daar Communications), a close friend of the current President Goodluck Jonathan. Dokpesi was involved with supporting democratic progress in Nigeria in the 1990s. It was the first privately owned Television network and was also said to be Africa's first satellite television station. He also owns the first private radio station called Raypower FM Nigeria. It is unfortunate that most media houses start off good but degenerate to become propaganda machines of any ruling government in order to receive largesse and contracts from government. This situation affirms the case of lack of integrity and consistency in objective journalism in Nigeria.

Dokpesi has as a politician been involved in Nigerian politics to an extent it is difficult to hope on unbiased news reviews and objective journalism from an establishment that has interest in leadership and affiliated to a particular political organization. For instance, he is associated with Dr. Bamanga Tukur, the former National Chairman of Peoples Democratic Party. Tukur was chairman for PDP from 2012 to January 2014. With the support of President Jonathan Tukur was elected National Chairman of Nigeria's ruling party, PDP, in March 2012. Stephanie Findlay affirms that "an informal online poll by AIT, a station belonging to one of Jonathan's close friends, showed Buhari winning the vote, with 76 percent of respondents." (Toronto Star Newspaper, Friday, January 30, 2015, A8).

forces exert some influences on media houses seen to be hard on government or not in line with government's propaganda expectations. Considering the financial pressure that some of these independent media organizations go through to continue to be in business, some of them have now closed down, and those still around are playing safe to avoid being clamped down by government agencies or hunted down through indirect intimidations.

One recalls the case of the media organization called *Next 234*, owned by Dele Olojede. He had experience in journalism, working at *Newswatch* Magazine and *Sunday Concord* Newspaper as a reporter. The reports he wrote for the New York *NewsDay* some years ago on Rwanda genocide won him a Pulitzer Prize in 2009 and other accolades around the world. Despite these awards and accolades, his media organization failed to stay in business. It closed down its regular print newspaper, but continued on for a while with online news. *Next 234* began with the purpose of distinguishing itself in quality journalism and publication of hard facts and changing Nigeria's journalism. We are not suggesting *Next 234* closed down because of government, but for them to still be operational and work with integrity, they will need a lot financial support. Practically, they do not have enough options to survive or be saved from bankruptcy other than getting along with some corrupt practices in government owned media organization, or allow themselves to be sponsored by powerful but influential politicians who may not be far from the ruling government or Boko Haram sponsors.

Boko Haram has attacked some media establishments they accused of distortion and false-reporting. On the 26th of April, 2012 headquarter of *This Day* Newspaper was bombed in Abuja. There were also bomb blasts in Kaduna that affected media organization like *The Moment* and *The Sun* Newspapers. Pat Utomi reported on this development in Nigeria. It was also alleged that Abul Qaqa, the spokesman for Boko Haram, at one point expressed the dissatisfaction of Boko Haram on inaccurate reporting by the Nigerian media organization and on being falsely accused, on some occasions, of certain attacks they (Boko Haram) do not take any responsibility for. This development kept some of the journalists and their newspaper owners in fear of giving accurate reports on the war against terrorism, or they try to distort as much information as possible to be in the good book of those in government. We have to recall *Nigerian Compass Newspaper*, a paper owned by former Governor Gbenga Daniel of Ogun State, and *Daily Independent* owned by former Governor of Delta State Mr. James Ibori (now serving a jail term in the UK for money laundry and corrupt practices). These two newspapers went down as soon as their owners lost significant links to political positions, contracts, and governmental influence. In such a situation, one wonders about the connection between attempts at quality news reporting/journalism, propaganda, and ownership of media organizations by people of high political clout with probable hands in information distortion. As Ellul points out, government could control the quality of information by indirectly distancing herself from media organisations that report on the real issues or insist in getting the objective truth to people. These are all aspects of the intrigue of propaganda in Ellul's view. He further explains that "[P]ropaganda…demands the exclusion of opposite trends and minorities—not total and official perhaps, but… partial and indirect exclusion." [142]

We now take a look on human communication and the politics of communication. In a related context Ellul discusses his concern about media ecology, how technology influence society and control many aspects of life, and the contemporary role of media in understanding society. For the purpose of this research, we shall focus on propaganda, communication, and Nigerian democracy/society.

c) **Propaganda and Democracy (Propaganda, Nigeria, and Ellul)**

Nigeria is richly blessed with human and natural resources. The crisis in the Niger Delta area because of oil control caused a lot of violence and oil war.[143] Amnesty was reached by the Nigerian government through the then President Musa Yar'adua to curb the escalating situation. He set up a Niger Delta Commission to address militancy and to provide some human rights needs to people in that oil region.[144] Will Ferguson recalled the report about Niger Delta region and their oil riches in his book. He notes, "Nigeria's here, at the bottom of the bulge. The Niger River runs through it, empties into the Atlantic Ocean at the Niger Delta. The Delta is a huge area, home to one of the riches petroleum fields in the world.[145] It's also one of the most dangerous places on earth. The

---

[142] Jacques Ellul, Propaganda, p. 247.
[143] Stanley Uche Anozie, "Human Rights and Terrorism: The Niger Delta Oil War," in Morality and Terrorism: an interfaith perspective, edited by Mahmoud Masaeli (Orange County, California: Nortia Press, 2012), pp. 206-208.
[144] Stanley Uche Anozie, "Human Rights and Terrorism: The Niger Delta Oil War," in Morality and Terrorism: an interfaith perspective, edited by Mahmoud Masaeli (Orange County, California: Nortia Press, 2012), pp. 215-216.
[145] A good historical commentary on the Niger Delta and its association with oil wealth and foreign oil trade is well articulated in Philip Curtin, Steven Feierman, Leonard Thompson and

militants and local warlords in the [Niger] Delta have declared war against the oil companies"[146] and government institutions. In a recent presentation by Tunde Bakare, the largest terror group in Nigeria "is the Movement for the Emancipation of the Niger Delta (MEND) with [a] membership strength of about 15,000 despite its having recorded much fewer attacks than Boko Haram."[147]

As in the above, the Boko Haram terrorists' acts started as an agitation against violent executions of their members and abuse of their fundamental human rights. Many considered the rise of Boko Haram was poverty and abandonment of the poor masses in the North. The teaming young people need jobs—dependable ones—to escape from poverty. We believe that if enough considerations and amnesty program provided to the Niger Delta militants[148] were extended to the unemployed youth in the North, some of them would not have chosen to support Boko Haram, or even attempted to associate with Al Qaeda, or contacted Islamic State of Iraq and Syria (ISIS or ISIL).[149] There has been a serious barrage of inconsistencies coming from Nigeria's leadership and spokespeople with regard to the direct relation between insecurity and unemployment. As Chukwudum B. Okolo puts it, unemployment could become "fatal when not controlled,"[150] and this is seen through the unemployed youth getting involved with terrorist groups like Boko Haram. The inconsistencies in finding out the cause of problems and the policies to address them have worsened the Nigeria terrorist narratives.

Jan Vansina, "The Commercial and Religious Revolutions in West Africa," in *African History* (London and New York: Longman Group UK Limited, 1978 (1992)), p. 381ff.
[146] Will Ferguson, 419: A Novel (Toronto: Penguin Canada, 2012), p. 112.
[147] http://saharareporters.com/2015/01/05/seven-signs-2015-elections-will-shipwreck-nigeria-pastor-bakare (Accessed on 5th of January, 2015) The Niger Delta Militants [MEND] have taken responsibility of some terrorist activities in Nigeria before the emergency of the Boko Haram terrorists. (Anozie, ibid., p. 220; p. 222).
[148] Some leaders of MEND group took responsibility for the bomb blasts on the 1st of October, 2010 in Abuja, Nigeria. "The Nigeria government, for political reasons, avoid[ed] giving MEND such a name." (Anozie, ibid., p. 220) See Stanley Uche Anozie, "Human Rights and Terrorism: The Niger Delta Oil War," in Morality and Terrorism: an interfaith perspective, edited by Mahmoud Masaeli (Orange County, California: Nortia Press, 2012), p. 220.
[149] Monica Mark has tried to associate Boko Haram and ISIS. The ISIS had suggested that kidnapping girls in Chibok is similar to kidnapping and selling the Yazidi women into slavery.
[150] Chukwudum C. Okolo, "Squandermania Mentality: Reflections on Nigeria Culture (Enugu, Nigeria: University Trust Publishers, 1994).

The inconsistencies in explaining the relation between the communication of security and youth employment policies in Nigeria, especially in the recent government of Jonathan, is a pointer to what Adebayo Oyebade stated in his article: "Reluctant Democracy: The State, The Opposition, and the Crisis of Political Transition, 1985-1993."[151] The flip-flop nature of Nigerian practice of democracy shows serious lack of determination to change the way things are going. This could be seen in the recent terrorists' attacks in Nigeria. The current government has stated that there are internal and external sabotage undermining the effort to overcome terrorism in the Northeast of Nigeria. Ellul will consider this as a result of the lack of the ability to communicate especially when confronted by daunting situations. This research presents the background to the transformation agenda promised Nigerians in recent years' elections promises and the lack of effectiveness by elected government in addressing terrorism and insecurity problems in various Nigerian states.

In the situation above, the Nigerian state itself seems to become an abstract concept. As we know, a democratic state may not exist in reality. It could be just a mere concept with fictitious essence; unreal or imaginary as well as false; an empty, dead and cold concept. It becomes in Nietzsche's view the "[T]he coldest of cold monsters."[152] When the values and principles that a state should maintain are not considered important, then Ellul considers such a state at this point, as were life is no longer protected, people are oppressed or hoodwinked into accepting propaganda, to be a distasteful state. Without a doubt, a citizen of a state could choose (not necessarily imposed by government) the above mentioned situation because of being susceptible to visionless existence and also fall unto "propaganda of his choice."[153] Technically speaking, the poor and the rich are free from certain forms of propaganda. Each member of socio-economic category could fall within the reach or is targeted by a specific or a certain form of an effective propaganda. In this case, as Ellul explains, propaganda "has precise objectives, it does not concern just anybody. To analyze whether such selective propaganda is effective, it would be

---

[151] Adebayo Oyebade, "Reluctant Democracy: The State, The Opposition, and the Crisis of Political Transition, 1985-1993," The Transformation of Nigeria (Essays in Honor of Toyin Falola) (Trenton, New Jersey: Africa World Press, Inc.,2002), pp.137--162.
[152] Jacques Ellul and Patrick Troude-Chastenet, eds., Jacques Ellul on Politics, Technology and Christianity: conversation with Patrick Troude-Chastenet, (Eugene, Oregon: Wipf and Stock Publishers, 2005), p. 23.
[153] Ellul, Propaganda, 104.

necessary to analyse only the target group or the particular that was to be modified."[154]

Society or the community of people and individuals are the targets of propaganda, political illusions and distorted leadership.[155] Everyday citizens are confronted by different and directed propagandas. This is especially so in a technological world where we are rattled and overwhelmed by the avalanche of socio-economic and political propaganda seeking to control our experience of the world and how we respond to things around us. There is an avalanche of myths of economic successes, hair-splitting political illusions, and structural oppression[156] as Nigerians head to 2015 elections, an election year and propaganda soaked political campaign. We will further develop these concepts when discussing Nigeria under Jonathan's leadership.

In an election year in Nigeria, Ellul's observation that some political campaigns are forms of modern propaganda—political propaganda[157] is not difficult to discern. His definition of propaganda is very comprehensive in that it includes all aspect of the act of influence of peoples' attitude. He considers propaganda as "a set of methods...to bring about the active or passive participation in its actions of a mass of individuals, psychologically unified through psychological manipulations and incorporated in an organization."[158] According to Ellul, the use of propaganda brings the propagandist and the propagandee in quite a close contact. This unhealthy contact is the basis for profound psychological influence in a democratic society. He notes, "[A] man who lives in a democratic society and who is subjected to propaganda is being drained of the democratic content itself—of the style of democratic life, understanding of others."[159] Propaganda can take away or help erode our

---

[154] Ellul, Propaganda, p. 270.
[155] Jacques Ellul and Patrick Troude-Chastenet, eds., Jacques Ellul on Politics, Technology and Christianity: conversation with Patrick Troude-Chastenet, (Eugene, Oregon: Wipf and Stock Publishers, 2005), p. 15.
[156] I discussed this in my article on how government support or sponsor structural terrorism to intimidate the masses. This also applies in the use of violence to compel people into accepting a manipulative approach in governance and information control or distortions. See Stanley Uche Anozie, "Human Rights and Terrorism: The Niger Delta Oil War," in Morality and Terrorism: an interfaith perspective, edited by Mahmoud Masaeli (Orange County, California: Nortia Press, 2012), pp. 218-222.
[157] Randal Marlin, Propaganda and the Ethics of Persuasion (Peterborough: Broadview Press Ltd, 2003), p. 36.
[158] Ellul, Propaganda: the formation of men's attitude, 1962/65, p. 6; Jacques Ellul, Propaganda: the formation of men's attitude, trans. by Konrad Kellen and Jean Lerner, (New York: Vintage, 1973), p. 61.
[159] Ellul, Propaganda, p. 256.

democratic values. That means democracy could become a "myth." As we noted above, when a democratic state becomes a mere concept, a fictitious essence, it loses purposefulness, and becomes the myth of democracy. In that case it is possible for "the citizen… [to] repeat indefinitely 'the sacred formulas of democracy' while acting like a storm trooper." [160]

For the people within a democratic society, it is difficult to discern this willful degeneration of democratic values because of the impact of propaganda. Propaganda, effective propaganda, takes root gradually. It brings changes in a society of community in order to change the whole landscape of our former independent faculties. Propaganda aims at modifying the content of an opinion or "change majority views, or destroy the morale of an enemy."[161] Unfortunately, the enemy that destroys morale in this case is the citizenry that is manipulated according to the interest of the propagandists.

The enemy—the citizenry—is the target of the information onslaught of the propagandists. It is a psychological warfare in which the citizens are turned into citizens of totalitarianism. If some of the people do not accept the policies of those in government, then they are classified among the oppositions (lovers of bad news) and enemies of government. Here is Ellul's explanation. Propaganda could be about auto-justification. It provides its own morality and justification. When self-justification is the basis for action then it manifests or creates the monster of totalitarianism. Anyone who is against or outside this totalitarian ideology or community is an enemy of the state. 'We' against 'them'! Ellul describes this as when the "modern man, the modern parties, want to be declared just."[162]

For the sustenance of any civilised democratic society, accuracy of information is important. Avoidance of misleading and distortion will be helpful to finding some peaceful solutions. For the current situation in Nigeria the questions are: what does government know? Are there suppressions of news or information? President Jonathan's Special Adviser on Media and Publicity—Dr. Reuben Abati— has applied some distortions and media-myth strategy in his services to the president. This is same with President Jonathan's Senior Special Assistant on Public Affairs (Special Adviser on Public Affairs)—Dr. Doyin

---

[160] Ellul, Propaganda, p. 256.
[161] Ellul, Propaganda, p. 259.
[162] http://ellul.org/ELLUL%20FORUM%20ARTICLES/ISSUE37.pdf (see p. 8). See the Jacques Ellul, "The Ethics of Propaganda," in Communication, 6 (1981), pp. 159-175. Translated from the French by D. Raymond Tourville.

Okupe[163]— in his BBC interview with Stephen Sackur on the Nigerian government and the rescue of the Chibok Girls. Okupe's uses the myth of propaganda by incessantly saying that "we [the Nigerian government] always get it right."[164] We understand this in light of Ellul description of 'myths of hero', 'myth of happiness' and 'myth of a great nation.'[165] (The myths of peace, freedom, progress etc). It means that the great 'hero' leader (President Goodluck Jonathan) will bring happiness and '*goodluck*' as his good name implies![166] Okupe suggested that even the President's inability to visit Chibok and the volatile Northeastern states was purposely shelved because of other urgent national issues (that means he was not really hindered by the terrorists).[167] As Ellul suggests these myths provide people with false hope through captivating and "activating images."[168] It is simply undeserving and flattering for the success of the Nigerian society/people to be based on unfounded hopes, miracles and mere *good-luck* charms in order to influence public opinion. In fact, for Ellul, as long as there is propaganda, there is no genuine public opinion.[169] We think that the opinion about the real reason for the President not visiting Chibok has since fortunately changed for a better understanding.

---

[163] There are other members of President Jonathan propaganda machinery but I have chosen to focus on officially prominent ones, but that does not mean they are most effective and most important propagandists in this aspect of governance. I have purposely avoided discussing names like Reno Omokri (effective with media technology propaganda, using Facebook, the blogosphere, twitter, etc). He is Special Assistant to President Jonathan on New Media.

[164] I associate Dr. Doyin Okupe's comment to a form of propaganda. Many people are of the view that Okupe knows that the best thing for him is to keep fighting for his pay cheques. This situation is similar to the one described by Louis Lochner, the bureau chief of the Associated Press in Berlin in the 1930s about how journalists are controlled. Lochner stated the policy of the German government as, "[T]o tell no untruth, but to report only as much of the truth without distorting the picture, as would enable us to remain at our posts." See David Halton, "I know Hitler will destroy Germany" in Toronto Star Newspaper, Saturday, 8th November, 2014, IN1 (The comment is related to excerpts from David Halton, *Dispatches from the Front: Matthew Halton, Canada's Voice at War*, (McClelland & Stewart, 2014).

[165] Ellul, Propaganda, pp. 39-40.

[166] Randal Marlin, *Propaganda and the Ethics of Persuasion* (Peterborough: Broadview Press Ltd, 2003), p. 34. Marlin describes them as "useful myths in the minds of a population." (p. 34).

[167] President Jonathan finally made a surprise visit to Maiduguri on the 15th of January, 2015. Some political analysts are of the view that it was a good idea to visit Borno State before the actual political campaign stopover in some of the Northeastern States. Meanwhile, the President is yet to visit Chibok where the kidnapping of 219 girls took place.

[168] Ellul, Propaganda, pp. 31; 31-32.

[169] Jacques Ellul on Politics, Technology and Christianity: a conversation with Patrick, USA: Wipf and Stock, p. 15.

Ellul holds this position by implying that there was no public opinion before Pierre Bourdieu.

Fortunately, against Okupe's BBC suggestions and responses, Jonathan himself acknowledged, several months later, that Boko Haram had prevented him from going to places he would have loved to visit, especially the communities and the victims of these senseless attacks.[170] Despite President Jonathan's argument that he had been prevented, one would like to think that he had no options other than to acknowledge that the terrorists hindered his necessary visit to the Northeastern States (he somehow will gain some sympathy votes against Boko Haram and the Oppositions parties). It could also mean he is certain that the effects of propaganda on the Nigerian masses are weakening so he prefers to be honest as a way out of failing propaganda. In this context Ellul observes, "[A]ll propaganda evaporates progressively when it ceases."[171] In many different times the federal government and some presidential spokespersons are numbed to learn that the Chibok girls' saga is almost a sudden-death case for their party (PDP). Their propaganda—to influence public opinion—by claiming that the secondary school girls will be back before Christmas 2014 is already flat and ineffective since the arrival of New Year 2015. Every form of propaganda set within the temporal relevance or limits of 2014 (to bring back the girls) is now obsolete, or did not happen as promised.

According to Ifeanyi Izeze, "since the girls were taken, all we have as at today are loads of propaganda, half-truths, misinformation and sheer falsehoods whose implication at best is outrightly misguided to steer us away from the real problem at hand which is even escalating to otherwise safe areas of the country."[172] A further reading on this situation in Nigeria is the article in the *Washington Post*. It says, "[H]ere is what you need to know about the kidnapped Nigerian girls, Boko Haram and how the US is getting involved."[173] In a recent report by Haruna Umar and Michelle Faul (*Toronto Star*), "Boko Haram has seized a score of towns and villages where it has declared an Islamic caliphate along the country's Northeast border with Cameroon. Thousands of

---

[170] See Lekan Adetayo, "Boko Haram restricts my movement-Jonathan" in Punch Newspaper, 28th June, 2014.
Ajibola Amzat notes also that the President sent "advanced party" to Maiduguri. See Guardian Newspaper, 28th June, 2014.
[171] Ellul, Propaganda, p. 296.
[172] Ifeanyi Izeze, "Bringbackourgirls: Tragedy of A Divided Nigerian People," in http. Saharareporters.com (Assessed 24th June, 2014).
[173] http://www.washingtonpost.com/news/post-nation/wp/2014/05/13/heres-what-you-need-to-know-about-the-kidnapped-nigerian-girls-boko-haram-and-how-the-u-s-is-getting-involved/(Accessed by 8th May, 2014).

people have been killed in the five-year-old Islamic uprising that has driven some 1.3 million from their homes."[174]

Following the failure of government to see to the return of the Chibok girls in 2014 after series of propaganda and misinformation, let us take note of some of the agencies of current propaganda machine. For instance, media people, politicians, etc. Nigerian politicians are beginning to understand that democracy is not considered a good propaganda object.[175] People are more willing to use their democratic rights to destabilize the forces of propaganda unlike in a military regime or where people have less access to freedoms and rights. People are easily swayed or manipulated to accepting a particular perspective about society (Ellul and Marlin describe it the willingness… to accept)[176] while some sections of society may firmly resist at any attempt to manipulate or use propaganda on them.

Propaganda is a menace that threatens the total personality. It persuades "man to submit with good grace."[177] It involves social psychology—on man's psychic mechanism, tendencies, desires, needs, etc. Modern propaganda is based on scientific analyses of psych and sociology. Modern propaganda must address the individual and the masses. It takes long to have effective propaganda on an individual. When dialogue ends, then propaganda starts![178] One type of propaganda may not be suitable for another situation or effective to influence every strata of society.[179] Propaganda succeeds because it takes advantage of the (a) need of the masses/society. As Ellul says, what should interest us in discussing propaganda and the administration of the state is "the mechanism of the process."[180] The mechanism determines the effectiveness or failure of propaganda among the target group of propaganda.

---

[174] Haruna Umar and Michelle Faul, "Boko Haram blamed for Nigerian attack," in Toronto Star, Friday, December 19, 2014, A18.
[175] Ellul, Propaganda, p. 6.
[176] Randal Marlin, Propaganda and the Ethics of Persuasion (Peterborough: Broadview Press Ltd, 2003), p. 34.
[177] Jacques Ellul, Propaganda: the formation of men's attitude, trans. by Konrad Kellen and Jean Lerner, (New York: Vintage, 1973), p. xviii.
[178] Ellul, Propaganda, p. 236.
[179] It is on record that Stalinist propaganda used Parlov theory of conditioned reflex. Hilter's was founded on Freud's theory of repression and libido. Americans was founded on Dewey's theory of teaching. See Ellul, Propaganda, p. 5.
[180] Jacques Ellul on Religion, Technology and Politics: Conversations with Patrick Troude-Chastenet (Oregon: Wipf and Stock Publishers, 2005), p. 24.

Let us take a look at the failure of propaganda crisis in Nigeria's war against terrorism. This failure was systemically exposed by the Chibok girls' kidnap and the series of propaganda crisis that followed it.

Chibok Girls' Kidnap Exposes Propaganda Machine

In this subsection, we will focus on the business of propaganda and distortion of truth through the agency of information manipulation in the Nigerian government. The failures to lead the Nigerian people with true, consistent facts after the kidnap have left the current leadership with a serious work of convincing the citizenry about their commitment to democratic values and security, and support the achievement of common well-being for all the Nigerian people.

The Nigerian Bar Association, through her president Okey Wali, on the 26th of June, 2014 criticised the weakness of leadership and inefficiency in communication by the Nigerian government in the face of terrorism. Mr. Wali noted that Nigerian government's war effort is so far not yielding results. The government ought to be at the "forefront of communication, information and interfacing in this Boko Haram and Chibok matter."[181] Government needs to speak with facts and stand by the facts. It should not attempt to politicize the war effort against terrorism. Indiscreet party politics must be avoided in addressing such issue of national importance or emergency.[182] As an emerging democracy, we have to avoid the "unfortunate politicization and trivialization of a serious national problem"[183] and work together to address this security and corruption problem.

Let us now take a look at some of the inhumane and indiscreet propaganda and politicization/politicking with life-threatening terror war in Nigeria.

Defence through Propaganda by Okupe

Propaganda, for Ellul, is a consistent part of every aspect of the public life. It destroys the citizen's capacity for individual constructive discernment. It

---

[181] The Sun Newspaper, online news, 9th June, 2014.
[182] See Government's White Paper on the Report of the Federal Government Investigation Panel on the 2011 Election Violence and Disturbances." Some PDP States also had some unrest.
[183] The Sun Newspaper, online news, 9th June, 2014. I am of the view that security and corruption problem is one problem (share a source).

is in this light that Okupe's recent comments on BBC emphasizing President Jonathan "had no shoes as a child"—meaning that the President grew up a regular Nigerian child and so is aware of the socio-economic situation of average Nigerians. Okupe also insinuated that the war by Boko Haram militants was because of the religious difference and ethnicity of the President.[184] This is an unfortunate propaganda approach in a damning political situation. The former Minister of Information, Mr. Labaran Maku (once supervising Minister of Defence) said to the Nigerian people that Boko Haram is Borno State's issue and part of the effort of the Opposition parties (i.e., All Progressives Congress and other political parties) to make Nigeria ungovernable for President Jonathan. This is a clear case of misinformation and distortion of fact [185] which must be avoided especially in an election year in Nigeria.

Still on that BBC interview, Okupe went on and on to persuade every Nigerian who cared to watch the interview that everything will be alright[186] with this administration since all current problems came from past leaders and the last government, yet Okupe was part of the past (Obasanjo's) government as a spokesman[187], although for a limited time. He continually spins the future of Nigerians by claiming that Nigeria will always get it right in way to showcase what one could refer as the idea of "deified guardians of life"[188]–in this case, their analysis of President Jonathan and his key cabinet ministers as true avant-garde or *politico-connoisseur* of a progressive Nigeria. This propaganda approach by media personnel of the government disallows "personal reflection and evaluation"[189] of what the real situation is for the people. It prevents people from taking a critical and constructive evaluation of the Nigerian society without being hoodwinked by Aso Rock's[190] propaganda machinery incredible illusions.

---

[184] According to Jibrin Ibrahim, a political analyst at the Centre for Democracy and Development in Abuja, "There is a general belief that Jonathan hasn't committed himself to fight against Boko Haram because he thought it was a political crusade against him and did not understand that it was a real terrorist movement." Stephanie Findlay in Toronto Star Newspaper, Friday, 30th January, 2015, A8.
[185] Randal Marlin, Propaganda and the Ethics of Persuasion (Peterborough: Broadview Press Ltd, 2003), p. 306.
[186] Plato calls "noble lie" in the light of our discourse on Ellul's approach to myths and half-truths. See Plato, *The Republic*, Book 111, 389c and Book V, 459c. Randal Marlin, Propaganda and the Ethics of Persuasion (Peterborough: Broadview Press Ltd, 2003), p. 146.
[187] Bayo Oluwasanmi refers to Doyin Okupe as an insider in Aso Rock Propaganda Empire.
[188] See James A. Fowler, A Synopsis and Analysis of the Thought and Writings of Jacques Ellul, 2000. www.christinyou.com/pages/ellul.html
[189] See James A. Fowler, A Synopsis and Analysis of the Thought and Writings of Jacques Ellul, 2000. www.christinyou.com/pages/ellul.html
[190] Aso Rock is the seat of governance of the federal republic of Nigeria in Abuja.

We have to recall that Ellul suggests that for propaganda to be really successful or effective it needs to be credible and devoid of illusions. The problem of denial of clear facts and falsification of information to justify the ruling government's perspective is a failure in Jonathan's political transformation agenda and political promises. In 2014 alone, there are too many incredible political illusions about economic progress in Nigeria. Some of the statistics from government agencies do not add up and the concrete situation reports on economic progress are so damning.[191] Within such a situation of propaganda and political illusions, David W. Gill explains, "[O]ne of the most remarkable insights of Ellul's reflections on propaganda is that propaganda does not just foist lies and falsehoods on its target audiences. It mobilizes its audiences to embrace and act upon accepted 'facts' and the orientation of their mythologies. Propaganda plays on prejudices, it doesn't just create them."[192] Propaganda makes use of prejudice and manipulative style to elicit compliance of the people. From the above one discerns that propaganda involves social scientific insights and psychological techniques to "sway over human affairs"[193] according to the interest of the propagandist. The interest that is served and is behind this manipulation of facts will like to control the ability of people to think. They do not want the people to think on their own and so sway them to stick to government's side.

As noted earlier, one of the serious cases of terrorism in Nigeria was the kidnap of Chibok Girls. When it happened, government/ruling party was taken unawareness and their initial response was to depict the Opposition parties as bearers of bad news or initiators of protests to set off a false alarm. According to Ifeanyi Izeze, "[A]t the beginning and heat of the *Bring Back Our Girls* protest, the PDP [Peoples Democratic Party] was busy accusing the APC (All Progressives Congress party) of politicizing the abduction of the girls by sponsoring the Oby Ezekwesili-led group, while the opposition in turn also accused the ruling party of coming up with the new group to counter the entire

---

[191] I am considering at this point the number of young people that died during the Nigerian Immigration Service Recruitment Test stampede in 2014. It is estimated that about 18 young people died. The huge number that participated in that shameful recruitment tests points to the high level of unemployment which has a role in driving the Boko Haram youth into unacceptable alliances with terrorism. This is poverty in action!

[192] David W. Gill, "The Word of Jacques Ellul," President, International Jacques Ellul Society, 2007, p. 23. http://ellul.org/ELLUL%20FORUM%20ARTICLES/ISSUE37.pdf (Accessed on December 12, 2014)

[193] Kluver, p. 101.

idea."[194] These activities at some point were pushed too far in order to sway society and the citizenry to the respective sides of the conflictual political parties. It was poorly managed by the government and her communication offices. Even some federal government agencies failed to show objectivity, consistency, and integrity in addressing the issue as Nigeria's State (as whole nation united) effort to rescue the abducted girls.

A federal government agency—the Nigerian security agency –Department of States Services (DSS), or State Security Services (SSS), on one serious occasion, as was alleged, showed lack of discretion when it almost prevented Oby Ezekwesili (a known advocate of the Chibok Girls' return), in June, 2014 from attending a BBC London interview. It was reported that the attempt was to prevent her from causing further embarrassment for the government with the Chibok crisis. At some point the military claimed that they have rescued the girls in order to give the impression that issues are getting resolved with regard to the girls. It was certainly embarrassing for Government not to secure the release or fulfill their promise on the girls' release. On another sad note, in spite of all these assurances by government to rescue or release the girls, Boko Haram was able to kill about 59 boys at the Federal Government College, Buni Yadi, Yobe State. Many other sad incidents have since happened after the Chibok catastrophic failures even when government and her media agencies have tried to orchestrate a well-guarded approach to issues of national importance. The mismanagement of the kidnap incident leaves one with heavy heart in disbelief on how government reported on the situation. This is a strong indication of weakness by those doing the communication duties for the President, and show of lack of accountability by those who are paid with tax-payers' money.

Another aspect of this weakness in leadership, poor communication and public relations was the case of the Commissioner of Police (Joseph Mbu) for the Federal Capital Territory banning the *Bring Back Our Girls'* march for the release of Chibok Girls. There is a blatant violation of the Freedom of Expression, Peaceful Assembly and Association (See the 1999 Constitution of Nigeria (as amended), Section 40 (Constitution Chapter 4).[195] A Human Rights organization in Nigeria, known as the Committee for Democracy and Rights of the People (CDRP) led by Comrade Saka Waheed had expressed in strong terms her dissatisfaction with the restriction of citizens' right to peaceful protest. A

---

[194] Ifeanyi Izeze, "Bringbackourgirls: Tragedy of A Divided Nigerian People," in http. Saharareporters.com (Assessed 24th June, 2014).
[195] Denrele Animasaun, "Talk is Cheap," Vanguard, Sunday, 8th June, 2014. http://www.vanguardngr.com/2014/06/talk-cheap/ (Accessed 8th June, 2014)

fiery Nigerian lawyer and a Senior Advocate of the Law, Femi Falana equally wrote against Police Commissioner Joseph Mbu's insinuations against the *Bring Back Our Girls'* campaign. These situations were not expected if the Presidency considered prosecuting the war against terrorism with the alertness and clarity that it demands. Those at the helm of affairs must be clear not to send any confusing signals to the Nigerian people and to the world. Now the issue is not about the imperfections bedevilling those in government and their probable honest desire to govern the best, but it has more to do with information management and the attitude to convince whoever is affected by the actions of the terrorists that his/her family's well-being is ultimately considered. The sensitivity of the situation, for a good leader, would require not preventing any honest and non-violent demonstration/protest by the people—as it is one of people's rights that must be respected and protected by all law enforcement agencies and all relevant state agencies.

James Fowler, reflecting on Ellul's view on propaganda, similar to the Nigerian government propaganda empire in Aso Rock led by Dr. Okupe, Dr. Reuben Agbati, Director General National Orientation Agency and Coordination of the National Information Center, Mike Omeri, and now former Minister of Information, Labaran Maku, Fowler notes, "it is the influencing of behavior in definable and predictable ways in order to provoke specific acceptable responses and actions which bring about the mass participation of individuals in the collective organizational structure."[196]

The levels of onslaught by Nigerian government media agencies, or what we have described above as Nigerian government propaganda empire in Aso Rock, and their maintenance of power, through socio-economic cum political illusions and opinion control, are part of what Ellul describes rhetorically and sarcastically as "[P]ower is based on opinion. What is a government are not supported by opinion? Nothing."[197] Certainly, power could be maintained through a regular use of "dirty trick" approach to defame opposition parties and dissenting views in order to sway voters/citizens to the side of the ruling government.

Ellul, in the light of the above, thinks that propaganda always has an effect. It does not really fail. What fails is the "surface propaganda, tactical

---

[196] See James A. Fowler, A Synopsis and Analysis of the Thought and Writings of Jacques Ellul, 2000. www.christinyou.com/pages/ellul.html
[197] Jacques Ellul, Propaganda: the formation of men's attitude, trans. by Konrad Kellen and Jean Lerner, (New York: Vintage, 1973), p. 123.

propaganda," but fundamental propaganda succeeds.[198] Propaganda overwhelms us to stay and wait until answers are given to us instead of finding them out ourselves. We are told what to believe! When to act! Propaganda is effective through public opinion (individual participates in public opinion) or "massified"[199] form of opinion.

The Chibok crisis: the height

When the Chibok girls' kidnap pressure and the consequent criticism of government's lack of leadership became strong, the Nigerian government inaugurated a committee on the 2nd of May, 2014 to gather facts about Chibok girls' kidnap. Presently, some facts of the Chibok kidnap have been officially disclosed by the Presidential Fact Finding Committee led by Retired Major-General Ibrahim Sabo. The committee states that 276 girls were abducted, 57 escaped, 119 students escaped from the school premises during the abduction. The actual number of missing students is 219.[200] This information is necessary to better understand the issues surrounding the abduction of the girls.

Following the sequence of events, one could see the difficulties of poor communication in the current leadership of Nigeria. It took a long period of doubting the kidnap and politicking by government to set up the committee that gathered the necessary facts about the Chibok girls' case. If the facts were immediately gathered and authenticated, then it is would show that government is committed to ensuring security of the people and the release of the girls. It is much more effective to lead the people with concrete facts and allow them educate themselves with the positive facts available from objective news reports in such a precarious situation, in fact, a war time situation. People are truly understanding and concerned with the war situation against terrorism, but they are not ready to see a system that is manipulative and over flooded with orchestrated false information.[201] The government has to communicate

---

[198] Ellul, Propaganda, p. 285.
[199] Ellul, Propaganda, p. 291.
[200] Haruna Umar and Michelle Faul, "Boko Haram blamed for Nigerian attack," in Toronto Star, Friday, December 19, 2014, A18. See Saharareporters online news, 20th June 2014. Stephanie Findlay affirms that President Jonathan's free fall started around this time. (Toronto Star, Friday, January 30, 2015, A8)
[201] The recent terrorist attack in Paris where 12 people were killed showed the preparedness of government in addressing the issues, getting at the three terrorists, and apologizing for failing to forestall the attack in spite of earlier intelligence reports. The incident was followed by about 1 Million march of world leaders and people of France. "Je suis Charlie" march—'I am

distinctively and humanly, without bias reporting or attempting to mislead the people despite the war situation.

The Boko Haram insurgency is a clear war time situation, at least for millions of Northern Nigerians whose communities have been taken over by the terrorists. Those directly affected are Nigerian citizens whose homes were destroyed and family members were killed, or kidnapped. According to Ellul, "[I]n time of war, everybody agrees that news must be limited and controlled,"[202] but in Nigeria's case it shows a colossal failure of propaganda and failure to communicate with the people by government. The situation is what Prof. Abiodun Salawu, Professor of Journalism, Communication and Media Studies, North-West University, South African described thus, "[T]he information/communication machinery of the president is not proactive and vibrant enough."[203] Ajibola Amzat, a Nigerian journalist, in a similar line argues that "disseminating inconsistent information that has placed credibility crisis on its integrity."[204] Thus the issue is not that the Chibok girls were not kidnapped but, at least, the President is willing to address the issue immediately to find if it is true or not, and if true, how does the military go about rescuing these girls. The commitment of the Presidency to national security in the face of territorial aggression and occupation by Boko Haram must be clearly communicated and, convincingly, too. In this light Prof. Ralph Akinfeleye, Department of Mass Communication, University of Lagos, notes, "the President's media are rather miscommunicating rather than communicating."[205] Despite the miscommunication or purposeful attempts to misinform the people, one fact is clear, according to Tunde Bakare, former APC Vice Presidential Candidate in 2011 election, "[I]n the recent Global Terrorism Index, based on 2013 incidents, Nigeria ranked 4th among 162 countries with 303 reported attacks, 1,826 fatalities and 457 injuries. Terrorism was said to have cost Nigeria $28.48 billion in the year 2013. Nigeria is surpassed only by Pakistan, Afghanistan and Iraq in this index. Given the dastardly activities of Boko Haram last year, the 2014 index would be even more damning for Nigeria."[206] Now let us take a brief look at Boko Haram (see above Boko Haram: the motif!)

Charlie'. The important point here is to avoid distortion or manipulation of facts. It demands giving the people the facts of the situation and in a good time.
[202] Ellul, Propaganda, p. 238.
[203] Guardian Newspaper, online news, 28th June, 2014.
[204] Ajibola Amzat, The Guardian Newspaper.
[205] Ajibola Amzat, Guardian Newspaper, online news, 28th June, 2014.
[206] http://saharareporters.com/2015/01/05/seven-signs-2015-elections-will-shipwreck-nigeria-pastor-bakare (Accessed 5th January, 2015)

The Boko Haram crisis in Nigeria has bedeviled the country for over 5 years now. The devastations are enormous and undeniable. It has already dragged the economy and lives of Northeastern Nigeria to a terrible halt. Some of these people are internally displaced persons (IDP)[207] and some are refugees in other countries sharing boundaries with that part of Nigeria. *Toronto Star* Newspaper report by Haruna Umar and Michelle Faul provides updates on level of devastation after 8 months of the kidnap of about 219 Chibok girls. The current report affirms that the, "Islamic extremists killed 35 people and kidnapped at least 185, fleeing residents said Thursday of an attack near the town where nearly 300 schoolgirls were taken hostage in April. Most of those kidnapped Sunday were young women, children and members of a vigilante group that is fighting Boko Haram, residents said…In a recent video, Shekau said the girls were "an old story," implying their release was no longer up for negotiation."[208] Of course, the leader of the Boko Haram in Nigeria—Mr. Shekau has been reported killed many months ago by the Nigerian military, even with purported pictures as evidence of his corpse. With this level of miscommunication and non-convincing approach to the use of propaganda, we shall now consider the impact of failed propaganda, this time, within the Nigerian military fighting Boko Haram.

Now let us take a look at some of the major highlights that buttress the failure of governance and failure to overcome the terrorists' group by the Nigerian military, and the inability of government to communicate humanly and convincingly for peace.

Ellul, Violence, and the Nigerian Military Mutiny

Oxford English dictionary describes violence, and by extension war, as the deliberate exercise of physical force against a person, group of persons, property, etc. It involves a physically violent behavior or treatment.[209] Violent behaviors could happen by the use of armed forces against foreign or opposing institution or party or state.

Meanwhile, Ellul states that the hostile contention or constrain used by a state in defence of her citizenry is rather called "force", not violence. He further

---

[207] There are about 4 million internally displaced persons Nigerians. About 1.5 million persons were displaced from the Boko Haram menace.
[208] Haruna Umar and Michelle Faul, "Boko Haram blamed for Nigerian attack," in Toronto Star, Friday, December 19, 2014, A18.
[209] Electronic Oxford English Dictionary (Oxford: Oxford University Press, 2015)

explains, "never acts by violence when it constrains, condemns and kills."[210] In the above, Ellul provides a leeway for the state in acts of force by describing "unjust force" which, for him, is not "violence", as such. The state has the legitimacy to go to war in defence of its reason for existence. The state makes it possible or it guarantees the existence of each individual members of the community/state. Any continual violence against the individuals and against the state will ultimately lead to its atrophification or gradual disintegration. In order to avoid the disintegration of a state which is a community of citizens that recognises a central leadership or control of power for the well-being and security of the entire citizenry, Ellul adds, "the state... must have the right to wage war,"[211] especially when there is a treat to the life of her citizens. In this situation "violence"—war—truly becomes the last resort to maintain the full enjoyment of human good, human dignity, social order, and peaceful existence. As Ellul affirms, this is when "[hu]man can retain control of violence, that violence can be kept in the service of order and justice and even of peace"[212]

For there to be peace and respect and mutual co-existence, any opposing elements, elements of violation and interference on the dignity of life or the quality of life of the other person or group of people raises the concern about violence in defence or war of attrition. Our current world situations make violence an often-talked-about theme.[213] Ellul considers "violence as 'one of the 'rudiments' (stoicheia) of this world."[214]

Psychological violence is a far-reaching or comprehensive form of understanding violence. In Ellul's perspective, it is that aspect of effecting violence on the other person or groups of persons in other to influence them or control them. As he states, "[P]sychological violence…is simply violence, whether it takes the form of propaganda, biased reports, meetings of secret societies that inflate the egos of their members, brainwashing, or intellectual terrorism."[215] Violence is easily related to terrorism depending on the situation and the purpose. Despite Ellul's contributions, he did not provide a precise

---

[210] Jacques Ellul, Violence: Reflections from a Christian Perspective (London: SCM Press, 1970), p. 3. Jacques Ellul, Contre les violents (Le Centurion, 1972).
[211] Jacques Ellul, Violence: Reflections from a Christian Perspective (London: SCM Press, 1970), p. 5.
[212] Jacques Ellul, Violence: Reflections from a Christian Perspective (London: SCM Press, 1970), pp. 5-6.
[213] There has already been a series of terrorist attacks since the beginning of the New Year (2015).
[214] Jacques Ellul, Prayer and Modern Man (New York: Seabury, 1970), p. 174.
[215] Jacques Ellul, Violence: Reflections from a Christian Perspective (London: SCM Press, 1970), p. 97.

definition of violence, but one of the experts on Ellulian socio-philosophical views thinks that Ellul will likely define it thus: as an act of "coercing someone in a way that violates his personhood."[216] This is exactly what Boko Haram terrorists aim to accomplish in Nigeria—the violation of other persons. Their ideology that they present to the world is the intention to establish Islamists civilization and a rejection of any form of Western democratic practices in Nigeria. This point does not undermine or obliterate our initial argument that socio-economic issues are at the back of the gradual growth of Boko Haram insurgency.

Poverty and unemployment made Boko Haram's fundamentalist Islamist ideology an easy sale to the teaming population of employable young people. As has been acknowledged by scholars on Nigeria politics, democracy, and war on terror, the confrontation between the Nigerian military was initially considered an attempt to flush out these so-called young disgruntled elements in the Northeastern States of Nigeria. Boko Haram was at this time considered a rag-tag that could be handled by the well experienced Nigerian military, experienced in the African Union Missions in Liberia, Sierra Leone, etc. Unfortunately, after close to 6 years the war against Boko Haram has grown to a full-blown war of self-embarrassment and infamy. The embarrassment that Boko Haram brought to the Nigerian government, and up until now, well respected Nigerian military, has led to a war fought without war ethics, but mostly to express derision, bitterness, and hatred. Hatred spurs on violence. Hatred sustains violence, the destruction of life and properties. Ellul affirms this unfortunate relation between violence and hatred. He notes, "violence is an expression of hatred, has its source in hatred and signifies hatred....It is absolutely essential for us to realize that there is an unbreakable link between violence and hatred"[217] Hatred has nothing to do with dignity and humanness, but violence in the context of war could be fought with dignity and humanness. This is the kind of war that Ellul considers a necessity, a necessary evil that is at the service of peace. As Ellul notes, war is naturally violent.[218]

Having established the connection between violence, terrorism and hatred, let take a look at the war effort in Nigeria. It is a good example of violence

---

[216] Kenneth J. Konyndyk, "Violence" in Clifford G. Christians & Jay M. Van Hook (eds), Jacques Ellul: Interpretive Essays (University of Illinois Press, 1981), p. 256. Konyndyk provides this enlightening comment.
[217] Jacques Ellul, Violence: Reflections from a Christian Perspective (London: SCM Press, 1970), p.104.
[218] Jacques Ellul on Religion, Technology and Politics: Conversations with Patrick Troude-Chastenet (Atlanta: Scholars Press, 1998), p. 39.

bound in hatred. This war situation has bred a form of disenchanted military, bereft of war ethics (human rights abuse) and bad records of mutiny because of lack of war equipment, poor motivation, and disillusionment.

Military and Mutiny

The war effort against Boko Haram, pursued with ill-motivated and disillusioned military, has helped uncover the weakness in Nigerian military and a clear indictment of the current Commander-in-Chief: President Jonathan. In war the leader of the group takes responsibility of failures associated with the prosecution of war by his/her group or battalion. The buck knows exactly where to stop: at the head! In a democratic state, the buck stops at the Presidency! The Commander-in-Chief!

The war against Boko Haram terrorism has exposed many anomalies and equally unveiled the failure of leadership within the Nigerian military. In recent times there have been news reports about corruption and lack of morale within the military, and reports about gross insubordination among the ranks and files of the armed forces. There are also cases of sabotage by insiders secretly providing security or classified information to Boko Haram. Unfortunately, for some time now, no deterrence and no names of senior officers involved in these have been published.

Not long ago, about 22 military officers were court-martialled in Lagos, Lagos State, while some young soldiers have been condemned by the military court for mutiny. The first group condemned to death by the military tribunal included about 12 soldiers following the mutiny at Maimalari Barracks in Maidugari in Borno State. According to Ifeanyi Izeze, "[T]he Nigerian military spokesman, Major General Chris Olukolade in Abuja gave a pacy account of what happened at the anti-insurgency command headquarters in Maiduguri where some soldiers of the newly created 7th Division of the Nigerian Army opened fire on the vehicle of the General Officer Commanding (GOC) the brigade. But this would surely satisfy only those who saw the incident the way he saw it, or, rather, the way he wanted them to see it (propaganda). As gathered, "some soldiers angered by the death of 12 of their colleagues during a Boko Haram ambush, Wednesday May 14th, 2014 opened fire on the vehicle of the General Officer Commanding (GOC) the newly created Maiduguri-based 7th Division of the Nigerian Army, Major General Ahmadu Mohammed and when he escaped, they proceeded to vandalise his official residence in

Maiduguri."²¹⁹ Izeze provides a clear narrative of Nigerian soldiers not receiving the emotional and psychological as well the full military equipment support to prosecute the war against terrorism. It takes a whole lot of pressure for soldiers to attack a senior officer not to say a General Officer Commanding (GOC). The consequences of such attack are obviously, and almost unimaginably, grave considering military laws.

Now, following grave military law court-marshalling process, a second group of about 54 young soldiers was in December 2014 condemned to death because of mutiny by the military court in Nigeria. Fortunately, these young soldiers have received the support of Nigerians for crying out against lack of equipment of war and adequate food. In these incidences, one could deduce that the soldiers are clearly ill-equipped, distressed, ill-motivated, and demoralized. These are major difficulties any dependable officers and soldiers do not need to deal with in prosecuting war of any serious magnitude. The difficult weaknesses in current Nigerian military, by implication, point to the weakness in the Commander-in-Chief, President Jonathan. The recent court martialing of military personnel is an indication of a bigger administrative cum political problem.

Most of the young soldiers condemned to die have taken to Facebook and other communication media to report on their conditions of operation, and expose how the operation of stamping out terrorism in Nigeria is prosecuted with ineffective weaponry and compromised security strategy. The young soldiers are sent-off to places were the Boko Haram terrorists are already lying in wait to attack the soldiers, especially having received prior information of how the Nigerian military commanders are moving the soldiers in the states.²²⁰ These young soldiers, without being properly equipped, are left with the only two options of either disobeying command and consequently court-martialled for insubordination or mutiny which amounts to death on the stakes. Since the war against Boko Haram terrorism got worse and deadly, the young soldiers have often found themselves between the devil and the hard place. It is in situations of these kinds that Binneh Minteh and Ashlie Perry insist that, "with a weak government unable to combat the threat from within, Boko Haram is

---

²¹⁹ http://saharareporters.com/2014/05/20/nigerian-soldiers%E2%80%99-revolt-7-div-jonathan-and-battered-espirit-d%E2%80%99-corp-ifeanyi-izeze (Accessed on 22nd of December, 2014)

²²⁰ http://www.bbc.com/news/world-africa-30547771; http://www.bbc.com/news/world-africa-30580578
(Accessed on 22nd December, 2014)

winning political support locally, obtaining training internationally."²²¹ According to Ike Willie Nwobu, Nigeria has become "wastelands of blood and despair…this new wave of insurgency and terror…is actually unprecedented in Nigeria." ²²² It seems the source of these wastelands of blood and disillusion is within the echelon of the Nigerian military. The military secret war strategies have been compromised.

The former Chief of Army Staff (COAS), Lieutenant General Azubuike Ihejirika, in 2013 complained that some sensitive military operations' information had been divulged by officers and soldiers sympathetic to Boko Haram terrorists.²²³ In June 2014, *Toronto Star* Newspaper noted that about 10 Generals in the military have been implicated.²²⁴ Even President Jonathan himself has confirmed that his own government's inner caucus has been infiltrated by people loyal to Boko Haram. If the president's inner security operatives are truly bugged by politicians/military officers sympathetic to the terrorist organization, then it is not difficult to deduce that the Nigerian military is in a terror war that it may never win, unless some serious challenges are addressed.

The Boko Haram terrorist group seems to be winning in every aspect of this asymmetrical war. It has succeeded in every aspect of their media and war propaganda in demoralizing the Nigerian government, military officers, and soldiers. The terrorists have used every visual propaganda means to bring to light their successes in confronting Nigerian military defence and might. The group seems to be strategically ubiquitous in the Northeastern states of Nigeria and have tactically infiltrated the war plans of government. A recent letter attributed to Lieutenant Colonel A. Wende of the 103 Battalion, currently serving in "Operation Zamani Lafiya" in Konduga²²⁵, addressed to the President Jonathan, duly points accusing finger on the rot in leadership (military and

---

²²¹ Binneh Minteh and Ashlie Perry, Terrorism in West Africa-Boko Haram's Evolution, Strategy and Affiliations, presented at the Mid-West Political Science Association's 71st Annual Conference Palmer House Hotel (Chicago Illinois, April 2013).
²²² Punch Newspaper, "Opinion" by Ike Willie Nwobu.
²²³ The then Lieutenant General Ihejirika made this point during his 2013 paper presentation at Army Transformation and Innovation Center in Abuja—a conference on personnel management and development.
²²⁴ Toronto Star, 3rd of June, 2014, A11. There are indications that the Nigerian military has suspended dismissing officers and carrying out the judgment of the military tribunal against soldiers involved in mutiny considering the sensitive political situation in the country. Many people predict a volatile political period because of the equal campaign strength of the ruling party (PDP) and the main Opposition party (APC).
²²⁵ Konduga is about 25 km to the Southeast of Maiduguri in Borno State.

national). The circulated letter appeared to have been accessed by the leaders of Nigerian military and possibly reached the presidency. The frustration is distinct and everywhere! It is not only the young soldiers and officers that are disillusioned about the war against terror. The Nigeria people, as we noted earlier under Chibok girls' crisis, are also frustrated with unsuccessful and endless war effort against Boko Haram. The Nigerian military is bedevilled by incessant news about internal crisis and mutiny. The Presidency--Commander-in-Chief –is perceived in some quarters to be clueless and psychological distraught, according to Gwynne Dyer. As Ellul acknowledges, "[T]error is always visual."[226] Boko Haram terrorists have taken advantage of visual propaganda to demoralize young Nigerian soldiers and officers. The way the Commander-in-Chief is seen in the international community as clueless and distraught emboldens the terrorists. The psychology behind terrorism is to inflict pain and create fear. These must be visible to the people whose lives are impacted. The devastations or carnages of terrorism really speak for themselves.

Boko Haram members repeatedly behead hostages and show tapes of such nefarious actions on YouTube, Facebook, and other communication media. Their recent invasion of a military barrack in one of the states in Northeastern Nigeria is a good example of their brutal use of terror, fear and visual tactics. Ellul states that this form of terrorism and its carnages tell us of "[S]uch terror results from the horror of reality."[227] For instance, the recent deadly attacks near Chibok—about 5 miles from Chibok—and around the village of Garkin Fulani caused the death of some women. The attacks took place in the villages of Danjara, Agapalwa, and Antagara (Gwoza district in Borno State). Mohamed Ali Ndume, a senator representing Borno State, confirmed this attack.[228] One has to recall that some of these Northeastern states are in the state of emergency, yet people are kidnapped or killed, and forced to embrace fundamental Islamist agenda. The most recent incident in Baga, near Nigeria's border with Chad, is estimated to have killed 150 to 2,000 people.[229] Honest efforts to find out the true situation and figures are ongoing.

---

[226] Ellul, The Humiliation of the Word (Grand Rapids, Michigan: William B. Eerdmans Publication co., 1985, Reprinted in 1988), p. 12.
[227] Ellul, The Humiliation of the Word (Grand Rapids, Michigan: William B. Eerdmans Publication co., 1985, Reprinted in 1988), p. 12.
[228] Mohammed Ali Ndume, in The Sun Newspaper, 11th June 2014. http://sunnewsonline.com/new/?p=66039 (Accessed on 3rd March, 2015)
[229] Amnesty International has reported about 2,000 people was killed. The Nigerian military is suggesting 150.

The situation of Boko Haram terrorism has caused some eminent Nigerians to express dissatisfaction with the failure of leadership and ineffective communication relationship between government and the Nigerian people. The former president of Nigeria Retired General Olusegun Obasanjo—an experienced leader and officer in his own right—has tried to weigh into the situation, and offer some critical assistance.

Propaganda and Ex-President Obasanjo's Assistance

The former President General Obasanjo made public to the Nigerian people a personal letter he addressed to President Jonathan criticizing Jonathan that he (Obasanjo) had access to Boko Haram leadership but not to the Presidency. Obasanjo is of the view that Jonathan leadership has isolated many prominent Nigerians who could have been useful in addressing the current security and unemployment problems. Obasanjo's first criticism against the Nigerian government war against terrorism is the inability of government to accept well-tested and credible authorities to assist in the war against Boko Haram, and to help mediate in the release of the kidnapped Chibok Girls's case. The government, according to him, have, in principle, aligned itself with some bad elements and corrupt politicians while excluding resourceful prominent ex-leaders who may not agree with Jonathan's unpopular policies and security approach. These accusations and other critical comments from Obasanjo were countered with firm propaganda by the spokesmen of the president. For Ellul, in line with the situation, states that "[P]ropaganda is by itself a state of war; it demands the exclusion of opposite trends and minorities—not total and official perhaps, but… partial and indirect exclusion."[230] Propaganda is not only meant to elicit cooperation from citizens, but also crush the ability (of citizens) to shape their lives and their understanding.

In December 2014, General Obasanjo said he had written a letter to the current President Jonathan, entitled "Before It Is Too Late." There he advised Jonathan to "[M]ove away from culture of denials, cover-ups and proxies and deal honesty, sincerely and transparently with Nigerians to regain their trust and confidence." He adds, "Nigerians are no fools, they can see, they can hear, they can talk among themselves, they can think, they can compare and they can act in the interest of their country and in their own self-interest. They keenly watch all actions and deeds that are associated with you if they cannot

---

[230] Ellul, Propaganda, p. 247.

believe your words. I know you have the power to save PDP[Peoples' Democratic Party] and the country. I beg you to have the courage and the will with patriotism to use the power for the good of the country."[231] He also requested that the current opportunity will serve to right the many wrongs of the current president and reassure Nigerians in the face of terrorism.

Ernesto Londono and Anne Gearan have this to say about President Jonathan's approach to terrorism. They said, "[A]ccording to Johnnie Carson, 'The Nigerians have shown a reluctance to accept not only our assistance but also a reluctance to accept some of our analytic advice.'"[232] It does not hurt for a current president to use some discretion in accepting some responsible advice from experienced authorities. Some eminent Nigerians have in one way or the other expressed the desire to assist especially in returning the girls to their family after the trauma of violence and possible abuses. As is a well-known, senior citizens and eminent political figures sometimes consider certain duties to their fatherland/motherland as an *opportune* call to duty[233]-- a duty of conscience! They may feel this need to offer a timeless political service for the common good of their people and to offer generous services to their nations in appreciation for what they have received in terms of honor and respect. In this light, Ellul rightly notes, "[N]othing is worse in times of danger than to live in a dream world. To warn a political system of a menace hanging over it does not imply an attack against it, but the greatest service one can render the system."[234]

The failure to accept the assistance of eminent Nigerians and other responsible authorities in prosecuting the war against terrorism by President Jonathan has left him with damning criticisms from international observers and commentators. For instance, Dyer expressed the incompetence of the current leadership in Nigeria, especially in its inability to prosecute the war against terrorism/Boko Haram. He sees the failure of leadership as making the disintegration of Nigeria a closed fact. He clearly indicts the federal government in these words "[I]n these circumstances, you would expect the federal

---

[231] http://saharareporters.com/2014/12/04/president-jonathan-sends-frontline-pdp-governors-beg-most-prominent-critic-obasanjo (Accessed on December 4, 2014)
[232] Johnnie Carson was the former assistant secretary of State for Africa. John Campbell, former US ambassador to Nigeria, said that President Goodluck Jonathan has "resisted help." See Washington Post, accessed 27th June, 2014.
[233] I presented a paper on *The Duty to Help and Duty to Responsible Justice in light of Alan Gewirth's The Community of Rights* at an Alternative Perspective and Global Concerns international conference. See Alternative Perspectives and Global Concerns, the sixth international conference at the University of Ottawa, 17th-18th October, 2014.
[234] Ellul, Propaganda, p. xvi.

government, and especially President Goodluck Jonathan, to be under constant attack for having failed to act decisively against Boko Haram, but nothing of the sort…Voters' expectation are so low that they are not even shocked by the quite plausible accusation that Jonathan has failed to fight hard against Boko Haram because the three northeastern states would probably vote against the PDP in the next election. And so the band plays on, as Nigeria drifts toward civil war and disintegration."[235]

This is the first time a logical and critical comment, to our knowledge, has expressed the necessity for concern in Nigeria's imminent disintegration. It almost seems like a plot that President Jonathan is perhaps unknowingly or covertly playing out. Hilary Clinton as then Secretary of States (USA) was alluded to have averred that Nigeria will cease to exist in the near future, include 2015. Mr. James F. Entwistle, current American ambassador to Nigeria, denies such a statement or any document to support it. In line with the argument for this paper on Ellul's communicative perspective, one cannot but agree with Dyer that "[T]he forthcoming election will not focus on the stunning incompetence and sheer inertia of President Goodluck Jonathan's government in the face of this [Boko Haram] threat. Boko Haram's rise to prominence has taken place entirely on Jonathan's watch, and at no time has he shown much interest in fighting it."[236]

While considering the above, the cat and mouse game and comments of President Jonathan's Media Advisers (Dr. Abati, Dr. Okupe, Mr. Omeri and others) it is clear that his propaganda machinery is collapsing like a pack of cards. The failure of governance in the face of terrorism is glaring before the people. People are determined to express their disappointment at the quality of leadership at this important time. Certainly, the situation does not suggest that the main Opposition party (APC) is being favored to replace President Jonathan. It also does not imply that those who speculate the possibility of the opposition winning 2015 presidential election are against the president because of baseless or founded arguments. About the recent news that the main Opposition party (APC) was planning to present a Muslim/Muslim Presidential and vice— presidential candidates, we firmly think that the Nigerian people have not shown

---

[235] Gwynne Dyer is an independent journalist based in London, England. See Gwynne Dyer, "Boko Haram not Nigeria's only problem," in The Peterborough Examiner, Thursday, December 4, 2014, Comment section, A4

[236] Gwynne Dyer is an independent journalist based in London, England. See Gwynne Dyer, "Boko Haram not Nigeria's only problem," in The Peterborough Examiner, Thursday, December 4, 2014, Comment section, A4

sufficient political maturity to prevent religious-politics gain support especially at a time when Boko Haram is described as a product of religious fundamentalism! It is satisfyingly interesting that the main Opposition party finally ditched the idea of a Muslim/Muslim to a Muslim/Christian—Retired Major-General Muhammadu Buhari/Prof. Yemi Osinbajo.

If the main Opposition party is having the difficulty of presenting a formidable presidential and vice-presidential candidates campaign, then the recent moves by President Jonathan to mend fence with the former President Obasanjo (his former party boss) may resuscitate his campaign as he is alleged to have sent some friends of Obasanjo to lessen the political damaged he (Jonathan) has incurred through poor leadership and negative propaganda. According to a well-known media platform on African news SaharaReporters, it [SaharaReporters] "learnt that the governors, who were protégés of Obasanjo during his tenure, had been asked to visit the former president to beg the former leader to tone down his opposition to Mr. Jonathan."[237]

This fence mending propaganda approach could be perceived in the recent statement released by Okupe with regard to the impeachment move against the President by some senators. According to these senators, high level incompetence in governance has led to continued terrorism, and the recent oil price crisis has not been adequately addressed either. Okupe seems to evoke the sense of nationalism and patriotism (with hidden distorted purposes) even in the face of crass incompetence and lack of leadership. Okupe's full statement reads, "[T]he Senate in the last four years has conducted its legislative functions and responded to issues that are of great national importance with commendable political sagacity…In this same period, the Senate has functioned as a stabilising force within the polity employing much political maturity that is required to guide and protect our nascent democracy…However, confrontation and strong disagreements are not uncommon phenomenon in Executive-Legislative relationship world-wide…The recent purported attempt by some senators to prepare impeachable offences against the President, as reported in some section of the media, is seen by us in this light….We strongly trust and believe in the leadership of the present Senate and the unwavering patriotism and commitment that have been shown by the distinguished members and we trust that ultimately it is this tendency towards true nationalism that will prevail in the Senate….It is our view that there are at present, serious fundamental issues of national

---

[237] http://saharareporters.com/2014/12/04/president-jonathan-sends-frontline-pdp-governors-beg-most-prominent-critic-obasanjo (Accessed on December 4, 2014)

importance such as winning the war against terrorism and stabilising the economy in the face of dwindling oil revenue which require the full attention, commitment and swift action of distinguished members of the Senate....We are of the opinion that all matters political can and will be resolved politically in the overall interest of our democracy and the wellbeing of our people."[238]

In the above, it appears as if Okupe is only playing to the gallery and have forgotten his divisive propaganda-filled attacks before this election time. He seems to be scheming out a way to praise all members of the Senate and dissuade them from going on with the impeachment move. The flip-flop approach of Okupe confirms this purposeful distortion of facts and propaganda taking place in Nigeria. Ellul advices, "propaganda cannot be anything other than what it is: an instrument of manipulation to obtain an objectively conforming behavior (orthopraxy). That is to say, that it obeys, exclusively, principles of efficacy, technical rules of a psychological or sociological nature, the usage of instruments which are themselves techniques."[239] The approach of the media magicians/propaganda machine of President Jonathan's government suggests an attempt to pummel the poor masses into believing that things are working and that they are truly considered in matters of good governance. Okupe's comment above was an attempt at resolving the political differences with displeased members of the Senate. It does not amount to astute leadership for genuine socio-economic transformation. Ellul states that "[P]ropaganda, in reality, includes in itself both the "apparatus" and "techniques" of propaganda and the message which is transmitted."[240]

The message transmitted is in order to hinder access to the facts and keep the people to conform to the political expectations of government's spokespersons. As Ellul notes, "it is precisely propaganda that prevents the facts from being perceived as such."[241] Prof. Pius Adesanmi described the whole situation of manipulative communication by spokespersons of government with

---

[238] http://www.punchng.com/news/jonathan-to-senators-focus-on-national-issues-not-impeachment/ (Accessed on December 4, 2014) It seems Okupe is running out of propaganda materials.

[239] http://ellul.org/ELLUL%20FORUM%20ARTICLES/ISSUE37.pdf (Accessed December 9, 2014). See the Jacques Ellul, "The Ethics of Propaganda," in Communication, 6 (1981): 159-175. Translated from the French by D. Raymond Tourville.

[240] http://ellul.org/ELLUL%20FORUM%20ARTICLES/ISSUE37.pdf See Jacques Ellul, "The Ethics of Propaganda," in Communication, 6 (1981): 159-175. Translated from the French by D. Raymond Tourville.

[241] http://ellul.org/ELLUL%20FORUM%20ARTICLES/ISSUE37.pdf See the Jacques Ellul, "The Ethics of Propaganda," in Communication, 6 (1981): 159-175. Translated from the French by D. Raymond Tourville.

a catch phrase as "career Jonathanism."[242] 'Career Jonathanism' is on the effort of people working for the Nigerian government to manipulate, clean-up, defend, rationalise, and wipe-out any dent of poor publicity by the current president. But to this one has to note that Ellul is not really after perfect accomplishments, but he demands a humane communication of the facts that will bring about peace and development in the society. It is on this note that we will like to take a look at the failure of propaganda in Nigeria, especially in light of President Jonathan's spokesperson—Dr. Okupe.

Failure of Propaganda Okupe's Ostrich Experience

Propaganda is "completely integrated and immersed in a social entity. It cannot be stripped in a bid to get a 'pure state.' "[243] It is always seen as an integral part of the state or community. As a sort of "psychological war"—it is a kind of onslaught against the citizens by hindering them from accessing the truth and the nature of governance. It is an essential aspect of the "breakdown of human communication"[244] since we have the difficulties of trusting our leaders and their appointed masters of communication/mercenaries of propaganda.

Jonathan's government and spokespersons[245] are of the view that Boko Haram is an instrument of the main Opposition party and of some Northern elements who feel they do not control government and thus use terrorism as the best way to get the attention of government. It seems to tally with what Ellul describes (he agrees with Marx) as, "when man realizes that he no longer has the means of influencing the situation he begins to revolt." [246] But one is not sure of the credibleness of such insinuations against the Opposition parties and some Northern elites. The gradual degeneration of the security situation in the country has clear indications of poor leadership, unemployment, lack collaboration between the ruling party and the main Opposition party in issues of national importance. The main Opposition party members are Nigerians whose contributions to governance must be considered and incorporated, without being

---

[242] http://saharareporters.com/2014/12/16/bastard-doyin-okupe-and-other-jonathanian-headaches-self-naming-pius-adesanmi (Accessed on December 17, 2014)
[243] Ellul, Propaganda, p. 264.
[244] Jeffrey P. Greenman, Read Mercer Schurchardt, Noah J. Toly, Understanding Jacques Ellul, (UK, Cambridge: James Clarke and co, 2013), p. 18.
[245] Some elder statesmen like Chief Edwin Clark (Ijaw Chief) have shared this opinion too about Boko Haram and the Opposition parties.
[246] Jacques Ellul on Religion, Technology and Politics: Conversations with Patrick Troude-Chastenet (Oregon: Wipf and Stock Publishers, 2005), p. 24.

badmouthed through dirty propaganda and divisive publications. It is the duty of those in government to show quality leadership in communicating with dignity and humanly for a peaceful society. This is what it means to have an inclusive democracy and governance. It is part of what former Secretary General of the United Nations Kofi Annan described as reaching out for political solution to the problem of insecurity and youth unemployment. Good governance, employment, national security are not a one-party responsibility, they are government's as well as all Nigerian in spite of political delineation. As we know national security and international security—war against every form of terrorism—is a global responsibility that needs not be compromised or undermined through dirty politicking and negative propaganda of divisive nature. Terrorism is against all humanity and requires everyone, the local and international communities' support.

With the current crumbling of the propaganda machinery of government, the failed negotiation for a peace deal with Boko Haram, the failed promises of returning the Chibok girls before the end of December 2014. The Nigerian people have to decide what is important to them. If the agent of propaganda pushes the poor masses to believe that they were manipulated by the people in government, then it is a direct declaration of war against the masses. As Wole Soyinka states the government of Nigeria failed to secure the prosecution of the war effort against terrorism "because [the] foreign countries were cynical of Nigeria's claim to fight insecurity."[247] In this case, Soyinka is proffering one of the reasons for US government non-active involvement in Nigerian government approach to dealing with Boko Haram terrorism. It is on record that the US will not to accept to sell certain ammunition to Nigerian military fearing compromise of security information. If the Nigerian government had secured these ammunitions and are in good collaboration with the US[248], it will have been one of the best ways to express the support of the international community and win the admiration of the entire Nigerian citizenry for a convincing approach to finish off Boko Haram terrorism. Maybe government would have been able to defeat Boko Haram and their alleged Opposition parties' sponsors (as alleged by the people in charge of government's media and communication).

But is it really the case that Boko Haram terrorists are the working of the Opposition parties? Could it be a sign of the failure of leadership, lack of

---

[247] http://www.punchng.com/news/jonathan-worse-than-nebuchadnezzar-soyinka-2/ (accessed on December 3, 2014)
[248] In 2014 the Nigerian government canceled the personnel training program of Nigerian military officers by the US military.

employment in a population of vibrant and enthusiastic youth? Recent reports from Niger (not Nigeria) confirm that young boys and girls from Niger have joined Boko Haram, not for religious reasons, but for economic reasons. This is not far from the situation in the Northeast of Nigeria. If what government's spokespeople are insinuating is mere propaganda to discredit the Opposition parties, then they have only succeeded in strictly using propaganda for a negative purpose. It is certain that those in charge of leadership with quality experience and knowledge could co-ordinate situations in a way to effectively communicate the facts of the encumbrance of governance without playing dirty game or distorting information to win political gains.

Ellul elaborates on this point while explaining the effectiveness of propaganda, especially dealing with the understanding that propaganda is neutral and we make it what it becomes—to serve the good or serve the bad. For him, "[I]n reality, nothing is further from the truth! No technical instrument is neutral; it carries its own logic within itself, and I have already shown in Propaganda that the most beautiful ideal, once it is carried by propaganda, is modified in its very essence and nature."[249] In reality, a positive 'ideal' has no meaning unless man personally accedes, conquers, and adheres to it through deep conviction and becomes himself a germ of this truth. Otherwise, he is nothing more than a robot, 'beyond dignity and freedom,' which removes all positive value to this adherence, and by this very fact, to the ideal to which one adheres. For if one adheres to an ideal in such a manner, this means that one could accept any other content, and could uphold, with the same conviction, the opposite ideal."[250]

With the primaries[251] of the various political parties in Nigeria now over, a good number of the ministers in Jonathan's government failed to make it in the primaries of their PDP party. This could be an indication of the failure of propaganda, especially in the case of former minister Maku, who was once a vivacious Minister of Information. He traveled all over Nigeria convincing people on the accomplishments of Jonathan's administration and suppressing some of Jonathan's leadership weaknesses. SaharaReporters states, "[T]he seven

---

[249] Jacques Ellul, Violence: Reflections from a Christian Perspective (London: SCM Press, 1970), p. 6. Violence has this neutrality since it could be used to achieve the good or the bad.
[250] http://ellul.org/ELLUL%20FORUM%20ARTICLES/ISSUE37.pdf See the Jacques Ellul, "The Ethics of Propaganda," in Communication, 6 (1981): 159-175. Translated from the French by D. Raymond Tourville.
[251] Primaries are election procedures for a political party to nominate her best candidates for the multi-party level campaign before elections. They could be related to US party conventions to select promising candidates to represent the party.

ministers, who resigned on 15 October [2014] included Information Minister, Labaran Maku, Health Minister, Professor Onyebuchi Chukwu and Nyesom Wike, Minister of State for Education. Others were Samuel Ortom, Minister of State for Industry, Trade and Investment; Musiliu Obanikoro, Minister of State for Defence; Darius Ishaku, Minister of State for Niger Delta and Chief Emeka Wogu, Minister of Labour and Productivity."[252] We could also look at other significant ministries once occupied by some of the ministers belonging to the ruling government PDP. Even a minister of health during the successful effort against Ebola Disease in Nigeria, Prof. Onyebuchi Chukwu, failed to be elected in his PDP party primaries.[253]

Following this massive lose by the former ministers of Jonathan's government, we are beginning to perceive how propaganda and poor communication in Jonathan's administration are affecting his former cabinet ministers and special advisers. One could say that using propaganda these ministers (especially Okupe) exposed his own too many inconsistencies and blatant misrepresentation of the facts. As Ellul states in this case "[T]he individual perceives only that propaganda that his personality lets him perceive, but his personality is changed by that propaganda."[254] Propaganda surely affects the propagandist like a fellow who is no longer seeing life as the reality. Our duty to society, according to Ellul, is to be aware of the conditions of reality, the conditions of our world. He calls it "the duty of understanding the world and oneself."[255] It is a duty also to disclose these effects of propaganda on propagandists and the people/society.

The failure of these former ministers who worked for the government of President Jonathan points to this failure of the duty to understanding Nigeria and our world. Most people who were involved in the distortion of facts for manipulation and influence deny morality (do have desire to create values made in time). The failure to emerge as their party's flag-bearers affirms that there is no greater obstacle to propaganda than history and philosophy. Propaganda is, therefore, destructive of the possibilities, of the foundations, of the basic premises of ethics the impediment that propagandee carry. At the time of truth,

---

[252] http://saharareporters.com/2014/12/10/5-jonathan-%E2%80%8Eministers-lose-out-governorship-primaries (Accessed on December 10, 2014)

[253] Ebola containment was a great success in APC controlled states. For instance, Lagos and Rivers States. With such a political divide is it alright to attribute such success to President Jonathan?

[254] Ellul, Propaganda, p. 264.

[255] Ellul, Presence, p. 98. See Jeffrey P. Greenman, Read Mercer Schurchardt, Noah J. Toly, Understanding Jacques Ellul, (UK, Cambridge: James Clarke and co, 2013), p. 17.

they crumble. Ellul puts it thus: "[T]here is no greater obstacle to propaganda than history (continuity of generations) and philosophy (explicative reflection on the experience of events). Propaganda is, therefore, destructive of the possibilities, of the foundations, of the basic premises of ethics."[256]

Soyinka recently criticised President Jonathan on his weakness in dealing with terrorism and corruption.[257] In a way, Soyinka is bursting the myth of success touted by Jonathan's administration. This is in line with Ellul's demands that we become "myth busters."[258] Our primary duty is to ask critical questions for the purpose of good governance and common good. While we articulate Ellul's notion of "myth busters", it is important to reconsider that "Doyin Okupe's myth" is denying the Nigerian citizens "human face" factor, humans are not mere numbers. Those who have been killed by Boko Haram are not mere statistics or figures. When humans are mere figures, then the influence of propaganda is at work.

The influence of propaganda is to sell the myth of success and well-being or of progress. Marlin brings this Ellulian perspective in these words, "[T]hese myths, of progress, happiness, work, race, the hero, and suchlike, operate on a broader spectrum than merely the political, but they can also diminish human freedom."[259] The goings-on in Nigeria are situations that people are interested in because their lives and their families are affected. We are dealing with human life, not mere calculation or political calculation covered up through propaganda.[260]

Okupe's (and now former minister Maku) rants do not get to people because as Ellul notes "modern integration propaganda cannot affect individuals who live on the fringes of our civilization or who have too low a living standard."[261] The poor could be pushed or subjected to agitation propaganda. However, it may be difficult to sustain such propaganda because most of the

---

[256] http://ellul.org/ELLUL%20FORUM%20ARTICLES/ISSUE37.pdf, see p. 8: See the Jacques Ellul, "The Ethics of Propaganda," in Communication, 6 (1981): 159-175. Translated from the French by D. Raymond Tourville.

[257] Sunday Didam Audu, "The Almajiri Institution, Boko Haram, and Terrorism in Northern Nigeria, "in Morality and Terrorism: an interfaith perspective, edited by Mahmoud Masaeli (Orange County, California: Nortia Press, 2012), p. 191. Didam Audu talks about the failure of leadership and disillusion from the political class in Nigeria.

[258] The Ellul Forum Archive (1988-2012), Spring, 2007, #37.

[259] Randal Marlin, "Problems in Ellul's Treatment of Propaganda," http://ellul.org/ELLUL%20FORUM%20ARTICLES/ISSUE37.pdf (online version) p. 9.

[260] Prof. Cornel West refers to Obama's effort on racism in America as guided by political calculation rather than by morality or conviction.

[261] Ellul, Propaganda, p. 105.

poor have no access to most information/communication technologies (expensive news means). It is important to communicate facts and true challenges of our world, especially to people who may lack access to the relevant information on issues concerning their society. As Ellul says, he is not against technology or suggests the elimination of technology, but rather to relate modern technology with concern for human dignity. As Marlin elaborates, it is "to recapture a space for human spontaneity, openness, and understanding of what is happening in the world."[262] We have to stand on course with the facts of our world to empower our people.

Most of the Nigerian populace lack the educational empowerment to make use of vital information, or critically analyze them for proper understanding and for their own good. This situation makes them simply "victims" of propaganda. In this era of massive media communication, with guidance of ethical communication, it is time to acknowledge that most people involved in terrorism in Nigeria are weighed down by the real problems of poverty and lack of employment in a massive scale. This is what Ellul means by saying that, "no propaganda can exist unless a mass can be reached and set into motion." [263] Most of the known "terrorists" in Nigeria are/were poor and unemployed youth that have been promised money for their family by their rich elite masters (who may be Muslims or non-Muslims).

Ellul concludes that it takes the efforts of both sides (the propagandists and the propagandee or citizens being influenced) to make propaganda effective. He affirms, "it has its roots and reasons in the need of the group that will sustain it."[264] (both groups need to work together for propaganda to be effective). The poor are very concretely and practically bound. They take what they see impact their lives. Perhaps this is why 'stomach infrastructure'[265] works in Ekiti State in Southwest of Nigeria, but again, it is not sustainable as a means of propaganda. As Ellul notes, "propaganda is particularly effective in the upper segment of the working class and in the middle classes."[266] It is predominant among those of

---

[262] Randal Marlin, Propaganda and the Ethics of Persuasion (Peterborough: Broadview Press Ltd, 2003), p. 34.
[263] Jacques Ellul, Propaganda: the formation of men's attitude, trans. by Konrad Kellen and Jean Lerner, (New York: Vintage, 1973), p. 104.
[264] Jacques Ellul, Propaganda: the formation of men's attitude, trans. by Konrad Kellen, (New York: Vintage, 1973), p. 121.
[265] Stomach infrastructure is the new political slogan said to have been used by PDP Governor Ayodele Fayose to win the incumbent APC Governor Kayode Fayemi in Ekiti State (past election in 2014).
[266] Ellul, Propaganda, p. 105.

"average standard of living." It succeeds with or among people with a certain store of ideas and a number of conditioned reflexes: average influence, affluence, education, etc.

Propaganda aims at the destruction of "truth and freedom.... "no matter what the good intentions or the good will may be of those who manifest it."[267] According to Randolph Kluver of Nanyang Technological University, "Ellul's greatest concern was not with mass media, but rather with the dramatic changes he witnessed in modern society, of which the mass media are a critical part, but more particularly, the ways in which society become 'dehumanized" by technology, politics and media."[268] Because these manipulations (through propaganda) lead to dehumanizing of the other person or society do not last, they somehow lead to a form of mental emancipation.[269] This is where many Nigerians have now found themselves.

Many eminent Nigerians, like Soyinka, Obasanjo, etc consider Jonathan too weak to lead the Nigerian people against Boko Haram. There seems to be a stronger air of support for Retired Major-General Muhammadu Buhari this time around than in 2011 (last presidential election). In his recent book: *My Watch* (an autobiography by Obasanjo), he notes that Buhari "will be a strong, almost inflexible, and a courageous and firm leader."[270] Nigeria needs a person of discipline and with a record of incorruptibility. These are the qualities needed to fight corruption, Boko Haram, poverty and unemployment.

We think it is prudent and relevant for one to borrow a commentary about terrorism in other parts of our world to buttress the nature of this devastation or destruction. Canada's National Magazine *Maclean's* describes the common intent and destructive purposes of all major Islamist terrorist organization as "a barbaric militant group that has murdered civilians and beheaded journalists in its pursuit of a new Muslim nation ruled by sharia law."[271] With this kind of organization hell bent in such barbaric mission, Nigeria truly needs a disciplined leader with clear incorruptible qualities. This person also needs the communicative skills and qualities that Ellul describes to be able to rally the people in a situation of war. Whether President Jonathan will revive these desirable potential he may possess to still be the president or whether the

---

[267] Ellul, Propaganda, p. 257.
[268] Kluver, Jacques Ellul: Technique, Propaganda, and Modern Media, p. 99.
[269] Kluver, p. 100.
[270] http://www.bbc.com/news/world-africa-12890807 (Accessed 13th December, 2014)
[271] "Terrorism: 'We Know Where They Are'," in Maclean's Magazine, October 27, 2014, Volume 127, Number, 42, pp. 26-27

incorruptible qualities needed to overcome Boko Haram are present in Retired Brigadier General Buhari to lead Nigeria, this is for history to record as from May 2015, if the elections hold. As Ellul envisions, we all need the ethics of communicating humanly to maintain a peaceful world and overcome terrorism that wants to wipe out our humanity. Any party that wins the forth-coming election will still need the collaboration of other parties to keep Nigeria's nascent democracy and maintain a common front that supports the values of intelligible democracy. We surely need a government that will, through Ellul's insightful perspective, eliminate any form of "dehumanize [ing] experience[s]... [that] undermine democracy and critical intelligence."[272]

Conclusion

Ellul desired a total approach to the critical problems of humanity. He did not focus on a singular problem. He talked about terrorism, propaganda, politics, etc all had a role to play in human total liberation, dignity, and enjoyment of common good. As he said, it is about "a total vision of human race, society and history."[273] The duty of the Nigerian government is to look at life from this same holistic perspective. That is, to address the real issues that likely will enhance the little success stories about Nigeria's nascent democracy.

Nigeria as a democratic state needs more than mere political sophistry and rhetoric, mere political action and propaganda to change the onslaught of terrorism sustained by corruption and unemployment. As Ellul notes, society is never better off when we rely on "political action."[274] So far, Boko Haram is after Nigeria's disintegration, but government needs to work with the Opposition parties in a way to showcase a strong, vibrant, and united front. The same applies to the media spokespeople of the Presidency. They must communicate in a way that does not denigrate the supporters of the Opposition parties in collaboratively building a cohesive Nigeria capable of tackling terrorism and corruption. No need to accuse the other of rights' abuse—to avoid worsening the situation. No need to rehearse the failing of Opposition parties' members in supporting a collective action for a true Nigerian society. We need

---

[272] Kluver, p. 99.
[273] Ellul, *Perspectives,* pp. 4-6. See Jeffrey P. Greenman, Read Mercer Schurchardt, Noah J. Toly Understanding Jacques Ellul, (UK, Cambridge: James Clarke and co, 2013), p. 4.
[274] Lovekin, *Technique, Discourse and Consciousness*, p. 121. See Jeffrey P. Greenman, Read Mercer Schurchardt, Noah J. Toly Understanding Jacques Ellul, (UK, Cambridge: James Clarke and co, 2013), p. 8.

to collaborate with Opposition parties and members in issues of national interest/security, especially against terrorism. Corruption and terrorism and unemployment are Nigeria's state-of-emergency problems!

Corrupt leadership, terrorism and unemployment are agents of the dehumanization of the Nigerian personhood. Ellul condemns in totality this aspect of indignity to people seen in democratic societies. He describes it the submergence of the person.[275] Communicating with dignity and sense of genuine purpose are what we need in building a community of rights and freedom. Persons and people in the community ought to be allowed to make their own judgment on socio-political situations without efforts to manipulate or distort the facts about the polity. While they make their own judgment, they are constructively able to work in co-operation with those at the helm of governance.

We conclude this section by borrowing[276] Ellul's recommendation to decentralize power so as to bring in creativity and co-operation in addressing the real issues of society rather than a very controlling and abstract State administration. We have to avoid the "inflexibility of institutionalization."[277] Multiple and diverse group should help the government figure out what the real issues of governance are and the best of ways to address the rampaging Boko Haram. It may not be out of place to consider reaching out for a political solution to Boko Haram, although this may not be the only way.

The sensitiveness of war must be acknowledged especially in such an asymmetrical form of warfare by Boko Haram. The issues inflaming the conflict are not beyond redemption when government, with all the resources available to her, pursues and communicates the exigencies of war in a humane manner without politicizing it. All Nigerian citizens, including representatives of government, members of the Opposition parties, and the entire citizenry ought to stand for peace and defend the survival of our emerging democracy.

---

[275] Ellul, *Presence of the Kingdom*, p. 25. See the book: Jeffrey P. Greenman, Read Mercer Schurchardt, Noah J. Toly Understanding Jacques Ellul, (UK, Cambridge: James Clarke and co, 2013), p. 15ff. (see google books)
[276] Ellul, *Perspectives,* pp. 15-16.
[277] Jacques Ellul on Religion, Technology and Politics: Conversations with Patrick Troude-Chastenet (Oregon: Wipf and Stock Publishers, 2005), p. 24.

Bibliography

Ellul, Jacques. *Violence: Reflections from a Christian Perspective*. London: SCM, 1970

--------..*Propaganda: the Formation of Men's Attitude*, trans. by Konrad Kellen. New York: Vintage, 1973.

---------.*The Humiliation of the Word*. Grand Rapids, Michigan: William B. Eerdmans, 1985, Reprinted in 1988.

---------.*The Technological Bluff*. Grand Rapids, Michigan: William B. Eerdmans, 1990.

---------.*On Religion, Technology and Politics*: *Conversations with Patrick Troude-Chastenet*.Oregon: Wipf and Stock, 2005.

Halton, David. *Dispatches from the Front: Matthew Halton, Canada's Voice at War*. McClelland & Stewart, 2014.

Glander, Timothy Richard. *Origins of Mass Communications Research During the American Cold War*. Language Arts and Discipline, 2000.

Greenman, Jeffrey, P and Read Mercer Schurchardt, Noah J. Toly. *Understanding Jacques Ellul*. UK, Cambridge: James Clarke, 2013.

Lasswell, Harold, D. and Dorothy Blumenstock. *World Revolutionary Propaganda*. New York: Alfred A. Knopf, 1939.

Marlin, Randal. *Propaganda and the Ethics of Persuasion*. Peterborough: Broadview, 2003.

Minteh, Binneh and Ashlie Perry. *Terrorism in West Africa-Boko Haram's Evolution*. Strategy and Affiliations, presented at the Mid-West Political Science Association's 71st AnnualConference Palmer House Hotel, Chicago Illinois, April, 2013.

Nasr, Seyyed Hossein. *Islam: Religion, History, and Civilization*. New York: HarperCollins,2003.

Okolo, Chukwudum, C. *Squandermania Mentality: Reflections on Nigeria Culture*. Enugu, Nigeria: University Trust Publishers, 1994.

Article by Ellul

Ellul, Jacques. "The Ethics of Propaganda." *Communication*. 6 (1981): 159-175. Translated from the French by D. Raymond Tourville.

Articles

Anozie, Stanley Uche. "Human Rights and Terrorism: The Niger Delta Oil War." *Morality and Terrorism: an interfaith perspective*, edited by Mahmoud Masaeli. Orange County, California, Orange County: Nortia, 2012.

Audu, Sunday Didam. "The Almajiri Institution, Boko Haram, and Terrorism in Northern Nigeria." *Morality and Terrorism: an interfaith perspective*, edited by Mahmoud Masaeli. Orange County, California: Nortia, 2012.

Dyer, Gwynne. "Boko Haram not Nigeria's only problem." *The Peterborough Examiner*, Thursday, December 4, 2014.

Findlay, Stephanie. *Toronto Star,* Friday, January 30, 2015.

Konyndyk, Kenneth, J. "Violence." *Jacques Ellul: Interpretive Essays.* Clifford G. Christians & Jay M. Van Hook (eds). University of Illinois Press, 1981.

Oyebade, Adebayo. "Reluctant Democracy: The State, the Opposition, and the Crisis of Political Transition, 1985-1993." *The Transformation of Nigeria (Essays in Honor of Toyin Falola).* Trenton, New Jersey: Africa World, 2002.

Part III:
African Hermeneutics of Ethics and Political Belongingness (Applied Ethics)

Chapter 6
Advancing an African Cosmopolitanism and Political Philosophy of Patriotism (The Hermeneutics of African Political Philosophy of Patriotism)

Stanley Uche Anozie

(Department of History, Philosophy and Political Science; Indiana University Kokomo, Indiana, USA, 2020)

Introduction

In advancing an African cosmopolitanism and political philosophy of patriotism, I articulated and established an African hermeneutic philosophy of the person that is centered on "I am because we are, and since we are therefore I am." I will argue that the recent democratic developments in some African countries like Nigeria, Ghana, South Africa, etc. affirm the need for a political culture that advances self-determination, self-regulation and self-actualization. The role of the political values or virtues of patriotism, African consciousness, honesty, dignity and integrity, in all these countries, especially in Nigeria, should be central in this narrative. In the period of Donald Trump's America, the "value of Patriotism" should be considered in relation to American cosmopolitanism and a revived discourse[278] on African cosmopolitanism and on political philosophy of patriotism.

In this chapter, I will develop my thoughts on the narrative of Donald Trump's America, especially within the background of recent true or untrue accusations against Trump. Some of these accusations suggest that he (Trump)

---

[278] The rich background of Kwame Nkrumah's political contributions through African Conscientism is important. The contributions of Professor P. L. O. Lumumba are inestimable.

was/is "a con man"[279], a cheat, and a bully. Former White House Press Secretary, under President Bill Clinton, Joe Lockhart directly described Trump by using words like "con man."[280] These attributes, although not conclusively and legally substantiated, are qualities that ethical agents could not associate with a president of a country, especially a democratically elected one. Political leadership is the highest level of patriotism, public service, and for Aristotle, one of the best excellences for a virtuous life in a virtuous society. The Presidency (the highest level of public service—for guaranteeing common good of all citizens) should reflect convincing/genuine honesty, dignity, integrity, respect, justice, etc.

With this historical background on the current political debates of our time (in/during a pandemic), my purpose is to strongly argue that any African country, including Nigeria, is capable of an African political philosophy of wellbeing that is sustainable through the political philosophy of patriotism. I had in my earlier article/chapter provided an introductory commentary to a political philosophy of patriotism by insisting on promoting the ethics of patriotism. My view is that political discourses should necessarily imply or involve an ethical dimension of ethical reasoning. Unfortunately, based on media resources, the majority of people (called politicians) are not living in accord with these established norms of political leadership shaped by patriotism and ethical/moral characters. The good-news for Nigeria, or generally speaking, for Africa, is that recent elections in Nigeria are still dependable instances of democratic discourse, engagement and success, although not sufficiently robust. From recent post-electoral reviews, the demand for integrity, accountability and truthfulness stood tall before the Nigerian people. In Jean-Paul Sartre's view,

---

[279] Rick Telander described Donald Trump in these words.
https://chicago.suntimes.com/2021/1/18/22237761/donald-trump-was-always-con-man-that-includes-time-usfl-generals-mccaskey-kelly-nfl-telander (Accessed December 28, 2021)

[280] https://www.newsweek.com/trump-tax-returns-con-man-1419474 (Accessed December 28, 2021). Joe Lockhart actually provided a time frame for such conducts by Trump. Lockhart noted that Trump has "played the long con now over 40 years."
https://www.newsweek.com/trump-tax-returns-con-man-1419474. Michael Bloomberg (a media billionaire from New York) identified Trump with similar words.
https://www.inc.com/chris-matyszczyk/expert-reveals-how-to-spot-a-con-man.html (Accessed December 28, 2021). Jay Sizemore entitled one of his subtopics as "Don the Con."
https://medium.com/politically-speaking/is-trump-the-greatest-conman-of-all-time-5a861438db6e (Accessed December 28, 2021). I have provided enough sources for our consideration of such controversial description of an American president.

choosing or not choosing to act or being indifferent to demand for integrity/accountability, is already making a choice. It is bad faith to act without considering the integrity, accountability and truthfulness or freedom of our time. Integrity or truthfulness is a form of freedom or justice in a democracy! It is an expressible, reasonable and realisation-*able* justice.

The main point of my paper/chapter is to suggest, and strongly so, that there is no *ONE* model of perfect democracy in practice. There is also no perfect justice (Amartya Sen[281] would describe this as *Transcendental Institutionalism* understanding of justice). The truth of democracy, especially in the practice of democracy, is in the awareness of its failures, the need for continuity of democratic discourse or public debates that fervently focus on the core political values and principles of life of patriotism.

The Background Problem: Pedagogy of Ethics of Patriotism

The United States, like other democracies of the world, is going through a learning curve of her own practice of democracy. Nigerians (including other Africans) can truly advance an idea of democracy that addresses their contemporary socio-political concerns. The central concern is, for any political leadership to be successful, the values of honor, honesty, dignity, integrity, justice, etc., must be commonplace. During the dispensation of Trump's America, the political atmosphere was fraught with troubles and was truly diminished. It was diminished because there was a lack of political guardianship from the top of her leadership structure. The required characters for political leadership in America was/is questionable and running deficit on administrative character and accountability. This concern is not only in the United States, there is an ongoing political concern in Canada (Trudeau's SNL-Lavalin crisis stinks of political corruption and the recent protests of Indigenous people in Canada against institutional or systemic racism or even genocide by Church and State). Without suggesting that these countries have politically failed, I am rather arguing that their views of a democratic-political paradigm are idealistic[282], exaggerated and misplaced. The notion that some particular political powers are political guardians or models for others to follow is always, and at present, inadequate and unsustainable. Thus, on this basis, African political philosophy

---

[281] Amartya Sen, *The Idea of Justice* (Belknap Harvard University Press, 2009), pp. 1-21.
[282] *Ibid.*, pp. 1-21ff.

of patriotism should have a place, a voice, and relevance in global discourse on human political wellbeing.

In my essay on: "Can Igbo Mysticism Fight Against Boko Haram" in *Responses of Mysticism to Religious Terrorism (Sufism and Beyond)* edited by Mahmoud Masaeli and Rico Sneller (2020), I presented my understanding and appreciation for an African concept of person--by way of African Igbo hermeneutic philosophy. I tried to build on the reflections of African sages in terms of the ramifications of self-understanding, self-determination and self-actualization of African people or African consciousness through advancing a metaphysical/ontological existence. This ontological existence should be one based on the ethics of patriotism (responsibility to political leadership and to convivial existence and continued interest in African consciousness). This ethics of patriotism is 'an essential other' of the hermeneutics of African political belongingness (convivial existence or ontological co-existent nature of a people). I explained that part of African Nigerian socio-political crisis is equally a crisis of the pedagogy of ethics of patriotism:

> a problem of ethical living (or capacity to moral agency). Corrupt leadership and lack of pedagogy of ethics of patriotism for community development in the leadership-followership relations gave birth to Boko Haram. Violence flavored the particular identity of Boko Haram. Unemployment sustained the destructive path of Boko Haram in a flavored atmosphere of hopelessness and poverty.[283]

As part of my considerations of the varied dimensions of the background problem of this discourse, it is my view that, in relation to the human person, there is African thought reflection on: a) beauty of life, and b) the relational nature of being, that have been undergoing gradual progress and polishing of content.[284] These two aspects are important in understanding African Igbo concept of person as well as brotherhood and sisterhood or communitarian notion of person (relational being of mutual support). I have advanced my thoughts on the person as brotherhood and sisterhood in my essay on *Maritain*

---

[283] Stanley Uche Anozie, "Can Igbo Mysticism Fight Against Boko Haram," *Responses of Mysticism to Religious Terrorism* (Belgium, Gompel&Svacina, 2019), p. 254. I have traced Nigerian political crisis to the problem of the pedagogy of ethics of patriotism.

[284] I am of the view that African political discourse and hermeneutical philosophy should be enriched as a body of scholarship. This is a basic way to make and advance African philosophical autonomy and competence in global discourse on any matters of public interests.

Studies conference paper proceedings published in 2017.[285] I noted that African thought advances:

> this relational being by developing the common good notions of, "hospitality, daily friendship, and dialogue with the members of other ethnic groups are vital laws admitting of no exception. One who is not a member of my own group is ultimately also the 'property' of the other just as I myself am, and this means that I owe him respect and esteem. Thus one is ultimately related to all human beings.' [286]

African philosophical ethics or thought has not been adequately promoted, even though the principles are already known. This is a significant background problem to African scholarship and practice/consciousness. As part of the background problem, I will argue that the socio-political sphere of Africa, and especially in Nigeria, has not promoted a culture and ethics of political patriotism. Political patriotism is different from merely demanding for political self-determination. It is more about protecting, promoting and advancing a political culture of African consciousness, wellbeing and sustainability. Political leadership (as a way of expressing political patriotism) is not a one-time thing. It is a philosophy of life, a way of living and preserving a politics of wellbeing and realization-focused justice. It is truly a politics of self-actualization (self-determination does not necessarily mean self-actualization).[287] Self-determination/independence or autonomy does not imply genuine well-being. However, genuine wellbeing or self-actualization cannot be accomplished without self-determination. Self-determination is a means to self-actualization. Self-actualization is the destination of self-determination.

Contemporary Historical Context: Donald Trump and Nationalism

The assault against philosophy (love of truth and wisdom for human wellbeing) and European/Western cultures' efforts to monopolize philosophical

---

[285] Stanley Uche Anozie, "Jacques Maritain's International Relations and African Philosophy of Personhood/Community," *Maritain Studies,* edited by Nikolaj Zunic (Vol. XXXIII, 2017), pp. 85-99.
[286] *Ibid.*, pp. 86-87.
[287] Self-determination or independence does not mean self-actualization. Self-determination is like political independence or autonomy after the colonial rule of some African countries. This does not imply genuine well-being for these African countries. For instance, in Nigeria, the Igboland is self-determined by Igbo politicians but the Igbo people have not accomplished genuine wellbeing or self-actualization. Self-actualization is not given by an external body or agency.

thinking or reason have diminished the growth of African Hermeneutic Philosophy[288] and even the effort to listen to African trend on cosmopolitanism of brotherhood and sisterhood or communitarian notion of person. Unfortunately, much of what we have as considerable reflections on African philosophical studies is reactionary articulations rather than ontologically and hermeneutically advanced considerations of African brotherhood and sisterhood. This point is encapsulated in my essay argument that:

> Scholarship is part of the politics of control/imperialism. The tradition of European/Western imperialism in relation to the quality of African Philosophy has been long and negative. There is the paralysis of African Philosophy. We have to find a proper grounding of African Philosophy. We have to avoid a 'philosophical agenda' imposed on us. The focus must be for an African audience. We have to overcome a form of philosophical welfa-rism. No human being is a stranger to the concept of humanity or human-ness.[289]

For this section, advancing an African political philosophy of patriotism (a self-help, self-determination, and self-actualization motivated approach), even more in a cosmopolitan worldview, means that: "The shared and pedagogical values of these [African] Igbo institutionalised groups should be revitalized in order to re-direct young Nigerians to becoming patriotic in community development (Nation-building and shared values)."[290]

The *au current* historical background to this chapter is the new socio-political movement of nationalism and protectionism supported by American President Trump and advanced by his non-cosmopolitan conservative agencies. I would be very precise in my consideration of the wave of moderate cosmopolitanism, nationalism and protectionism in America. I would be of the view that Trump's *Trump-ism* is a prevalent but a parochial phenomenon of America. It is not really a *Trump effect*. It is rather what America has chosen to be since, before, and after Obama's Democrat presidency. Kelly Brown Douglas[291] has identified the problem as emerging from American

---

[288] This could be expressed as African sage philosophy or African philosophy.
[289] Stanley Uche Anozie, "African Hermeneutics of Illuminating Consciousness: The Intercultural Problem of Language and Hermeneutics," *Cosmic Consciousness and Human Excellences: implications for Global Ethics*, Mahmoud Masaeli, ed (Cambridge Scholars Publishing, 2019).
[290] Stanley Uche Anozie, "Can Igbo Mysticism Fight Against Boko Haram," *Responses of Mysticism to Religious Terrorism* (Belgium, Gompel&Svacina, 2019), p. 267.
[291] Kelly Brown Douglas, *Stand Your Ground* (Orbis Books, 2015), pp. 1ff.

exceptionalism and manifest destiny political culture (of White supremacy, Anglo-Saxon superior identity, and the new World Order ideology) in Western societies.

Societies are like individual persons, who wish to review their positions or worldviews as often as possible in light of their self-interests. Ayn Rand considered the virtue of self-interest (in my interpretation, not virtue of selfishness) as fundamental to wellbeing in reflective beings. It means that reflective beings are disposed to pursue their own self-interest at all times, and so are not really altruistic creatures. Rand defined altruism as: "Any action taken for the benefit of others is good, and any action taken for one's own benefit is evil. Thus, the beneficiary of an action is the only criterion of moral value and so long as the beneficiary is anybody other than oneself, anything goes."[292]

In Rand's book *The Virtue of Selfishness*, she noted that:

> If a man accepts the ethics of altruism, his first concern is not how to live his life, but how to sacrifice it… Altruism erodes men's capacity to grasp the value of an individual life; it reveals a mind from which the reality of a human being has been wiped out…Altruism holds death as its ultimate goal and standard of value—and it is logical that renunciation, resignation, self-denial, and every other form of suffering, including self-destruction, are the virtue of its advocates.[293]

Rand continued, "Man's proper values and interests, that concern with his own interest, is the essence of a moral existence, and that man must be the beneficiary of his own moral actions."[294] It is also Rand's position that "The creed of sacrifice is a morality for the immoral."[295]

In light of these statements, pre-Trumpian seeming altruistic American democracy is superficial and redundant. Altruism is contrary to European/Western human moral nature/existence. In other words, people truly and really act for their own primary benefits or goods. Of course, there could be some secondary benefits that other individual persons could experience and enjoy but not as primary beneficiaries. Throughout history, United States of America's socio-political terrain was influenced by political narratives that

---

[292] Louis P. Pojman, *How Should We Live? An Introduction to Ethics* (USA: Wadsworth/Thomson Learning, 2005), p. 25.
[293] Ayn Rand, *The Virtue of Selfishness* (New York: New American Library, 1964), pp. vii, 27-32.
[294] *Ibid.*, p. ix.
[295] Ayn Rand, *Atlas Shrugged* (New York: Dutton, 1957), p. 102-9.

positioned her as an altruistic-interventionist super-power. Clearly, the United States of America would be running on self-depreciating capitalist deficit if it has to continue in that direction. Trump understandably agreed that the United States of America needs to focus on herself and her citizens' interests. As is common, most countries of the world, including the so-called super-powers were good at directing international policies to suit their overall strategic national interests. As is well-known, the financial costs of some international organizations were borne by most of these super-power nations but they balance their accounts by dictating the policy directions of these international organizations through immense, intense and soft diplomacy approaches.

Trump's presidency and his army of conservatives (this delineation cuts across Democrat and Republican Parties) have prevailed on the American people to re-focus on a Randian "self-interests" of Nationalism and Protectionism and Exceptionalism. The era of seeming altruistic super-power is, for the present, over. The United States of America has to care for America and Americans first. But this is true. It has been the *Geist* and *Motif* behind European/Western and American history. It is America *First* (just as it means Europe *First* or Western culture/civilization *First*). America *First* is a euphemism for American exceptionalism[296], Manifest destiny, and Anglo-Saxon superior culture identity. America *First* is about America's strategic national self-interests and it is anti-altruistic Western cultural hegemony.

With America *First* ideology, one could easily discern the depth of influence from psychological egoism and ethical egoism (anti-altruism) views and how these views could have influenced a non-globalist or non-cosmopolitan approach to political governance and socio-cultural hegemony. One could also understand the non-cosmopolitan direction of American socio-economic and political policies. My recent reading on Pat Buchanan (a former aid to Richard Nixon) who was a former presidential candidate in the United State of America (in 1992, 1996, and 2000) confirmed this obvious ideological position in United States of America's socio-political structure and perspective in the past 25 years. Buchanan supported nationalist system, he encouraged a restricted immigration policy as good as walling of America, and called to change America's interventionist approach:

> In an article published in the spring of 2017, Alberta points out that many of the policies President Trump ran on, and is [are] now implementing, were first proposed by Buchanan more than twenty years ago. These

---

[296] Kelly Brown Douglas, *Stand Your Ground* (Orbis Books, 2015), pp. 3-47.

policies include secure borders instead of open borders, fair trade instead of free trade, nationalism instead of globalism, foreign policy restraint instead of interventionism, and America first instead of NATO first, among other things.[297]

The point about secured borders and nationalism (the New England, the New World) was clearly communicated in Douglas' book *Stand Your Ground*.[298] According to Douglas, "America's grand narrative of exceptionalism is the narrative of America's identity. To be a chosen nation is to be an Anglo-Saxon nation. To be an Anglo-Saxon nation is to be a chosen nation."[299] Unfortunately, a good number of the American people think that American Nationalism is only as a result of *Trumpian* politics. It was set by the first Americans and shaped by the founding fathers.[300] Obviously, *Trumpian* politics personified what was historically a nationalist ideology or a seeming prevalent faceless ideology that was part of the "dawning of America."[301] American-driven patriotic nationalism is an expression of American exceptionalism.

Trump's American Patriotism: The Crisis of Leadership Character and Socio-Political Values

According to David Brooks, a columnist on *New York Times* 'Morality and Michael Cohen Wednesday's testimony and the crisis of American conscience':

> Trump, personifying the worst elements in our culture, is like a providentially sent gong meant to wake us up and direct us toward a better path. Nonetheless, his kind of life has an allure for other lonely people who also live under the illusion that you can win love and respect with bling and buzz. Michael Cohen was one of these people. He testified that in serving Donald Trump he felt he was serving a cause larger than self. Those causes were celebrity and wealth.[302]

---

[297] https://www.lifesitenews.com/news/former-presidential-candidate-on-vigano-testimony-this-is-a-homosexual-scan (Accessed December 13, 2021).
[298] Douglas, *Stand Your Ground*, pp. 1ff.
[299] *Ibid.*, p. 16.
[300] *Ibid.*, p. 15.
[301] *Ibid.*
[302] https://www.nytimes.com/2019/02/28/opinion/michael-cohen-testimony.html?action=click&module=Opinion&pgtype=Homepage (Accessed March 1, 2019).

Brooks continued:

> Normal people have moral sentiments. Normal people are repulsed when the president of their own nation lies, cheats, practices bigotry, allegedly pays off porn star mistresses. Were Republican House members enthusiastic or morose as they decided to turn off their own moral circuits, when they decided to be monumentally unconcerned by the fact that their leader may be a moral cretin?[303]

Before we got to this point, one needs to revisit the history of the political emergence of Trump's presidency.

Trump's emergence as the democratically elected president of the United States of America has significantly marked the upsurge of homegrown epithet of socio-economic and political views of "making America Great again." Certainly the political stream that supported the emerging socio-cultural, economic and political views of nationalism contributed to the defeat of the Democratic Party in Trump and Clinton presidential contests. Trump's socio-economic political agenda and appeal epitomized the desire for patriotic nationalism: *America First* socio-economic political agenda. One had to recall that America *First* is not just a socio-economic political agenda. It has to be culturally *European* or *Western* for it to be *American*. It is everything about wellbeing –and is "America First." On my interpretation, America *First* puts the United States of America's national interest in its place among the *comity of nations*, and does not necessarily make the United States of America less of a "superpower," as they say. On my view also, Trump's "business-focused politics" approach addressed the excessive admiration for American superpower/American exceptionalism ideology of the last 50 years (and more). The idea that attracts my attention in this comparison is because of change between an American-driven patriotic nationalism of the last 50 years and the current drive (especially in Trump's model of Nationalism or non-Cosmopolitanism or moderate Cosmopolitanism, American First) for a positively parochial socio-economic, cultural cum political approach, in which the non-altruistic strategic national interests of American citizens are considered first, rather than that of global citizenship.

During September 2018 convention of leaders at the United Nation in New York, Trump affirmed before the global community that America is against 'globalism'. America, according him, is focused on American Patriotism. It is a

---

[303] https://www.nytimes.com/2019/02/28/opinion/michael-cohen-testimony.html?action=click&module=Opinion&pgtype=Homepage (Accessed March 1, 2019).

patriotism that first considers the needs of American people, the interests of America in global trade deals, an America that does her barest minimum in funding the United Nation. It is an America that is not involved in the *Americanization* of other countries but respects the religious liberty, the political interests and cultural worldviews of other nations of the world. Trump suggested that America does not focus on institutions that are "unelected" and lack "accountability" to her own people. America has and is obligated to her elected offices and to institutions that are accountable to America. In Trump's United Nation's speech, it appeared that there was an undertone of a demand for United Nations and her systems/structures to be accountable to America. The fascinating aspect of Trump's non-globalist patriotic America is that Trump himself recognized or rather identified what he described as the failures of Socialist Nicolás Maduro in Venezuela, the corrupt dictatorship in Iran (Trump asked the global community to sanction and isolate Iran), ISIS as blood tasty terrorist organization, the Syrian crisis (regime), etc. Trump made reference to his first United Nation's proposal for global agenda that promotes "a vision for a brighter future for all of humanity" [304] in the world. Trump emphasized that America stands for her people and the world. For him, United States of America will not tell other nations or countries and peoples how to live, or work or to worship. America asked and demanded the world to respect her values and honour her sovereignty. America has a distinct culture and rich history. America chose independence and cooperation.

Trump's socio-political and economic comments to these nations or countries suggest a clear level of patriotic political nationalism. In a system that is not necessarily exclusivist to United States of America, and for lack of a better term, one may refer to Trump's patriotic political nationalism—as a *Moderate Cosmopolitanism* (with a mixed bag of nationalistic, non-altruistic, and globalist superpower intents) in relation to *Extreme Cosmopolitanism* or Globalization supported in over 100 years by capitalist economies of the world. This is significant because of Trump's reference to "a vision for a brighter future for all of humanity"[305] (a moderate cosmopolitanism). As is politically necessary, it is up to the citizens of the United States of America, through democratic elections, to define and re-define their interests and political narratives.

---

[304] https://www.youtube.com/watch?v=rewri7OdEZA (Accessed December 14, 2021).
[305] https://www.youtube.com/watch?v=rewri7OdEZA (Accessed December 14, 2021).

Based on the recent United States presidential elections results, the political narrative in America aligns with Brooks' analysis above on ethical leadership and citizenry. There was an obvious circumstantial[306] need for citizens to change the political narratives of America during a pandemic. Whether this narrative would predicate a new political system that is not solely based on America *First*, American Exceptionalism, Manifest Destiny, Anglo-Saxon Superior Race Identity, etc. requires a good enough time for genuine review or evaluation.

At this point, I will take a brief look at the forms of cosmopolitanism in the history of ideas and the relationship between the different forms of cosmopolitanism.

Forms of Cosmopolitanism in the History of Ideas

Cosmopolitanism is the view that all humanity comes from one source of existence and so are citizens of the world. One could relate cosmopolitanism to "moral objectivism"—the idea that for a universal moral principle to apply to all persons it ought to be traced to the argument that there is something like "universal humanity," which is same as "citizens of the world" or fellow-citizens under the guide of one ethical universal principle or core objective principles. The notion of universal humanity implies that there ought to be universal moral principles or guidelines that equally apply to all persons as persons/people of the world. The universal moral principles or moral objectivism is possible because there in one universal principle/law/standard of existence or source of all beings.[307] We are all connected to this one "source" of all beings and one "source" of the world/universe of human affiliations. Aristotle is attributed to have said in Nicomachean Ethics 1135a—One may also observe in one's travels to distant countries the feelings of recognition and affiliation that links every human being to every other human being.[308] According to Louis P. Pojman, in reflecting on the source of the concept of cosmopolitanism:

---

[306] Some changes in political history are based on circumstantial embarrassment or shame. Between 2019 and 2020, most Americans were ashamed of frequent stories of racist nationalism expressed by persons occupying political leadership positions. How deep the shame was has to be verified with historical consciousness.

[307] Douglas, *Stand Your Ground*, p. 62. The narratives about cosmopolitanism could have relevance in mono-genetic and poly-genetic theories (on all human creation and source).

[308] Aristotle, *Nicomachean Ethics* 1135a. See also Pojman, *How Should We Live? An Introduction to Ethics*, p. 65.

Humans obey these laws because they can perceive the laws' inner reasonableness. This notion enabled the Stoics to be cosmopolitans ("people of the cosmos") who imposed a universal standard of righteousness (*jus naturale*) on all societies, evaluating various positive laws (*jus gentium*—"laws of the nations") by this universal standard of reason.[309]

There are different forms of cosmopolitanism, especially based on diverse socio-political and philosophical traditions. The well-known cosmopolitanism of ancient Greek society was promoted by stoics.

Stoic cosmopolitanism--It considers all human beings as citizens of the world. It sees human relationships in a concentric circle. This means that each circle of human relationship–like a globe—accommodates various groups of the society. For instance, there is a circle around the self/person, a circle around immediate families, a circle of immediate communities, a circle of immediate country people, and a circle of humanity, etc. Each of these circles is a circle of identity. For stoicism, we live in the circle of identity in the city-state of our birth and the circle of deliberations/debates/human arguments and aspirations. Our human aspirations expose us to the necessity of human interconnected-ness or the consciousness of understanding of our common humanity. This concentric circle illustrates human affinity, affiliation[310], interconnectedness, orientation, etc. We are all fellow-citizens of the human world or city. The basis for being "fellow-citizens" is the affiliation of human solidarity, and less on reason and principle.

Natural Law (based) cosmopolitanism--It is based on the law of nature. According to the law of nature, we are all humans and it is natural for us to be cosmopolitans. In ancient Greek philosophy, Socrates felt that Athens provided him with the values to speak about socio-political values. "Whether Socrates was self-consciously cosmopolitan in this way or not, there is no doubt that his ideas accelerated the development of cosmopolitanism and that he was in later antiquity embraced as a citizen of the world."[311] I have added an interesting read from Plato about Sophist Hippias' address at Callias' house in *Protagoras* (337c7-d3):

---

[309] Pojman, *How Should We Live? An Introduction to Ethics*, p. 65.
[310] Martha Nussbaum, "Kant and Stoic Cosmopolitanism," *The Journal of Political Philosophy* (Volume 5, Number 1, 1997), pp. 1-25.
[311] https://plato.stanford.edu/entries/cosmopolitanism/
(Accessed August 6, 2018). (Gorgias 461e1–3; cf. Apology 37c5–e2 and Meno 80b4–7).

Gentlemen present… I regard you all as kinsmen, familiars, and fellow-citizens — by nature and not by convention; for like is by nature akin to like, while convention, which is a tyrant over human beings, forces many things contrary to nature.[312]

This appears to be the form of cosmopolitanism promoted by Pope Francis in his encyclical *Fratelli Tutti*. This form of cosmopolitanism is based on the narrative of our common humanity, social love and social friendship. It promotes the values of social fraternity, that we are all brothers and sisters, the principle of humanity and the universality of our humanity. It also promotes equality and liberty for all human beings as rational beings. It is a form of cosmopolitanism that is associated to the principal being behind nature and the law of nature. Nature operates based on the principles/laws/standards of the creator of nature: the Universal Being/Necessary Being (the First Cause).

Enlightenment concept of cosmopolitanism--The idea of cosmopolitanism of the Enlightenment period and Modern period was based on capitalism and on the anthropological 'discoveries' of the then new world. It is also connected to the emergence of human rights' narratives and surge for human capacity to reason. Human capacity to reason is directly associated with the attitude of open-mindedness and impartiality/rational objectivity. One has to recall that this demand for the capacity to reason was mainly about the rational identity of European people, not about other cultures, including Africans.[313] I explained this point in my earlier essay that Eurocentric philosophy assumes that we live: "in a world obsessed with globalized monoculture of capitalism and materialism and individualism. Global capitalism and materialism and individualism, by their nature, obliterate the focus on integral humanism…of person-within-social harmony."[314] The implication of this assumption is that to be under the influence of any other culture except European and the Enlightenment era is not to be cosmopolitan. It is to live under an irrational cultural prejudice. European culture was rational, enlightened, urbane and universal (at home everywhere and desirable everywhere).

---

[312] https://plato.stanford.edu/entries/cosmopolitanism/ (Accessed August 6, 2018). Protagoras 337c7-d3.

[313] Scholars like Rene Descartes, G. W. F. Hegel, and Immanuel Kant were promoters of this view of European/Western human capacity to reason. This point has been developed and expressed in my essay on Jacques Maritain and African Christianism. I argued that much about Western cosmopolitanism—just like Western Christianity, is a form of promotion of European cultural imperialism and monopolization of rationality.

[314] Anozie, "Jacques Maritain's International Relations and African Philosophy of Personhood/Community," p. 98.

As was attributed to Georg Wilhelm Hegel and others like him. They used words like 'primitive,' 'native,' 'tribe,' 'backwardness,' and 'savagery' to describe African culture or to suggest the real qualities of Enlightenment cosmopolitanism. Joseph McLaren affirms that: "These ideas were inheritances of the eighteenth century, passed down by such thinkers as the German philosopher Georg Wilhelm Hegel, who viewed African societies as outside of history, in a 'completely wild and untamed state,' and… lacking … developing any culture."[315]

In an attempt to briefly advance on this discussion of diverse forms of cosmopolitanism, I have adapted a summary of the **Enlightenment concept of cosmopolitanism** from Stanford Encyclopedia. It stated that:

> In the eighteenth century, the terms 'cosmopolitanism' and 'world citizenship' were often used not as labels for determinate philosophical theories, but rather to indicate an attitude of open-mindedness and impartiality. A cosmopolitan was someone who was not subservient to a particular religious or political authority, someone who was not biased by particular loyalties or cultural prejudice. Furthermore, the term was sometimes used to indicate a person who led an urbane life-style, or who was fond of traveling, cherished a network of international contacts, or felt at home everywhere. In this sense the… 'cosmopolitan' was often used to signify a "man of no fixed abode, or a man who is nowhere a stranger."[316]

Enlightenment concept of cosmopolitanism is approached from the point of view of mental liberation against the religious authorities that dominated at the time or even abused their power at the time. Based on the abuse of power, moral corruptions and social injustice that contradicted basic human equality, there was another consideration of cosmopolitanism from a moral perspective.

Moral cosmopolitanism--It holds that all humans are brothers and sisters. The purpose is "to indicate the fundamental equality of rank of all humans, which precluded slavery, colonial exploitation, feudal hierarchy, and

---

[315] Joseph McLaren, "Things Fall Apart: Cultural and Historical Contexts," *Critical Insights: Things Fall Apart*, ed. M. Keith Booker (Pasadena, California: Salem Press, 2011), p. 23. See Selden Rodman, "The White Man's Faith," *Review of Things Fall Apart, by Chinua Achebe*, New York Times Book Review 22 February, 1959, p. 28; p. 93; p. 98; See McLaren, op. cit., pp. 23-24.
[316] https://plato.stanford.edu/entries/cosmopolitanism/ (Accessed August 6, 2018).

tutelage of various sorts."[317] It means that all persons stand in certain moral relations to one another. This is the strict demand of this form of cosmopolitanism. Moral cosmopolitanism is akin to Natural Law cosmopolitanism very vividly articulated in *Fratelli Tutti* of Pope Francis. This distinctive point is that other forms of cosmopolitanism could be moral without necessarily being based on Natural Law reasons or justifications. Natural Law cosmopolitanism is universal and objective for all communities and cultures. It is not suitable in addressing the subjective conditions of human existence, especially on the continent of Africa and other non-European parts of the world. Africans and their thoughts on their conditions of existence are part of the thoughts of the citizens of the world or world citizenship. For instance, Immanuel Kant is known for his moral cosmopolitan approach that focuses on the principles of universalizability, humanity, autonomy, and rationality, and the basic right of resort/space of existence. Unfortunately, Kant's 'morality' was not generously extended to Africans (some Europeans seem to think).

In Kant's universal principle of hospitality and what will bring a sense of common humanity to all, he talks about what will "finally bring the human race ever closer to a cosmopolitan constitution."[318] Kant's position is correct but its application to all human being, including Africans, was poorly thought out or rather not thought out at all. In relation to Kant and the limitations of his moral cosmopolitanism, there may be situations/philosophical positions that do not promote cosmopolitanism in African communities, especially in cases of violations or crimes committed against people of other ethnic nationalities or cultural identities. There are also some African social-ethical policies that do not directly promote the wellbeing of persons. There are also situations that were caused by individual person in a community and were against the wellbeing of that community.[319] For instance, a person's choice to suicide goes contrary to the community's sense of cosmopolitanism or understanding of common humanity. Suicide is considered to be a desecration of the earth or a crime against the earth (Earth goddess--*Ala*).[320] It is a crime against human solidarity with the earth. Suicide requires rejection of the body of the suicide victim and

---

[317] https://plato.stanford.edu/entries/cosmopolitanism/ (Accessed August 6, 2018).
[318] Immanuel Kant,"Toward Perpetual Peace," *Practical Philosophy* – Cambridge Edition of the Works of Immanuel Kant, trans. M. J. Gregor (Cambridge University Press, Cambridge, 1999), p. 329.
[319] I could relate this to the argument promoted by former President Donald Trump that some immigrants and migrants are dangerous people from crime-infested countries.
[320] African Igbos explained that as a crime against "Ala" (Earth goddess). It is a crime against the "Universe."

the punishment of the person's family members as a part of performing some purification rituals. In such situations, for purification purposes, some of the personal rights/individual human rights are suppressed by collective/community's rights. The common interests or rights of the community override the interests or personal rights of the citizen of a community. In African hermeneutical philosophy on person, family, and community; the place of family in the community of mutual existence is the basis of our ethics, at least domestic ethics. These facts remain central in the ethical life of the people and the formulation of moral principles people communicate to younger generations. Kant's form of moral cosmopolitanism would be critical of these specific African cultural-ethical approaches or activities that are not universally affirmed. Meanwhile, one has to decipher if these African moral principles are religious- or humanistic-driven.

Beyond Kant's approach to moral cosmopolitanism, generally speaking, moral cosmopolitanism is also very critical of the exploitation and colonization of other people/cultures, especially the African people and other cultures. Exploitation and colonialism may not necessarily be the sole basis of *Fratelli Tutti* by Pope Francis. Other moral cosmopolitans' scholars are Emanuel Levinas and Jacques Derrida. I would think that African cosmopolitanism can survive in this context of moral cosmopolitanism experience. Moral cosmopolitanism naturally connects to African cosmopolitanism of brotherhood and sisterhood. However, one has to spell out the distinctions if there are any.

African cosmopolitanism of brotherhood and sisterhood is anchored on *African Ethics* because of the natural relation between African metaphysics of person, the metaphysics of brotherhood and sisterhood and African Ethics. To affirm the place of African ethics, Kwame Gyekye argued that humanism or good of humanity is at the center of African traditional religion and ethics. I will further explain that African Igbo hermeneutical ethics:

> is not dependent on African religions but they mutually support each other in metaphysical subtlety. This explains the place of person as an ethical cum relational being. …Africans' ethics is non-revealed and non-individuality based ethics. It is thus an ethics based on solidarity, political belongingness/well-being, and deep in common humanity.[321]

---

[321] Anozie, "Jacques Maritain's International Relations and African Philosophy of Personhood/Community," p. 91.

African Cosmopolitanism and Political Philosophy of Patriotism

The historical condition for this essay is the symbolic place of Trump's American patriotism. Trump's presidency and policies have necessitated the political philosophy of patriotism. Trump made use of every opportunity of his presidency to put "American First" and "Make America Great Again" as the mantras that shaped American exceptionalism and democracy. I have identified this as Trump's *American Patriotism* (that by its nature only accommodates moderate cosmopolitanism). This is not unique to Trump's presidency. It has been an integral part of American "Manifest Destiny" democracy/socio-economic and political culture. This new understanding/socio-economic and political culture or political demand for *Moderate* cosmopolitanism in the United States of America is instructive for political introspection in other countries and continents, especially in Africa. I consider African Political Philosophy of Patriotism as the clarion call to commitment for African renaissance (or African continued consciousness). It is an invitation, and fervent demand, for Africans and African countries to define and re-communicate and re-transmit the core values of their notion of cosmopolitan brotherhood and sisterhood. It requires continued revisit, renewal and resurgence in the application of African socio-economic and political values to African experience. The framework and ethics of this patriotism should be based on the excellence of research, intensity of purpose and deliberate advancement of enduring African excellences/virtues that emerge through introspective political re-evaluation and consciousness.

The crux of this introspective political re-evaluation and consciousness is that African political belongingness[322] is a necessity to every forms and facets of African development initiative. Political Belongingness is a requirement for any patriotic progressive society. I identify political belongingness as an intrinsic aspect of self-determination, autonomy and basic wellbeing. Political Belongingness equates to or same as political rights. Without political rights all other human rights (economic, social, cultural and religious rights) are not functional or they would not have enduring transformational capacities. The benefits of political belongingness, expressed through introspective political re-evaluation, are clearly seen in the effort to reviving African cosmopolitanism of brotherhood and sisterhood, especially following colonial distortions of African

---

[322] For a contextual relevance, I would describe the term as "African Political Belongingness"--which is a requirement for any patriotic progressive society. Patriotism—in this case-- demands the actualization of African political belongingness. It sets the framework and pace for diverse cultural and civilizational experience.

mode of existence and thought. African people and scholars should be able to patriotically tell their own stories and communicate the richness of their philosophical reflections. This richness should be repeated, reviewed, reintroduced and re-developed. These are the ways to promote and advance African scholarship. In my earlier scholarship (introductory contributions to African philosophy), I have called this body of work or literature *African Hermeneutic Philosophy* (or even African Hermeneutics Studies).[323] African Hermeneutic Philosophy encapsulates the hermeneutics of African political belongingness, the hermeneutics of political philosophy of patriotism, the ethics of patriotism, the concepts of person and person as a rational being, African cosmopolitanism of brotherhood and sisterhood, etc.)

African cosmopolitanism of brotherhood and sisterhood is about African people being aware of other people (as *Others*, not merely as a collection of individuals or *otherness* as strangers with strange language, or described in German as–*Auslaender/Fremder, Fremden*, with *fremdsprache*--foreign languages). African cosmopolitanism has been famously articulated through *Ubuntu* (African) view of the world.[324] African cosmopolitanism is same as *Ubuntu* cosmopolitanism. *Ubuntu* cosmopolitanism is anchored on the notion of "I am because we are, and because we are therefore I am."[325] A person is a person because of the other person. It means that our personhood is ontologically intertwined. It is ontologically and anthropologically an "I-We" cosmopolitanism. *Ubuntu* is about re-affirming human interpersonal relationship. This relationship is core to our nature and the basis for our ontological duty to one another as human persons. With particular reference to African Igbo hermeneutical philosophy, I have associated *Ubuntu* to *Umunna* in African Igbo worldview. In African Igbo religious and philosophical worldviews, *Umunna* describes the notion of inclusive human connectedness and our communitarian nature. *Umunna* lays the foundation for *Ikwu-na-Ibe*

---

[323] African scholars and people should tell and re-tell their own stories for the promotion of their wealth of views of the world. I preferred to identity the scholarship as African Hermeneutic Philosophy. See Stanley Uche Anozie, *Hans-Georg Gadamer and African Hermeneutic Philosophy* (Chisinau: Generis Publishing, 2020).
[324] Edwin Etieyibo (University of the Witwatersrand) argued that *Ubuntu* is a form of strict moral cosmopolitanism. It is an African Cosmopolitanism, which he associated with global justice. https://philpapers.org/rec/ETIUCA (Accessed December 20, 2021). See Edwin Etieyibo, "Ubuntu, Cosmopolitanism, and Distribution of Natural Resources," *Philosophical Papers* 46 (1) (2017):139-162.
[325] Stanley Uche Anozie, *Hans-Georg Gadamer and African Hermeneutic Philosophy* (Chisinau: Generis Publishing, 2020), p. 172. See John Samuel Mbiti, *African Religions and Philosophy* (London: Heinemann Educational Books Ltd, 1969), p. 113.

(near and far human fraternity or human family). *Umunna* (like *Ubuntu*) encapsulates the inherent virtues or excellences of our common humanity.[326] We have this excellence just for being human and in sharing human-ness.

These enriching views about the excellence of our common humanity are based on the premise of non-revealed African religions and cultures. In this case, African religions and cultures are not about conversion or colonization or domination of other people/cultures but for the genuine existence and expression of the person and the community. African religions are spirituality. African religions, like spirituality, are not imposed on anyone. They do not place emphasize on membership or on the census of adherents. In this sense they are cosmopolitan—because they allow the interaction of the diverse cultures as versions/expressions of one human culture. For instance, indigenous Igbo culture is not set to establish that it is better than indigenous Yoruba culture, and there is no place for proselytism or conversion for each of these original and indigenous cultures. There is no undue emphasis on one particular culture being against the other. It is about identifying the fundamental values of existence in our diverse cultures, which could essentially be ONE (as directed by the Supreme Being—in Igbo is—*Chukwu okike*). African Igbo or indigenous Igbo culture would say: *Nku di na mba na ehere mba nri* (The firewood in each community or culture is suitable to cook their own food. Every culture is sufficiently and adequately enriched.

Every culture or worldview has the capacity to bring a life of excellence to her people. This does not mean that every culture is perfect. It rather accentuates the point that cultures have the capacity to enrich the people or are dynamic in promoting the life of excellence. Human beings are cultural beings. We live and speak culture, and we are the product of culture. We create culture and culture cultivates us. African Igbo people refer to culture as: *Ome-na-ala* or *Odi-nala*. *Ome-na-ala di n' odi n' odi*—meaning—Cultures are diverse. Cultures abound.[327] This notion of Africa Igbo *Ome-na-ala* or *Odi-nala* and the ethics of *Umunna* (living according to the standard/principles of *Ome-na-ala* or *Odi-nala*) illustrate a cosmopolitan approach that is not selfish or exclusivist in perspective. It does not place emphasis on African Igbo *First*, Nigeria *First*, or Africa *First*.

---

[326] Anozie, "Jacques Maritain's International Relations and African Philosophy of Personhood/Community," p. 91. Prof. P. Iroegbu identified this African ethics as the ethics of *Umunna*. (*Ibid*. p. 91).

[327] Cultures are diverse. Cultures abound. Cultures are rich. Cultures renew or revive themselves.

The idea of Africa *First* or Nigeria *First* is not the interest of African Hermeneutic Philosophy or African Sage Philosophy; rather it is about promoting our political obligations or responsibilities and contributions:[328] Igbos can make Igboland great. Nigerians can make Nigeria great. Ghanaians can make Ghana great, etc. by establishing their cultural or socio-philosophical values or thought and sharing the understanding that people are willing to adopt or learn from them. We promote cultures just like in Aristotelian virtue ethics, which is the excellence of each culture; each culture should shine and thrive.

In the above, I have tried to make a clear distinction between "America First" (Nationalism) and "Make America Great Again" (American Patriotism) or even "Make Nigeria Great Again" as the basis for enriching discourse on African cosmopolitanism of brotherhood and sisterhood or that of open-mindedness and human fraternity. The most challenging aspect of this discourse is the cosmopolitan direction of its narrative. It is challenging because being cosmopolitan is essentially aligned to the principle of humanity or common humanity or world citizenship. The values of world citizenship, cosmopolitan humanity, common humanity, etc. are not necessarily taught. They are intelligibly discerned. They are ontological to the people because of the values of open-mindedness and impartiality. These positive values are not taught; they are rather naturally discerned and adopted for their usefulness for building our human community or human solidarity. It is commonly said: "The good speaks for itself." African Igbo people will express this as *Ahia oma na-ere onwe ya* or *Mma ugo no ugo n' ahu* or *Mmiri maru ugo na asa ugo aru* (the context determines the suitability of this proverb).[329] Another English expression is: "Charity begins at home" –that could be translated as— *Ana amarama site na-ulo maram fuo na-ama*. African cosmopolitanism is humanist and humanitarian. It must to be humanist before it could be humanitarian. This means that it is not merely humanitarian (not merely outward looking). The resounding point of this

---

[328] In this context, I think about the work of Howard W. French, *Born in Blackness* (USA: Liveright Publishing Corporation, 2021). The problem of single stories diminishes the ability to read and understand African views of the world or reality. I consider this quotation important: "one that reveals a long-concealed history of trivialization and, more often, elision in depictions of African history throughout the last five hundred years. As French shows, the achievements of sovereign African nations and their now-far-flung peoples have time and again been etiolated and deliberately erased from modern history."
https://www.harvard.com/book/born_in_blackness/ (Accessed December 19, 2021). The idea above sustains my reason for African perspective in history and philosophy.
[329] This Igbo proverb implies that the beauty of the Eagle/bird (*Ugo*) is enhanced by the rain. The beauty of the Eagle/bird is *inside* the bird or it is an inherent part of the bird. Expressions like "Agwa bu mma" (Character is beauty or good character beautifies one) could also be contextually suitable or appropriate.

narrative is that African cosmopolitanism of brotherhood and sisterhood is not in exclusion of other people (unless the people are not genuine and not welcomed members of the community). However, one could argue that in African societies or communities' people's rights were sometimes neglected or violated.[330] This concern about possible abuses against human rights and dignity could be related to *Nwa-diala* or *Diala* (an Igbo word for an indigene, a full-fledged community member) and *Nwa-osu* or *Nwosu* (an excommunicated person or one dedicated to an isolated to a god or goddess, an ex-indigene). For clarity sake, the challenges caused by *Nwa-diala* and *Nwa-osu* distinctions should be considered and addressed as part of African socio-ethical crises. African ethics explains what her ethical principles or moral standards are, who did what in the past, and who was banished or should be punished by the community. With regard to these ethical crises, abuses and lack of clarity, I recommended that:

> one understands that that there is an obvious obstacle to individual person's freedom and well-being but the desire to question the values of the community is part of the ongoing discourses between individual person's and their communities for a better society....This is why critical or reflective thinking should be a part of every human organization, even when it is denied or the opportunity is frustrated. The demand for well-being should be at the core of political agitation (leading to consideration of political personhood in a community).[331]

Certainly there are narratives suggesting abuse of political rights, freedom, and unfairness to some of the persons who were banished in the communities. Within African[332] Igbo socio-ethical context, everyone is welcome. Everyone is part of the *Umunna* unless one has committed a heinous crime (*Imeru ala*—violated the peaceful land or earth). Everyone is welcomed until they violate the peace of the land. If there is no violation committed, the person could stay as long as the purpose of their visit is honorable or noble. We feel at home everywhere. African Igbo express this thus: *Obia ra ngam abiagbulam* (Let my guest not kill me). Generally, the guest is always a part and parcel of the community. The guest enjoys universal hospitality.[333] (*Onye obia m*

---

[330] See my work: African Ethics: Human Being is Beautiful –for further reading.
[331] Anozie, "Jacques Maritain's International Relations and African Philosophy of Personhood/Community," p. 85.
[332] Kwame Anthony Appiah, *Cosmopolitanism: Ethics in a World of Strangers* (London: Penguin Books, 2006).
[333] Immanuel Kant expressed a similar understanding in *his Perpetual Peace: A Philosophical Sketch* (1795). He argued that everyone has a place on earth. The earth is place of shared

or *Onye obia anyi*---Our guest).[334] The guest enjoys our fraternal solidarity. No one is always a stranger. No one is anywhere a perpetual stranger.[335] To be a "stranger" is not a permanent status. The shared humanity of everyone, including the guests is communicated through the ethical framework of *Onyegbula* (Do not kill) and *Onyeghala* (*Onyeghala ibe*) (Do not abandon the other).[336] The other person is an essential part of who you are or the other person is *a core* of your beingness/being human. We are ontologically co-dependent beings. Our affiliation to life and sustained existence are expressed through Igbo names like *Ndubusi* or *Nduwuisi* (Life is ultimate. Life is primary. Life has primacy), *Ugo-ndu* (The excellence of life or Pride of life), *Uju-ndu* or *Obia-na-uju* (Coming with the fullness of life or the bountiful life). We have a duty to protect the other.[337] We also have a duty to promote and guarantee the bountiful life---living truly well. Meanwhile, my only task here is to justify and sustain the narrative and scholarship on African cosmopolitanism of brotherhood and sisterhood. I am primarily interested in the 'ought', not in the 'is', questions: What were the ethical ideals and values that Africa set out to accomplish? What are the values that we live by? These are the central concerns of this paper/chapter.

In addressing the central concerns of this paper/chapter, my goal is to argue that African cosmopolitanism of brotherhood or sisterhood is better embraced by African mind through its regular consideration and rigor of intellectual exercise on what it truly is. Africans have to progress from "who" they are and "what" they do to "what could" be done to become better. One cannot truly become better without knowing "Who" and "What" and "How" his/her original views/thoughts of the world should be understood or communicated in the world.

In African thought, especially Igbo socio-political thought/culture, every member of the community participates in all that are good for the community. What is good for the community includes the moral values, socio-cultural

---

humanity. It is a shared-space. It is a communal space. For this communal space, everyone has a basic right of resort.

[334] Jacques Derrida expressed this view that is in line with African Igbo ethics of hospitality.

[335] https://plato.stanford.edu/entries/cosmopolitanism/ (Accessed August 6, 2018). Although the quotation is Western, it adequately captured the point about African Igbo philosophy.

[336] Emanuel Levinas communicated a similar thought in *Other*. The *Other* invites to us/you his/her vulnerabilities. Ethics is care, caring or taking care of the Other's vulnerability.

[337] Ulrich Beck, *The Cosmopolitan Vision* (Cambridge: Polity Press, 2006), p. 45. For Beck, traditional nation-state politics is opposed to the expectations of cosmopolitanism. Nation-states are particular. Cosmopolitanism is global or universal.

values, economic values and systems, religious values of the community (including the accepted diversities—*Onye na-chi ya* or a person's uniqueness). Meanwhile, the central point of African cosmopolitanism is the natural relation of all human beings (*Nwanne di na mba*---Brotherhood and sisterhood are found in other lands/cultures/communities). *Igwebuike*—meaning—"we are better together," or "being a team is better for us", or "we are greater by being one people." Some scholars have attributed this similar approach to cosmopolitanism in Socrates[338] (a Greek scholar) who did not travel outside his community most of his life but connected to all human beings—familiar and unfamiliar, citizens and foreigners—as part of his Athenian freedom of expression and freedom to live well (being human well).

Let me now take a look at the theme "African cosmopolitanism is African ethics," and also an essential part of ethics of patriotism.

African Cosmopolitanism is African Ethics

African cosmopolitanism is African ethics. It is the ethics of our common humanity that explores the riches of shared-values, share-existence, shared-experience, shared-lifeworld, shared-beingness, etc. Shared-values determine ethics of a community. African ethical principles or reasoning justify the form of ethics and the shared-values for human wellbeing in the community. Some of these ethical principles are based on intrinsic religious reasoning and consequentialist/utilitarian reasoning or justifications. Of course, as I pointed out, there could be various reasons to see failures of individual person in recognizing these common humanity or human solidarity qualities and shared values in words and actions. One thing so clear about the integrity of African ethics is that the foundations are similar (not exactly the same) to Deontological ethics or ethics of duty, Consequentialist ethics, and Aristotelian Virtue ethics or ethics of character.

Ethics as character-based is an important point in African philosophy and African cosmopolitanism. Ethics does not imply perfection in actions. It is much of practicing, nudging, reviewing, and re-engineering.[339] What we do is acquired through time, through practising, and through observing respected people in the community. Most of these respected people in the community are members of social groups, cultural groups, age-grade groups that positively influence the

---

[338] *Gorgias* 461e1–3; cf. *Apology* 37c5–e2 and *Meno* 80b4–7.
[339] See my African Ethics: Human Being is Beautiful--- essay for further reading.

lives of the young. For instance, African Igbos would say: *Onye agwa oma* or *Onye agwa mara mma*—meaning—"a person with sound character, a good-natured human being." *Onye agwa ojo*—meaning—"a person with/of bad characters."

In my earlier work, I noted that Kwame Gyekye's essay on 'African Ethics' and its relation to the idea of "individual" and "person" are laudable.[340] I averred that:

> The individual is that human being who persists in a series of bad practices (unethical behaviors) and does not recognize the dignity of the other person. However, this individual does not lose his/her essential personhood based on the mere bad or ill wishes of the other who wants it so, rather one becomes an individual by continually participating in inhuman action….In Igbo Nigerian African ethics [African Igbo ethics], there is a distinction between a moral person (truly a person), a human being (children, sick fellows, mentally challenged people, intellectually challenged people) and an individual (evil and unethical subject). As Gyekye notes, 'it does not imply at all that an individual considered 'not a person' loses his rights as a human being or as a citizen or that people in the community should cease to demonstrate a moral concern for him or display the appropriate moral virtues in their treatment of him; only that he is not considered a morally worthy individual.[341]

There lies the essence of African cosmopolitanism of brotherhood and sisterhood. African Ethics captures the core values of African cosmopolitanism of brotherhood and sisterhood. It is helpful for imparting ethical ideas of Africans to young generations of Africans, especially in the context of our common humanity or global citizenship. African lifeworld is determinative of our African cosmopolitan ethics of patriotism. It is within these diverse lifeworld of socio-cultural-economic-political-religious factors that life is truly meaningful for a patriotic African person. For me, "[T]his is why an integral global ethics is a necessity in our co-mutually-existent world."[342] It is also why African Igbo hermeneutical ethics (as part of African hermeneutical philosophy of cosmopolitanism and African political philosophy of patriotism) is worth advancing. For now, American notion of cosmopolitanism, or

---

[340] Anozie, "Jacques Maritain's International Relations and African Philosophy of Personhood/Community," p. 93.
[341] http://plato.stanford.edu/entries/african-ethics/ (Accessed November 5, 2017)
[342] Anozie, "Jacques Maritain's International Relations and African Philosophy of Personhood/Community," p. 95.

European/Western approach to it, does not address all aspects of cosmopolitanism. In other to suggest a one-sided articulation of cosmopolitanism, some European/Western scholars have tried to distort other cultures' views of our common human life and our common world citizenship.

I would like to address the need for the rehabilitation of African cosmopolitanism of brotherhood and sisterhood.

Western Hegemony and the Rehabilitation of African Cosmopolitanism

My take on African cosmopolitanism of brotherhood and sisterhood is that the African concept of the human person is deeper and more enriching than is often presented. African philosophy of person as a relational being and African communitarianism are same as African cosmopolitanism. The long period of Western colonialism and monopolization of reason provided a context for African' loss of the richness of their values and the perfidy of cultural erosion. The reinvigoration of African frame of mind or African consciousness is a central issue that I deliberately promote in this essay/chapter.

The idea of cosmopolitanism, in a modern theorist perspective, has been used to defend the colonization of Africans, African cultures and other cultures. This means that Western cosmopolitanism is about aligning all humanity to Western categories and conceptual framework. The idea is that people who are unable to conform are compelled through wars and conquests and unhealthy international policies. Sometimes the people of other cultures were accused of violating the natural social order that is based on cosmopolitanism:

> In fact, the very notion of a natural sociability was sometimes used instead to legitimate war against peoples elsewhere in the world who were said to have violated this common bond in an 'unnatural' way, or who were easily said to have placed themselves outside of the domain of common human morality by their 'barbaric' customs.[343]

Are there a level of cosmopolitan mode of thinking and existence in African hermeneutical philosophy? This mode of thinking is different from a form of cosmopolitanism that recognises a single state in which all peoples and cultures are subsumed. Western/European form of cosmopolitanism is at the

---

[343] https://plato.stanford.edu/entries/cosmopolitanism/ (Accessed August 6, 2018).

core of colonialism and capitalism. One could reference French policy of *assimilation* and British policy of *association* as examples of this form of cosmopolitanism.

The African perspective of cosmopolitanism is that our common humanity (may be related to ethical objectivism) is true whether people recognize it or not. The metaphysical dimension in African discourse is that the process of human consciousness is a gradual one. Each culture at some point achieves this self-realization. For the African people, it is part of their metaphysics of existence. Unfortunately, the path of this human consciousness has been truncated by slavery and colonialism. The restoration of African philosophical thought essentially deserves a quality hermeneutical orientation so as to outline the metaphysical content in African ideas. In light of this demand, I relate my task to the idea of "Hermeneutical Orientations" in African philosophy that Samuel Oluoch Imbo, Tsenay Serequeberhan, Marcien Towa and Okonda Okolo have been associated with. The essential advancement of African philosophy must be through hermeneutical enterprise.[344] It is a hermeneutical enterprise that is centered on African unitive world of existence.

The Unitive Nature of Existence in African Philosophy

Existence is one. Our existence is in coherence with other existences or world of existence. Life is one. Life is the vital force. Life is same as consciousness because without consciousness something cannot be said to live. Consciousness may be different from self-consciousness but existence or life affirms consciousness (rational or irrational consciousness). African people, especially African Igbo, recognize life or consciousness in almost all that we see or perceive. The human person embodies this rational consciousness even when culture plays a role in the conception of human nature or the conception of personhood as part of nature. Gyekye explains, "The type of social structure or arrangement evolved by a particular society seems to reflect –and be influenced by –the public conceptions of personhood held in the society."[345]

---

[344] Samuel Oluoch Imbo, *An Introduction to African Philosophy* (Maryland: Rowman and Littlefield Publishers, Inc., 1998), p. 27ff. See also Tsaney Serequeberhan, *The Hermeneutics of African Philosophy: Horizon and Discourse* (New York: Routledge, 1994).
[345] See Kwame Gyekye, "Person and Community in African Thought," *Person and Community*, Kwasi Wiredu and Kwame Gyekye, eds (Washington, D. C.: The Council for Research in Values and Philosophy, Vol. 1, 1992), p. 101.

From an African [Igbo] philosophical perspective, Africa has lost most of these cultural awareness and spiritual well-being as essential aspects of existence as consciousness because of colonialism, slavery, neo-colonialism, globalism, etc. According to Samuel Oluoch Imbo, "the real African has been distorted by Western scholars beyond recognition...European narratives rendered these African stories primitive and barbaric."[346] The generations of African people have been lost in the mode of thought. Unlike the gradual development of what is essentially considered as Western Philosophical Thought, what we see as African philosophy is filled with doubts[347] about its authenticity and originality.

Frantz Fanon adumbrates this doubt on genuine African philosophical thinking because of the implications or effects of the psychological damage from colonization, slavery and Eurocentrism (Western hegemony). For Fanon, unfortunately, the heart of African intelligentsia is to replicate Western Philosophy according to the approval of the *Masters*. There is nothing to justify that world philosophies must be "mono-cultural" and "Eurocentric." Our vision of reality should be variedly considered because of our diverse conditions of existence or lifeworld. These diverse conditions have to identify that "African consciousness in the first two decades of the century was further fed by a variety of sources. The quest for democratic government, even where pursued by multi-racial pressure groups, almost inevitably harboured racial undertones. The governments were mostly white, while the disfranchized masses were mostly African." [348] The restoration or rehabilitation of our diverse experience of the world (one world) is the path to a unitive knowledge and the unitive nature/metaphysics of human existence since life is one. Life or existence is continuity (continuity with discontinuity). As I noted in my unpublished work on *African Philosophy of Dance as a Mode of Existence*: "[W]hat unfolds is the consciousness of history and consciousness of our historical situation. It unfolds not as a totally new project but as a cultural discontinuity as well as an ontological continuity in a new mode of being for authentic intercultural

---

[346] Samuel Oluoch Imbo, *Oral Traditions as Philosophy: Okot P'Bitek's Legacy for African Philosophy* (USA: Rowman & Littlefield Publishers, 2002), p. 2.
[347] http://www.unesco.org/culture/caribbean/pdf/ghc_onlinechapter_vol5_chap6_en.pdf (Accessed December 23, 2021).
[348] http://www.unesco.org/culture/caribbean/pdf/ghc_onlinechapter_vol5_chap6_en.pdf (Accessed December 23, 2021) See Tony Martin, "African and Indian Consciousness," *General History of the Caribbean* (United Nations Educational, Scientific and Cultural Organization, Volume V, Chapter 6, 1996), p. 261.

relations within a global world determined by diverse socio-cultural, socio-economic and philosophical factors."[349]

Conclusion

My chapter reflection on African cosmopolitanism of brotherhood and sisterhood is an invitation to articulate beyond the demands of African notion of personhood to that of African cosmopolitanism. African political philosophy of patriotism is the conscientious agency for promoting African consciousness and cosmopolitanism. This chapter is an invitation to a new understanding and a new mode of existence in relation to humanity in general. Has African philosophical world and thought any agenda to accommodate the vision of common humanity without boundaries? Or is African philosophy of cosmopolitanism and political philosophy of patriotism one that fits African narrative of person—an African person in an African world alone? My considerations of some unfolded views of African cosmopolitanism, which is a moral, as well as metaphysical, call for being-with-others, not just the African other but the global or World Other (not Order). Trump's moderate cosmopolitanism and rigorous affirmation of America *First*/American Exceptionalism and Manifest Destiny are sufficient justifications to revive and rehabilitate African cosmopolitanism of brotherhood and sisterhood, which is no less an advancement of the hermeneutics of African political philosophy of patriotism (of preserving and continually applying our philosophical views of the world or African consciousness[350]). African epistemological resources and categories or framework need to be applied and challenged based on African world experiences. This (I may describe as *epistemic and political patriotism*) is the basic route to identifying and preserving African political philosophy of patriotism. African political philosophy of patriotism is a conscientious mechanism to achieving African political belongingness, especially as a core aspect of self-determination and autonomy/political right.[351]

---

[349] Stanley Uche Anozie, African Philosophy of Dance as a Mode of Existence (an unpublished work on the Hermeneutics of Person, Diversity and Belongingness).

[350] http://www.unesco.org/culture/caribbean/pdf/ghc_onlinechapter_vol5_chap6_en.pdf (Accessed December 23, 2021) See Tony Martin, "African and Indian Consciousness," *General History of the Caribbean* (United Nations Educational, Scientific and Cultural Organization, Volume V, Chapter 6, 1996), p. 258ff. In 19th Century, Henry Sylvester Williams (a Trinidadian), was said to be the first to convene the world's first Pan-African Conference. This is considered as a significant part of African consciousness narratives. (Ibid., p. 259).

[351] Anozie, "Jacques Maritain's International Relations and African Philosophy of Personhood/Community," p. 85.

Bibliography

Anozie, S. U. (2017). The Paradox of Non-Violent Religions and Violent Cultural Practices. In M. Masaeli and R. Sneller (Eds.), *The Root Causes of Terrorism: A Religious Studies Perspective*. UK: Cambridge Scholars Publishing.

----------(2017). African Esoterism with a Concentration on Igbo tradition. In M. Masaeli (Ed.), *Spirituality and Global Ethics*. UK: Cambridge Scholars Publishing.

----------(2017). Jacques Maritain's interpersonal relations and African philosophy of personhood/community. In *Maritain Studies* (Volume XXXIII). Edited by Nikolaj Zunic. Published by the Canadian Jacques Maritain Association.

----------(2020). *Hans-Georg Gadamer and African Hermeneutic Philosophy*. Chisinau: Generis Publishing.

Bujo, B. (1998).*The Ethical Dimension of Community: The African Model and the Dialogue between North and South*. Nairobi: Paulines Africa.

----------(2001). *Foundations of an African Ethic: Beyond the Universal Claims of Western Morality*. New York: Crossroad.

Cole, H. and Chike A. (1984). *Igbo Arts: Community and Cosmos*. Los Angeles: Museum of Cultural History.

Dzobo, N. K. (1992). Values in a Changing Society: Man, Ancestor and God. In Kwasi Wiredu and Kwame Gyekye (Eds.). *Person and Community*. Ghanaian Philosophical Studies. Washington D.C.: The Council for Research in Values and Philosophy.

Gikandi, S. (1991). *Reading Chinua Achebe: Language and Ideology in Fiction*. Portsmouth: Heinemann.

Gyekye, K. (1992). Person and Community in African Thought. In *Person and Community*, edited by Kwasi Wiredu and Kwame Gyekye. Vol. 1.Washington, D. C: The Council for Research in Values and Philosophy.

Imbo, Samuel Oluoch. (1998). *An Introduction to African Philosophy*. Maryland: Rowman and Littlefield Publishers, Inc.

---------(2002). *Oral Traditions as Philosophy: Okot P'Bitek's Legacy for African Philosophy*. USA: Rowman & Littlefield Publishers.

Kant, Immanuel. (1999). "Toward Perpetual Peace." In *Practical Philosophy – Cambridge Edition of the Works of Immanuel Kant*. Translated by M. J. Gregor. Cambridge University Press, Cambridge.

Martin, Tony. (1999). "African and Indian Consciousness." In *General History of the Caribbean*. United Nations Educational, Scientific and Cultural Organization. Volume V, Chapter 6.

McLaren, Joseph. (2011). "Things Fall Apart: Cultural and Historical Contexts." In *Critical Insights: Things Fall Apart*, edited by M. Keith Booker. Pasadena, California: Salem Press.

John Samuel Mbiti. (1969). *African Religions and Philosophy*. London: Heinemann Educational Books Ltd.

Rand, Ayn. (1957). *Atlas Shrugged*. New York: Dutton.

----------(1964). *The Virtue of Selfishness*. New York: New American Library.

Serequeberhan, Tsaney. 1994. *The Hermeneutics of African Philosophy: Horizon and Discourse*. New York: Routledge.

Other sources:

http://plato.stanford.edu/entries/african-ethics/

https://plato.stanford.edu/entries/cosmopolitanism/

https://www.lifesitenews.com/news/former-presidential-candidate-on-vigano-testimony-this-is-a-homosexual-scan

Chapter 7
African (Igbo) Ethics of Rights' Discourse: Theory and Practice

Stanley Uche Anozie

(Philosophy Department, Boston College, Chestnut Hill, MA, USA, 2022)

Introduction

The United States of America, like other democracies of the world, is going through a learning curve in her own practice of democracy. The theories of justice and rights by Thomas Hobbes, John Locke, John Rawls, Amartya Sen, etc. having been adopted to build on American democracy, especially on fundamental human rights, justice, dignity, liberty, equality/equity, fraternity or social solidarity and happiness or human wellbeing. Amartya Sen in his work: *The Idea of Justice* challenged the abstract and institutional approach to justice and rights in Rawls, Locke, Hobbes, etc. Sen's approach to justice and rights is through a discourse- or dialogue-based approach. He advocated for a public discourse or public debate approach to understanding justice and rights in a democracy or a political institution. He placed emphasise on the general efforts to reduce injustice and enhance a culture of rights or justice. One could describe this as a comprehensive, collaborative, comparative and communicative culture approach to achieving justice and human rights in a democracy or a political institution. This form of achieving justice and human rights Sen identified as realization-focused approach to justice and rights. It is a consequentialist approach to justice—i.e., the justice as outcomes enjoyed by most number of people or minimizing injustice for the most number of people in a community. In other words it is communitarian. Sen distinguished this realization-focused approach to justice from the abstract-transcendental institutionalism approach. In light of this realization-focused and comparative culture approach to justice and right, and with the historical and political situations of our time, I would like to reflect on the topic: *African (Igbo) Ethics of Rights' Discourse: theory and practice,* since it is based on African hermeneutic or discourse culture. I would make references to African Igbo culture as *a context* for my reflections. It has a humanity-based form of discourse and a communitarian discourse ethics on rights.

African ethics or African discourse ethics involves many diverse socio-political theories of rights, justice, dignity, equity, solidarity and happiness or wellbeing. Based on some democratic challenges in some African countries and their practice of democracy, I would argue that African scholars should pay a close attention to African scholarship on African socio-political philosophy and African discourse ethics. I have elaborated on this point in my recent works on "African Cosmopolitanism of Brotherhood and Sisterhood" and the "Hermeneutics of African Political Philosophy of Patriotism." The present essay is a core aspect of my research on the "Hermeneutics of African Political Belongingness." Rights, Justice and Equity are important themes in socio-political philosophy and ethics. One could truly advance an idea of African ethics of rights' discourse (theory and practice) that addresses contemporary African (Igbo) socio-political leadership and political rights' concerns. The main requirements for a successful political leadership are that the values of rights, justice, dignity, integrity, equity, social fraternity, etc., must be commonplace as shared-moral values in a community. Let me take a look at the significant historical dispensations, political atmosphere, situations or background influences to African (Igbo) ethics of rights' discourse.

Background to African (Igbo) Ethics of Rights' Discourse

During the presidential dispensation of Donald Trump's America, the political atmosphere was fraught with troubles and was truly diminished. It was diminished because there was a lack of political guardianship from the top of American leadership structure to the American people. The required characters for political leadership in America was/is questionable and running deficit on administrative character, acuity and accountability. This concern was not only in the United States. There is also an ongoing political concern in Canada on the recent protests by the indigenous peoples of Canada against institutional abuse of the human rights of the indigenous people or systemic racism or even genocide by Church officials who collaborated with the federal government of Canada. Without suggesting that these countries—established on Western transcendental-institutionalism approach to rights and justice—have politically failed, I am rather arguing that their views of a democratic-political paradigm are idealistic, exaggerated, assumptive, and focused on a view of the world that is abstract, universalistic and transcendental institutionalist. The notion that some particular European or Western political theories on human rights and justice are universal political paradigms or universal categories for others cultures and civilizations to follow is always, and at present, inadequate and unsustainable. Thus, on this basis, I will argue that African political philosophy of patriotism as an aspect of the hermeneutics of political belongingness should have a place, a voice, a different perspective or dimension to reality, and relevance in global comparative discourse on human rights, justice and wellbeing, especially within the context of the chosen topic for this essay: *African (Igbo) Ethics of Rights' Discourse: Theory and Practice.*

In my earlier essay on: "Can Igbo Mysticism Fight Against Boko Haram" in *Responses of Mysticism to Religious Terrorism (Sufism and Beyond)*, edited by Mahmoud Masaeli and Rico Sneller (2020), I presented my understanding and appreciation for an African concept of person--by way of African Igbo hermeneutic philosophy. African (Igbo) concept of person is a good basis or foundation to define what rights and justice mean in African Igbo world. I tried to build on the reflections of African Igbo sages in terms of the ramifications of self-understanding, self-determination and self-actualization of African Igbo people or African consciousness through advancing a metaphysical/ontological and hermeneutical existence. This ontological and hermeneutical existence should be one based on the ethics of patriotism (from responsibility to political leadership and to convivial existence and continued interest in African consciousness). This ethics of patriotism is necessary "other side" of the hermeneutics of African political belongingness (convivial existence and ontological co-existent nature of a people). I explained that part of African-Nigerian socio-political crisis of rights and justice is equally a crisis of the pedagogy of ethics of patriotism, which is "a problem of ethical living (or capacity to moral agency). Corrupt leadership and lack of pedagogy of ethics of patriotism for community development in the leadership-followership relations gave birth to Boko Haram...Unemployment sustained the destructive path of Boko Haram in a flavored atmosphere of hopelessness and poverty." (Anozie, (2019), p. 254)

As part of my considerations of the varied dimensions of the background problem of this discourse, it is my view that, in relation to the human person and the problem of pedagogy of ethics of patriotism, there are African Igbo reflections on the person: a) beauty of life, and b) the relational nature of being. These reflections have been undergoing gradual progress and polishing of content. African Igbo discourse ethics and hermeneutics of African political belongingness (socio-political philosophy) should be enriched as a body of literature and scholarship. This is a basic way to make and advance African Igbo philosophical autonomy and competence on any matters of public interests.

These two aspects (African Igbo discourse **ethics** on rights/justice and the hermeneutics of African **political** belongingness) are important in understanding African Igbo concept of person--human dignity and rights, African cosmopolitanism of brotherhood and sisterhood, African political philosophy of patriotism and the ethics of patriotism.

Human Person, Patriotism and Human Rights

My thoughts on the person as brotherhood and sisterhood in *Maritain Studies* conference paper proceedings published in 2017 emphasized on the relational nature of the person. African Igbo worldview advances: "this relational being by developing the common good notions of, 'hospitality, daily friendship, and dialogue with the members of other ethnic groups are vital laws admitting of no exception. One who is not a member of my own group is ultimately also the 'property' of the other just as I myself am, and this means that I owe him respect and esteem. Thus one is ultimately related to all human beings.' "(Anozie, (2017), pp. 86-87) (Bujo, (1998), pp. 5-6)

African Igbo philosophical or discourse ethics has not been adequately promoted, even though the principles are already known among African scholars. As part of the background situation, the socio-political sphere of Africa, and especially in Nigeria, has not promoted a culture of rights and ethics of political patriotism due to Eurocentric and colonial-epistemic paralysis. Political patriotism is different from merely demanding for the right to self-determination. It is about protecting, promoting and advancing a political culture of African Igbo consciousness, wellbeing and sustainability. Political leadership (as a way of expressing political patriotism) is not a one-time thing. It is a philosophy of life, a way of living and preserving a political right of wellbeing and realization-focused justice. It is truly a right to self-actualization (self-determination does not necessarily mean self-actualization). Self-determination/independence or autonomy alone does not imply genuine well-being. However, genuine wellbeing or self-actualization cannot be accomplished without self-determination. Self-determination is a *means* to self-actualization. Self-actualization is the *destination* of self-determination. Self-determination or independence does not mean self-actualization. Self-determination is like a right to political independence or autonomy after the colonial rule of some African countries. This does not imply genuine wellbeing for these now independent African countries. For instance, in Nigeria, the Igboland is "self-determined" by Igbo politicians but the Igbo people have not accomplished genuine wellbeing or self-actualization. Self-actualization is not given by an external body or agency. Self-actualization comes through autonomy and political philosophy patriotism.

I consider African political philosophy of patriotism as the clarion call to commitment for all African renaissance (or African continued self-consciousness). It is an invitation, and a fervent demand, for Africans and African countries to define and re-communicate and re-transmit the core shared-values of cosmopolitanism of brotherhood and sisterhood. It requires continued revisit, renewal and resurgence in the application of African socio-economic and political values to African experience. The framework for this resurgence and the ethics of patriotism should be based on intensity of purpose, excellence of research, and deliberate advancement of enduring African excellences/virtues that emerge through introspective political re-evaluation and consciousness.

The crux of this introspective political re-evaluation and consciousness is that African political belongingness is a necessity to every forms and facets of African development initiatives. African political belongingness is a requirement for any patriotic progressive African society. I consider political belongingness as an intrinsic aspect of the right to self-determination, autonomy and basic wellbeing. Political Belongingness is inclusive of all forms of political rights. Without political rights all other human rights (economic, social, cultural and religious rights) are not functional or they would not have enduring transformational capacities. The benefits of African political belongingness, expressed through introspective political re-evaluation, are clearly seen in the effort to revive African cosmopolitanism of brotherhood and sisterhood, especially following colonial distortions of African mode of existence and worldviews. African people and scholars should be able to patriotically articulate their views of the world, tell their own stories, and communicate the richness of their philosophical reflections. This richness should be repeated, transmitted, reviewed, reintroduced and re-developed. These are the ways to promote and advance African scholarship. In my earlier scholarship (introductory contributions to African philosophy), I have called this body of work or literature as African Hermeneutic Philosophy (or even African Hermeneutic Studies). African scholars and people should tell and re-tell their own stories for the promotion of their wealth of views of the world. I preferred to identity this entire scholarship as African Hermeneutic Philosophy because of the importance of narratives and interpretation to understanding other people. (Anozie, (2020), p. 1ff) African hermeneutic philosophy encapsulates the hermeneutics of African political belongingness, the hermeneutics of political philosophy of patriotism, the ethics of patriotism, the concepts of person and person as a rational being, and African cosmopolitanism of brotherhood and sisterhood.

African cosmopolitanism of brotherhood and sisterhood is about African people being aware of other people (as Others, not merely as a collection of individuals or otherness as strangers with strange language, or described in German as–*Auslaender/Fremder*, *Fremden*, with *fremdsprache*--foreign languages). African cosmopolitanism has been famously articulated through *Ubuntu* (African) view of the world. African cosmopolitanism is same as *Ubuntu* cosmopolitanism. *Ubuntu* cosmopolitanism is anchored on the notion of "I am because we are, and because we are therefore I am." (Mbiti, (1969), p. 113) A person is a person because of the other person. It means that our personhood is ontologically intertwined. It is ontologically and anthropologically an "I-We" cosmopolitanism. *Ubuntu* is about re-affirming human interpersonal relationship. This relationship is core to our nature and the basis for our ontological duty to one another as human persons. With particular reference to African Igbo hermeneutical philosophy, I have associated *Ubuntu* to *Umunna* in African Igbo worldview. In African Igbo religious and philosophical worldviews, *Umunna* describes the notion of inclusive human connectedness and our communitarian nature. *Umunna* lays the foundation for *Ikwu-na-Ibe* (near and far human fraternity or human family). *Umunna* (like *Ubuntu*) encapsulates the inherent virtues or excellences of our common humanity. (Anozie, (2017), p. 91) We have this excellence just for being human and in sharing human-ness. These enriching views about the excellence of our common humanity are based on the premise of non-revealed African religions and cultures. In this case, African religions and cultures are not about conversion or colonization or domination of other people/cultures but for the genuine existence and expression of the person and the community.

African religions are spirituality. African religions, like spirituality, are not imposed on anyone. Every person has a right to practice his or her own spirituality. The primary goal of spirituality is humanity (or human wellbeing). African spirituality do not place emphasize on the number of members or on the census of adherents. In this sense, they are cosmopolitan in their understanding of cultural and peoples' rights—because they allow the interaction of the diverse cultures as versions/expressions of one human world. For instance, indigenous Igbo culture is not set to establish that it is better than indigenous Yoruba culture, and there is no place for proselytism or conversion for each of these original and indigenous cultures. The absence of proselytism or conversion is indicative of indigenous African response to freedom of association or right to association and freedom of expression. There is no undue emphasis on one particular culture being against the other culture or culture as human responses to nature and the effects of nature. Culture is conventional. Culture is human-made. It is to this extent that culture is *artificial* in relation to *nature* itself. Culture is a subjective response to nature. Nature is universal and objective. African Igbo people, like other people, are cultural beings as well as culturally subjective. They express this cultural subjectivity through their thought perspective, language and their fundamental values of existence.

African Igbo through thoughts, language and culture identify the fundamental values of existence in their diverse cultures, which could essentially be ONE (as directed by the Supreme Being or in Igbo is—*Chukwu okike* or *Onye kere uwa nile*). African Igbo or indigenous Igbo culture would say: *Nku di na mma na ehere mba nri* (The firewood in each community or culture is suitable for its people). People create culture and culture creates a people. Culture addresses all the concerns and needs of a people. Every culture is adequately enriched. Every culture or worldview has the capacity to bring a life of excellence to her people. This does not mean that every culture is perfect or perfect in the capacity to bring a life of excellence. It rather accentuates the point that cultures have the capacity to enrich the people or are dynamic in promoting the life of excellence as long as these cultures observe the objective universe or nature. Culture affirms the aspirations or rights of a people. As cultural beings, we live and speak culture, and we are the products of culture. For African Igbo people, 'being cultural persons' and 'culture cultivating us' are the two sides of human rights and dignity. We have the right to culture and the right to be cultivated by our cultures. These two sides are co-dependent and inseparable. One of the abuses or violations by Eurocentrism, cultural hegemony, Christianization, colonial-epistemic paralysis and colonial culture impoverishment is that they violated the cultural essence, identity, and rights of the African people. (Mutua (2002, pp. 113-118) The right to cultural identity is at the core of possessing human dignity. We create culture and culture cultivates us. African Igbo people refer to culture and tradition as: *Ome-na-ala* or *Odi-nala*. *Ome-na-ala di n' odi n' odi*—meaning—Cultures are diverse. Cultures abound. (French, (2021)) Africa Igbo *Ome-na-ala* or *Odi-nala* (culture and tradition) and the ethics of *Umunna* (living according to the standard/principles of *Ome-na-ala* or *Odi-nala*) illustrate a cosmopolitan approach to human rights and justice that is not selfish or exclusivist in perspective. Right is not exclusivist. Right is not absolute. Right is dialogical and discursive. Right is communitarian and mutually edifying as illustrated in African Igbo proverb: *Egbe bere, Ugo bere* (Live and Let Live). It also implies that our life together is best for all. Culture and tradition do not place emphasis on African Igbo *First*, Nigeria *First*, or Africa *First* even though we are culturally subjective.

The idea of Africa First or Nigeria First is not the basic interest of African Hermeneutic Philosophy or African Sage Philosophy; rather it is about promoting our political rights to self-determination, political rights to self-actualization, and fulfilling our other obligations or responsibilities. Igbos can make Igboland great. Nigerians can make Nigeria great. Ghanaians can make Ghana great, etc. by establishing their cultural or socio-philosophical values or thought and sharing their understanding that people are willing to adopt or learn from them. Africans and African Igbo promote cultures just like in Aristotelian virtue ethics, which is the excellence of each culture; each culture should shine and thrive.

In the above, I have tried to make a clear distinction between "America First" (Nationalism) and "Make America Great Again" (American Patriotism) or even "Make Nigeria Great Again" as the context for enriching discourse on African ethics of rights' discourse, the hermeneutics of African political belongingness, African cosmopolitanism of brotherhood and sisterhood or that of open-mindedness and human fraternity and African political philosophy of patriotism or ethics of patriotism. The most challenging aspect of this discourse is the cosmopolitan direction of its narrative. It is challenging because being cosmopolitan is essentially aligned to the principle of humanity or common humanity or world citizenship. The values of world citizenship, cosmopolitan humanity, common humanity, etc. are not necessarily taught. They are intelligibly discerned for African Igbo people. These mean that cosmopolitanism and our sensibility to common humanity are natural rights. They are rights that we have because we are human beings or persons within nature. They are not positive rights (made and protected by societies and conventions). For Africans, especially African Igbo people, natural rights are ontological rights. They are ontological to the people because of the source of such natural rights, and the values of open-mindedness and impartiality, especially from that *ONE* Supreme Creative Source (*Chukwu okike* or *Chi okike*). These positive values open-mindedness and impartiality are not taught; they are rather naturally discerned and adopted for their usefulness in order to build our human community of rights or human solidarity. African Igbo people emphasize this point in expressions like: *Ala wu otu* (The world, nature or earth is one. ONE World from ONE Supreme Creative Source), *Nkechinyere or Chinyere* (What God has given to humanity), *Egim nke-onye or Nkemdirim* (Everyone has his or her human uniqueness or individuality), *Nkemakolam* (May I not miss what is my right or may mine be there for me), *Ahamefula* (May my name never be lost. My name is indicative of my personal rights), *Onye na chi ya* (human uniqueness or fate), etc. Our uniqueness (as our right to self) speaks for itself.

Our uniqueness speaks the good about us. It is commonly said: "The good speaks for itself." African Igbo people will express this as *Ahia oma na-ere onwe ya* or *Mma ugo no ugo n' ahu* or *Mmiri maru ugo na asa ugo aru* (the context determines the suitability of this proverb). *Mmiri maru ugo na asa ugo aru* --Igbo proverb implies that the beauty of the Eagle/bird (Ugo) is enhanced by the rain. The beauty of the eagle/bird is inside the bird or it is an inherent part of the bird. The beauty of the eagle is the "right" of the eagle to be beautiful. It is the "essence" of the eagle. Expressions like *Agwa bu mma* (Character is beauty or good character beautifies one) could also be contextually suitable or appropriate. Another English language expression is: "Charity begins at home" –that could be translated as— *Ana amarama site na-ulo maram fuo na-ama*. African cosmopolitanism of brotherhood and sisterhood is humanist and humanitarian. It must to be humanist before it could become humanitarian. This means that it is not merely humanitarian (not merely outward-looking). The resounding point of this narrative is that African cosmopolitanism of brotherhood and sisterhood is not in exclusion of other people (unless the people are not genuine and not welcomed members of the community). However, one could argue that in some African societies or communities' people's rights were sometimes neglected or violated. This concern about possible abuses against human rights and dignity could be related to *Nwa-diala* or *Diala* (an Igbo word for an indigene, a full-fledged community member) and *Nwa-osu* or *Nwosu* (an ex-communicated person or one dedicated to an isolated to a god or goddess, an ex-indigene). For clarity sake, the challenges caused by *Nwa-diala* and *Nwa-osu* distinctions should be considered and addressed as part of African socio-ethical crises. African Igbo ethics explains what her ethical principles or moral standards are, who did what in the past, and who was banished or should be punished by the community. With regard to these ethical crises, abuses and lack of clarity, I explained that: "one understands that that there is an obvious obstacle to individual person's freedom and well-being but the desire to question the values of the community is part of the ongoing discourses between individual person's and their communities for a better society....This is why critical or reflective thinking should be a part of every human organization, even when it is denied or the opportunity is frustrated. The demand for well-being should be at the core of political agitation (leading to consideration of political personhood in a community)." (Anozie, (2017), p. 85)

Certainly there are narratives suggesting the abuse of political rights, freedom, and unfairness to some of the persons who were banished in the communities. Within African Igbo socio-ethical context, everyone is welcome. Everyone is part of the *Umunna* unless one has committed a heinous crime (*Imeru ala*—violated the peace of the community or land). Everyone is welcomed until they violate the peace of the land. If there is no violation committed, the person could stay as long as the purpose of their visit is honorable or noble. We feel at home everywhere. African Igbo express this thus: *Obia ra ngam abiagbulam* (Let my guest not kill me). Generally, the guest is always a part and parcel of the community. The guest enjoys the right to universal hospitality (*Onye obia m* or *Onye obia anyi*---Our guest). This is another socio-political right. It is a right to hospitality (a duty not to be hostile), and a right to human solidarity or human friendship. We have a right to peace and peace on the land. Land goes with peacefulness. Land brings peace. People are connected with the land in a very intricate way. Possessing land is to have a space of genuine existence. "Possessing" (not dominating) the land is part of being connected to the earth and to be indigenous (autochthonous). Immanuel Kant expressed a similar understanding in his *Perpetual Peace: A Philosophical Sketch* (1795). He argued that everyone has a place on earth. The earth is place of shared humanity. It is a shared-space. It is a communal space. For this communal space, everyone has a basic right of resort. The guest enjoys our fraternal solidarity. No one is always a stranger. No one is anywhere a perpetual stranger. To be a "stranger" is not a permanent status of a person. The shared-humanity of everyone, including the guests is communicated through the ethical framework of *Onyegbula* (Do not kill) and *Onyeghala* (*Onyeghala ibe*) (Do not abandon the other). One has a right to life or a duty to protect the life of another person. Everyone has a right not to be hindered or left behind. Again, this emphasizes our common humanity. We are better together. The other person is an essential part of who you are or the other person is a core of your beingness/being human.

We are ontologically co-dependent beings. Our rights to life and right to affiliation to life and sustained existence are expressed through Igbo names like *Ndubusi* or *Nduwuisi* (Life is ultimate. Life is primary. Life has primacy), *Ugo-ndu* (The Excellence of life or Pride of life or the Glory of life), *Uju-ndu* or *Obia-na-uju* (Coming with the fullness of life or the bountiful life). We have a duty to protect the other. For Ulrich Beck, traditional nation-state politics (in this case ancient Greek city-states or a closed society) is opposed to the expectations of cosmopolitanism. Nation-states are particular. Cosmopolitanism is global or universal. (Beck, (2006), p. 45) We also have a duty to promote and guarantee the bountiful life---living truly well as a fundamental right of a person in African ethics of rights' discourse.

Meanwhile, my main task here is to justify and sustain the narrative and scholarship on African ethics of rights' discourse, African cosmopolitanism of brotherhood and sisterhood and the ethics of patriotism. I am primarily interested in the 'ought', not in the 'is', questions: What were the ethical ideals and values that Africans set out to accomplish? What are the values that we live by? These are the central concerns of this paper. Let me take a look at the implications of not working on the beautiful (natural) dispositions we have. Could we lose our right to moral agency (and so lose our purposeful existence)?

In my earlier cited work: "Jacques Maritain's Interpersonal Relations and African Philosophy of Personhood/Community" in *Maritain Studies* (Volume XXXIII), I noted that "Gyekye's essay on 'African Ethics' and its relation to the ideas of 'individual' and 'person' are laudable." (Anozie, (2017), p. 93) I also addressed the purposive development of a moral person, the notions of human being and individual. There is a clear distinction between the moral or ethical person and the non-ethical individual. I argued that even though an individual could persists in a series of unethical behaviors and may not respect the dignity or beauty of the other person, "[H]owever, this individual does not lose his/her essential personhood based on the mere bad or ill wishes… rather one becomes an individual by continually participating in inhuman actions....there is a distinction between a moral person (truly a person)... and an individual (evil and unethical subject)." (Anozie, (2017), p. 93) African Igbo people will consider the person as morally bankrupt or losing his/her purposiveness (to lose the right to his/her purpose or one's natural right to human essence)—to imply any of these: *Onye agwa rere ure* or *Onyeagwa ajo* or *Onye ndu ojo* or *Onye na-enweghi uju nke ndu*. I argued that the ethical person (whose human rights and dignity are intact) as the beauty of life "is extended as the beauty of nature, which suggests the purposiveness of nature. The beauty of nature--the beauty in nature--is because nature is a continuum, continuity, being-in-existence. Being-in-existence is to be essentially purposive/ purposeful. Without purpose, there is no existence." (Anozie, (2017), p. 79) Here lies the essence of African cosmopolitanism of brotherhood and sisterhood: "I am because we are, and because we are, therefore I am" (*Umunna* or *Ikwu-na-ibe* or *Onye aghala nwanne ya* or *Igwebuike*—I-We community for African Igbo people).

In addressing one of the central concerns of this paper, my goal is to argue that African cosmopolitanism of brotherhood or sisterhood is better embraced by African mind through its regular consideration and rigor of intellectual exercise on what it truly is. Africans have to progress from "who" they are and "what" they do to "what could" be done to become better. One cannot truly become better without knowing "Who" and "What" and "How" his/her original views/thoughts of the world should be understood or communicated in the world.

In African thought, especially Igbo socio-political thought/culture, every member of the community has a right to participate in all that are good for the community. What is good for the community includes the moral values (rights), socio-cultural values (rights), economic values (rights) and systems, religious values (rights) of the community (including the accepted diversities—*Onye na chi ya* or a person's uniqueness). Meanwhile, the central point of African cosmopolitanism is the natural relation of all human beings. This means *Nwanne di na mba*---brotherhood and sisterhood are found in other lands/cultures/communities. *Igwebuike*—meaning—"we are better together," or "being a team is better for us", or "we are greater by being one people." Some scholars have attributed this similar approach to cosmopolitanism in Socrates (a Greek scholar) who did not travel outside his community most of his life but connected to all human beings—familiar and unfamiliar, citizens and foreigners—as part of his Athenian freedom of expression and freedom to live well (being human well). (Gorgias 461e1–3; cf. Apology 37c5–e2 and Meno 80b4–7)

Let me now take a look at the theme "African cosmopolitanism and ethics of rights' discourse," as an essential part of the ethics of patriotism.

African Cosmopolitanism and Ethics of Rights' Discourse

African cosmopolitanism is African ethics. African ethics is an ethics of discourse. In this essay, it is the ethics of rights' discourse. It is an ethics that emerges through communitarian public discourse or public deliberations, especially since we are not dealing with a revealed form of ethics or morality. The ethics of discourse is discernably humanist and humanitarian (Not revelatory, idealistic and abstract). It is the ethics of our common humanity that explores the riches of shared-values, share-existence, shared-beingness, shared-experience, shared-lifeworld, etc. This is the shared-lifeworld of *Umunna*. Shared-values determine ethics of a community. African ethical principles or reasoning justify the form of ethics and the shared-values for human wellbeing in the community. Some of these ethical principles are based on intrinsic reasoning and consequentialist/utilitarian reasoning or justifications. Of course, there could be various reasons to see failures of some individual persons in recognizing these common humanity or human solidarity qualities and shared-values in words and actions. One thing so clear about the integrity of African (Igbo) ethics is that the foundations are similar (but not exactly the same) to Deontological ethics or ethics of duty, Consequentialist ethics, and Aristotelian Virtue ethics or ethics of character on rights and justice. Each of these ethical theories may be a particular articulation of universal concepts. In Kwasi Wiredu's view, African scholars should overcome conceptual colonization, especially by challenging Western conceptual framework by using indigenous African critical conceptual schemes. (Wiredu, (1996), p. 136)

Ethics as character-based is an important point in African philosophy and African cosmopolitanism. Ethics does not imply perfection in actions. It is about practicing, nudging, reviewing, and re-engineering. What we do is acquired through time, through practising, and through observing respected people in the community. Most of these respected people in the community are members of social groups, cultural groups, age-grade groups that positively influence the lives of the young. For instance, African Igbo people would say: *Onye nze, Ndi ozo,* or *Ndi nze-na-ozo*—meaning—"A titled person/people with sound character, a person/people of truth and honesty or integrity." These are the people to be emulated in the community. Their job is to speak out against evil and promote human rights and justice for all. Traditional rulers are custodians of culture, tradition and rights. Parents are custodians of rights in the families. Age grades are custodians of rights and promoters of justice. Some of these rights, among others mentioned above, are: right to life, right to association, right to political participation in community service, right to freedom thought, right to innocence (until proven guilty), right to land from ancestral holdings as an adult from a community/clan, etc. These rights are similar to Akan people of Ghana in Kwasi Wiredu's reflections. (Mutua, (2002), p. 66; pp. 188-189)

In summary, African ethics of rights' discourse captures the core values of African theory of rights and justice, African cosmopolitanism of brotherhood and sisterhood, and the ethics of patriotism (all under the hermeneutics of African political belongingness). It is helpful for imparting ethical ideas of Africans to young generations of Africans, especially in the context of our common humanity or global citizenship. African Igbo worldviews provides a specific cultural context to explain African ethics of rights' narratives. African Igbo lifeworld on rights and justice is determinative of our African cosmopolitanism and the ethics of patriotism. It is within these diverse lifeworld of socio-cultural-economic-political-religious factors that life is truly meaningful for a patriotic African and Igbo person. "This is why an integral global ethics is a necessity in our co-mutually-existent world." (Anozie, (2017), p. 95) It is also why African Igbo discourse ethics (as part of African hermeneutical philosophy of cosmopolitanism and African political philosophy of patriotism) is worth advancing.

Conclusion

African ethics of rights' discourse: theory and practice is an important aspect of understanding the place of human person and rights in African worldview, especially with reference to African Igbo world. African Igbo hermeneutical ethics (as part of African hermeneutical philosophy of cosmopolitanism and African political philosophy of patriotism) is rich and enrichening. For now, Western notion of rights, justice, equality, equity, dignity, cosmopolitanism, etc. does not address all aspects of these global values. There are cultural categories and frameworks suitable for Western practice of democracies on human rights. In other to suggest a one-sided articulation of cosmopolitanism, some European/Western scholars have tried to distort other cultures' views of our common human life, human rights and our common world citizenship. This essay recommends the revival and rehabilitation of African ethics of rights' discourse as part of encouraging a philosophy of diversity, equity and inclusivity or an inter-cultural discourse philosophy on rights and justice.

Bibliography

Anozie, Stanley Uche. (2017) "Jacques Maritain's International Relations and African Philosophy of Personhood/Community," *Maritain Studies*, edited by Nikolaj Zunic (Vol. XXXIII).

----------(2019) "Can Igbo Mysticism Fight Against Boko Haram," *Responses of Mysticism to Religious Terrorism*. Belgium: Gompel&Svacina.

---------(2020) *Hans-Georg Gadamer and African Hermeneutic Philosophy*. Chisinau: Generis Publishing.

Beck, Ulrich. (2006) *The Cosmopolitan Vision*. Cambridge: Polity Press.

Bujo, Benezet. (1998) *The Ethical Dimension of Community: The African Model and the Dialogue between North and South*. Nairobi: Paulines Africa.

French, Howard W. (2021) *Born in Blackness*. USA: Liveright Publishing Corporation.

Mbiti, John S. (1969) *African Religions and Philosophy*. London.

Mutua, Makau. (2002) *Human Rights: a Political and Cultural Critique*. University of Pennsylvania Press.

Wiredu, Kwasi. (1996) *Cultural Universals and Particulars: an African perspective*. Bloomington: Indiana University Press.

Chapter 8
African Perspectives on Global Development

Stanley Uche Anozie

(The College of the Humanities (Religion), Carleton University, Ottawa, Ontario, 2017)

Introduction

The important issues for consideration here are: a) what is really Global Development? b) how does Africa look at Global Development as an achievable ideal-that is inclusive of Africa? How does one relate the significant pointers in history that show that Global Development might be an illusion for Africa (considering the so-called Arab Spring, the assassination of Gadaffi, the continued destabilization of Libya, mono-linguisticality of Anglo-Saxon/Western languages, colonization by use of the language of development?) Development, as an integrative project—is a duty for all, development means peace, world without peace is not a developed world.

In this work, I am interested in articulating how Africa looks at global development, and how African people could participate in determining the direction of this global development. The questions that need answers are: Is Africa a 'recipient continent' that depends on the generosity of rich Western nations in order for her to continue to exist? Could it be that a systemic structure has been put in place to guarantee or ensure that Africa has no role in understanding, in enriching dialogues, or in contributing to whatever it is that could be considered as an African view on Global Development?

For my discourse on Global Development, I will focus on how the West or Western societies/economies define "Global Development?" Do we really have 'global development'? If there is global development, the excessive socio-political conflicts of our time beg the question about 'global peace.' Global Development should be another concept for Global Peace. Global development proceeds out of global peace. Global peace rewards global development efforts.

Global Development is not possible without Global Peace. Peace is mutually inclusive with Development. To truly have peace is to have development, and vice versa. As is now common knowledge, another name for peace is development. In that sense, do we really have peace? A related and further reading on this point could be found in my *Ethics of Duty Reassessed: Alan Gewirth's Community of Rights Critical Perspective*.

There has to be a moral debate to identify the relations between poverty and underdevelopment. While poverty and underdevelopment are indications of dissatisfactions or lack of peace, development is the new term for peace and requires the interplay of ethical theory and practice. For development to be humane and integral there should be an ethical aspect that requires comprehensive and relevant actions. These actions, among others, involve a duty to help, and not only the responsibility (duty) to justice as a primary ethical duty, especially for those who are incapable of accomplishing/maintaining their well-beings for themselves. These actions are highly recommended in a globalized society.

The seeming perpetual situation of poverty, suppression and dependency, have given rise to the question of intellectual and psychological bases for development. Is the issue of lack of development not truly a question of intellectual and psychological bases for development? One could translate this intellectual basis for development as a philosophical basis while the psychological is the emotional side effects of history of colonization and slavery (mental colonization to decolonizing the mind) to African/Global development.

Intellectual and Psychological Bases for Development

For me, without a philosophical base, then Africans will bear the brunt of negative development. Thought gives birth to technology and policies of development. John Henrik Clarke has argued that colonization and cultural imperialism contributed to Africans losing their frame of mind as a psychological basis for "poor development" or even African people's poor interest in self-development and their value of their self-worth.

In *African Hermeneutics of Illuminating Consciousness*, I stated that "Frantz Fanon's work is also a good area to find the implications or effects of this psychological damage or imperialist distortion. Fanon reflects on the 'Black Skin, White Masks' phenomenon-the phenomenon of lack of the authentic self.

At the centre of the mind-set of some African intelligentsia is the effort to replicate Western Thinking/Philosophy according to the approval of the Masters—the Colonial Masters! But truly, there is nothing to justify that our world philosophies must be [imperially] 'mono-cultural' or 'mono-linguistic.'" (Anozie, African Hermeneutics of Illuminating Consciousness (2017)). Meanwhile, the linguistic categories of understanding the world are present in every culture and may be considered as coded messages for the people. (Anozie, S. U. (2017). "African Esotericism with a Concentration on the Igbos," p. 168). The visions of reality should be variedly considered because of our diverse contexts of experience or conditions of being or lifeworld.

My position is that there is no true development if there is 'no genuineness of the person.' The main goal of development begins as the 'development of the person' in terms of the person as the central target of well-being. When development, in other words, well-being of the person is not directed essentially to actualized personhood, then development becomes an assumption, a distraction, a chimera, a distortion, etc.

The distortions in socio-anthropological narratives were promoted by some Western scholars. There was or is the great divide between the so-called 'barbarity of Africa' and the 'nobility of Europe.' In *African Hermeneutics of Illuminating Consciousness*, I affirmed that, some Western social anthropologists promoted and advanced, and solidified this dichotomy of primitivity and reality. Africa is synonymous to barbarity and primitivity while Europe/North America is known for civility/nobility/reality. Some social anthropologists through time became "the 'handmaid' of colonialism, domination, and civilization/cultural decimation of the African Mind. This made it possible for the West to overlook 'genuine' African identity and reality and what African is capable of offering (a preconceived model of society) (Imbo, (2002), p. 3). This is in line with "imperialist historiography" programmed to see and present Africa in an unfortunate light (Imbo, (2002), p. 3). The mind-set was determined to do a bad job of "pathological dichotomous framework" (Imbo, (2002), p. 3)." (Anozie (2017)).

It is in this light that I will make references to recent MIGRANT CRISIS in Libya/Lampedusa –a new African graveyard Europe. Young Africans are queuing into the narrative that the best is found in Europe (in the colonial psychological and ideological narrative on the nobility of the global North and the barbarity of the global South). Some of these young Africans are brain-washed into believing that they are 'better dead trying to get to Europe rather than strive in Africa'. The population of young Africans illegally traveling to Europe through Libya to Lampedusa, Italy is alarming. Most of them end up on the waters of Mediterranean. The situation brings to mind the narratives of African slavery, in which some sick and recalcitrant slaves were thrown overboard to die. According to Ann Marie Bahr, about 15 million people were forced out of Africa. Chinweizu Ibekwe and others have suggested over 40-100 million African slaves. I am of the view that the number of young African slaves taken from African to the New World were more than 40 million, especially in term of the duration of approved slavery in African by Europeans (in collaboration with agencies of Western Christianity). The population and age-class of these young African taken into slavery were among the best and brightest of Africa. It is in a similar vein that the current Libya slavery crisis involving youthful Africans is a repeat of the sad narrative of 'brain drain' of some good and dynamic and productive age groups for African Development or African Development workforce in a time of high expectations on technological development/globalization.

Muammar Gadaffi, International Organizations and African Development

In this age of technological development and globalization, if globalization is effective for the well-being all humanity, then its application will need not have any geographical bounds of operation. African youth could access these resources from any time and any place of the world without having to travel desperately to Europe. One may argue that the migration crisis was worsened by the demise of the strong man of Libya-Colonel Muammar Gadaffi. The assassination of Gadaffi as well as the destabilization of Libya contributed to the collapse of the wall of security in Libya and the collapse of the borders of some African countries close to the north of the continent (many West Africans flood to Libya in hope of migrating to Europe). President Muhammadu Buhari and Lawyer Femi Falana, a Senior Advocate of Nigeria, have attributed the recent Herdsmen crisis in Nigeria as a result of the effects of the war in Libya. Some of the weapons used to prosecute the war in Libya are been purchased by Boko Haram and armed herdsmen to cause maximum havoc in Nigeria. A destabilized Nigeria has many implications for human development and migration in African.

At this time in history, the global situation points to an unequal understanding and application of 'Global Development'. The nature of recent insurgencies and wars in our world are indicators of the absence of global development (as another name for peace) in a universal sense. The war in Iraq alluded to this fact. The war in Syria is also an indication of the complex factors and interests in relation to the pursuit of global development even a divisive world order of: the developed and the underdeveloped; the global north and the global south, etc. The basis of Global Development is a theme that academics and global leaders must be engaging themselves in for enlightening dialogues on global societal existence or human well-being. One could relate the situation to NAFTA/politico-economic crisis in North America.

In my view, within the context of the politics of NAFTA, Donald Trump - former US President- is advocating for fair trading/business relationship between US and her neighbours. These are, in light of Trump's perspective, strong and deliberate reasons for a renegotiation of the most global deals that negatively impact on the African people. In current socio-political dispensations, most of global deals were anchored on aids to Africa rather than on collaborative initiatives and agenda for reciprocity-mutuality well-being of persons from the different continents. One can relate the situation to the conditions of grant of loans to 'Developing Countries.' The conditions of IMF Loan and other grants are based on "control" of the structure of governance of most African countries. According to former South African President Jacob Zuma, to be African and to be black is a double jeopardy. There is a combination of race and inequality in world political or political economy agenda.

Recently, the UN General Assembly rebuked US President Trump because of his stand on recognizing Jerusalem as the capital of Israel by moving US Embassy from Tel Aviv to Jerusalem. The UN General Assembly voted 128-9 (35 abstention) in favour of rejecting as invalid Trump-US recognition of Jerusalem as the capital of Israel. The relevant point in this work is that Trump through his UN Ambassador Nikki Haley asserted American Power Politics of dominance and domination by confirming that US will withdraw its support of the UN and that US position in the matter at stake is "final" (despite the stand of other countries of the world). The Peterborough Examiner of Friday December 22, 2017 reported, "Nikky Haley, the American ambassador to the UN, said…the U.S. decision to move its embassy is final. She raised the prospect of the U.S. not continuing its financial support of the UN, noting that her country is by far the largest contributor to the UN and its agencies, helping to feed, clothe and educate people, sustain fragile peace, and hold outlaw regimes accountable. 'We also have a legitimate expectation that our goodwill is recognized and respected,' Haley said." ('Canada abstains from UN vote' in *The Peterborough Examiner*, Friday, December 22, 2017). This reflects the tragedy of globalization of control by America as the power of the West (although in this case not every Western country supported US moves.) But the significant defiance of the US to punish countries that did not support her recognition of Jerusalem as the capital of Israel sufficiently affirm the dominant control that considers less good the position of the other, especially in threatening to withdraw support to an international organization whose role is mainly to address global peace or development. One could liken the situation with former Israeli's Prime Minister- Benjamin Netanyahu- who asked his Israeli UN diplomat to stay out of UNESCO (we can extend this discussion to UN commission on human rights and their role in developing diverse international human rights/values).

What are the roles of UNESCO in International Development, especially African Development? We could relate this to other international organizations and the quality of global contributions to human development. When one relates the situation of the US (Trump) and Israel (Netanyahu) to global development and peace, then the situation indicates the real cog in the wheel of progress. It is at this level that one has to review the acceptance of international organization in global development if her goals could be challenged or threatened by 'so-called' global powers. For a moment, let us take a look at the UNESCO and it roles in relation to Language and Education (on the background of threats of global threats to its roles). For any country or body to control the goals/initiatives of an organization in support of culture, diverse language, education, etc. is worrisome for equity in global development ideas.

We could also argue from UNESCO to Language and Education: Effective pedagogy leading to transformational development is only possible through an integrative learning process. This process ought to recognize the role of cultures (the diverse cultures) of other people and the ability to use their own language to communicate the complex nature of science and technology. No matter how intelligent an African person is in his/her field, without a home grown language of his/her understanding and doing arts and sciences, his/her education will not be 'truly' transformational. I perceive this in the number of African intelligentsia who have studied in Europe and America but are unable to truly capture the essence of education to benefit themselves and their own people. In fact, to control language is to control the 'content' of thinking (some scholars argue that we think with others, we do not think alone, thinking is thinking with-the-other. I associate this point with Martin Heidegger's view of

Dasein, *Mitsein*, or Being-with-the-other), the direction of global development and what it really means. To control language is to determine the section of society that will be the final beneficiary of the dividends of such pedagogical process, articulated through a specific language. I will like to take a good look at my most intriguing scholars on language: Hans-Georg Gadamer and Ngugi wa Thiong'o's reflections in this regard.

Gadamer's Theory of Language: the Politics of Language and the Liberation of the Mind

Language itself has a universal character to communicate the reality of its world. Every language epitomised or captures this capacity to universality. Every language attempts in its own unique way to encapsulate the abstract universal idea that it considers at a time. From Gadamer's reflections on the theory of language we can advance further into Thiong'o's perspective/inter enlightening perspective on the relevant capacity of an African language.

For Gadamer, language was always central. Language is at "the center of philosophical concern. Language is the fundamental mode of operation of our being-in-the-world and the all-embracing form of the constitution of the world." (Gadamer, *Philosophical Hermeneutics*, (1976), pp. 3-4). Language as an essential structural element of understanding is present in all acts of understanding. Understanding is the central issue in hermeneutics that is carried out through the medium of language. The problem of language is central to understanding the problem of hermeneutics and as a consequence at the center of philosophy and global development. Gadamer adds that language is central because it has an interpretative use in terms of the inner structural element of understanding.

Understanding is linguistic and is present in every human endeavor. We exist within a linguistic world and language retains its purity in the experience of the world without enclosing us within relativity. Gadamer puts it thus:

> Understanding is language-bound... It is indeed true that we live within a language... While we live wholly within a language, the fact that we do so does not constitute linguistic relativism because there is absolutely no captivity within a language. (Gadamer, *Philosophical Hermeneutics*, (1976), pp. 15-16).

In hermeneutics language plays a fundamental role. Language goes beyond the statements we utter through it, but this does not affect the fundamental importance of language. It is often the case that language is at times unable to exactly communicate what our thoughts are. Gadamer explains, "the task of expressing in words what they say to us seems like an infinite and hopeless undertaking....But this does not alter the fundamental priority of language" (Gadamer, *Truth and Method*, (2004), p. 402; Gadamer, (1975), p. 362.) Language has intellectual quality and every language has the capacity to express reality. For him each language does it by itself in its own way. Language connects us to the world and is part of our being in the world. In hermeneutics, we develop the linguistic world since we all are "always already at home in language." (Gadamer, *Philosophical Hermeneutics*, (1976), p. 63). Through language we express, acquire universal concepts and we articulate our philosophical views about the world and reality. Language and philosophy go to together.

Gadamer in his own way criticizes the neglect of language. For him, our being-in-the-world is primordially linguistic and we live in a linguistic community. In language the reality that is beyond every individual consciousness becomes visible and it plays a role that moves beyond a phenomenological experience to a hermeneutical consciousness of the worldviews of cultures. Through language we transmit meaning and understanding. It is in this same way that the art of understanding unfolds through language following the interaction between the past and the present experiences.

For us to understand the past and the present experiences in hermeneutics there ought to be a constitutive relation between language and reality (the world in light of development). This constitutive relation through language is a basic condition of understanding. The possession of language "is the ontological condition for our understanding of the texts that address us." (Gadamer, *Philosophical Hermeneutics*, (1976), p. xxix.) Understanding presupposes our immersion in tradition of "total language dependence." (Gadamer, *Philosophical Hermeneutics*, (1976), p. xxix.) Language mediates between us and reality. As a medium of understanding language is not reduced to the status of mere tool of understanding. It is always constitutive of the world we understand. Gadamer observes:

> it must be emphasized that language has its true being only in dialogue, in coming to an understanding. This is not to be understood as if that were

the purpose of language. Coming to an understanding is not a mere action, a purposeful activity, a setting-up of signs through which I transmit my will to others. Coming to an understanding as such, rather, does not need any tools…It is a life process in which a community of life is lived out (Gadamer, *Truth and Method*, (2004), p. 443; Gadamer, *Truth and Method*, (1975), p. 404.)

Since language is constitutive, then it is not merely instrumental to understanding. It is always present in the act of understanding and does not at any point become irrelevant to the quest for meaning. That means that in the knowledge of the world or of ourselves we are always involved in the use of our own language (Maurice Merleau-Ponty, *Signs* (Evanston, Illinois: Northwestern University Press, 1964), p. 59; Gadamer, *Philosophical Hermeneutics*, p. xxix.) As linguistic beings we are spoken to through our languages.

It is through language that human being engages with the world and whoever has language "has a world." (Gadamer, *Truth and Method*, p. 440.) Although language is the universal medium of understanding through which we perceive the world, it does not focus on itself. This is the transparent nature of language since it makes it possible for the subject matter to be understood among people. Language reveals reality, and reality in turn does influence the use of language. Every language reveals reality from a horizon and reality takes place within language. It is in this way that language presses beyond established conventions or the societal assumptions about language. Gadamer adds, "[L]anguage is the medium in which substantive understanding and agreement takes place between two people." (Gadamer, *Truth and Method*, p. 386; Gadamer, *Truth and Method* (1975), pp. 345-346.) The knowledge of language involves being open to an active participation in a transformation dialogue with others which consequently broadens one's initial horizon. In speaking we dialogue through language and we share our thoughts with some other person. This is the dialogic and disclosive nature of language which does not emphasize the individual person, but presents and reveals the object of communication "before the eyes of the other person to whom I speak." (Gadamer, *Philosophical Hermeneutics*, (1976), p. 65.)

As Gadamer often repeated the being that is understood is language. There is no other autonomous being outside language and this being is said through language itself. Language is always present in the disclosure of being, yet there is the "forgetfulness of language that its real being consists in what is said in it." (Gadamer, *Philosophical Hermeneutics*, p. xxx). It discloses the real being of existence through what is said to us and it also reflects the self-transcending nature of language. Every language is a medium of understanding. Every language reveals of being and all attempt at language is for the disclosure of truth, the world and to express man himself. Historical situations express the world in language. Gadamer explains that language describes "a realm as indispensable to human life as the air we breathe. As Aristotle said, man is truly the being who has language. For we should let everything human be spoken to us." (Gadamer, *Philosophical Hermeneutics*,(1976), p. 68).

Language is the basis for the different cultural worlds to understand each other. Within language we merge into a common understanding of the world. There is no place for a mutual exclusive existence within language. This fusion is the ground for the encountering of the other world that stands over against us. As Gadamer notes, "the other world that we encounter is not only foreign but is also related to us. It has not only its own truth in itself, but also its own truth for us." (Gadamer, *Truth and Method*, (2004), p. 439. Gadamer, (1975), pp. 399-400.) This view is important in understanding other linguistic worlds. Every language is a view of the world (Gadamer, *Truth and Method*, (2004), p. 439. Gadamer, *Truth and Method*, (1975), pp. 399-400.) The use of language is not a privilege for human beings and so we possess language because we have a world of existence that is a linguistic world. This world of existence is a world of development and well-being. The existence of a world is unique to human beings. Gadamer elaborates:

> Language is not just one of man's possessions in the world; rather, on it depends the fact that man has a world at all. The world as a world exists for man as for no other creature that is in the world. But this world is verbal in nature… languages are worldviews… language maintains a kind of independent life vis-à-vis the individual member of a linguistic community; and as he grows into it, it introduces him to a particular orientation and relationship to the world as well. But the ground of this statement is more important, namely that language has no independent life apart from the world that comes to language within it. (Gadamer, (2002), p. 440. Gadamer, *Truth and Method*, (1975), pp. 401-402.)

He notes also that our knowledge of the world and all knowledge of us are always intrinsically influenced by the language we speak. We cannot understand and give meaning to relations in the world without language. Gadamer's hermeneutics emphasizes the all-encompassing nature and the universality of language. It is universal since it involves every person and every circumstance of humanity. As universal, language is constitutive of every culture and each culture expresses itself through language. It is also infinitely used through ongoing dialogue or conversation such that even a break in conversation through language remains an ongoing process of dialogue.

Every society has its own language that presents or addresses it (the society, or the world of that society). In Gadamer's hermeneutics, language helps express the fact that we have a world. He makes reference to the use of an African language. An African language has its originality and addresses its world, like any living language it equally has a conceptual universality and pragmatic meaning. This pragmatic meaning is important for universality of hermeneutics. The use of a concept in different particular contexts presents different connotations in interpretation. Gadamer observes:

> There is an African language that has two hundred different words for camel, according to the camel's particular circumstances and relationships to the desert-dwellers. The specific meaning that "camel" has in all these different denominations makes it seem an entirely different creature. In such cases we can say that there is an extreme tension between the genus and the linguistic designation. But we can also say that the tendency towards conceptual universality and that towards pragmatic meaning are never completely harmonized in any living language. (Gadamer, *Truth and Method*, (2004), p. 434; Gadamer, (1975), pp. 394-395.)

Following the above, the language of each people communicates their worldviews and each person lives in language. The language we speak as part of the world is capable of describing our world. Using a foreign language may not provide one with the appropriateness that a homeland language could provide. Gadamer's comment about the multiple words one African language uses to describe 'camel' because of the slightest change of circumstances in relation to part of the camel applies to this discourse on translation (into another language). In this way he explains the capability of any language to describe its reality in the most appropriate way more than that another language could translate it in original sense. Gadamer opines:

> When a person lives in a language, he is filled with the sense of the unsurpassable appropriateness of the words he uses for the subject matter he is talking about. It seems impossible that other words in other languages could name the things equally well. The suitable word always seems to be one's own and unique, just as the thing referred to is always unique. The agony of translation consists ultimately in the fact that the

original words seems to be inseparable from the things they refer to, so that in order to make a text intelligible one often has to give an interpretative paraphrase of it rather than translate it." (Gadamer, *Truth and Method*, (2004), p. 403.)

The discussion so far relates the problem of language and hermeneutics. All forms of interpretation are truly linguistic and reality is understood linguistically. It is not contrary to understanding to talk of language when discussing hermeneutics. We cannot overlook the role of language when attempting to understand hermeneutics. As Gadamer affirms that in all forms of interpretation whatever that is intelligible is communicable through language. Language is constitutive of our experiences and our understanding of our experience. However, whatever that may not be linguistic still has the capacity to be interpreted linguistically. Our tradition, in a general sense, may not be linguistic but everything is explainable or could be explained through language. If hermeneutics is the discourse of understanding, then language makes understanding possible. Hermeneutics as understanding does not mean that language is a meaningful windowless isolation such that a translation from one language to another is impossible. The point is the following:

> Understanding is essentially linguistic, but in such fashion that it transcends the limits of any particular language, thus mediating between the familiar and the alien. The particular language with which we live is not closed off monadically against what is foreign to it. Instead it is porous and open to expansion and absorption to ever new mediated content (Gadamer, *Philosophical Hermeneutics*, (1976), p. 99.)

The hermeneutical process of questions and answers is an essential part of interpretation. We have to inquire for more information from utterances, explanation etc in order to understand an author or a text. Gadamer recognizes that in narratives and dialogue with an interpreter the author or speaker involves the fusion of perspectives. Even any momentary stop of a conversation does not mean that dialogue is over.

Gadamer considers the role of hermeneutics in literary texts and the communication of truth to be classified within the human sciences rather than the natural sciences. The truth of hermeneutics is not like the fixed knowledge common in the natural sciences. The interpretation of texts offers one the opportunity of accessing different standpoints in which new perspectives –the perspective of African development-are heard. He observes the unique nature of human sciences as distinct from natural sciences. As part of the human sciences, modern historical research is about the transmission of meaning /tradition. The object of historical research is man in his changing circumstances or conditions, not determined purely by the law of science and scientific verifications. Human sciences are guided by what is given and what the interests in tradition by the generations of interpreters are. Every new voice has something new to tell us and every new experience of history is a new voice that ought to be listened to.

With the above discourse, I articulated the universality of language and hermeneutics and how we understand when we encounter other people, other language, or other text in our discussions on global development.

Thiong'o and Language

Gadamer's theory of language, discussed above, and well repeated in this book, will be used to justify my view on using African language(s) to communicate African perspective on Development. Language determines the strength of communication, and any form of development begins with communication or understanding the idea or the content of what development one is dealing with. Development or self-advancement cannot happen without it being linguistically possible or conceivable in a language most appropriate to the culture or world of existence of the recipient of well-being arising from development. It is in this sense that Thiong'o's theory of language and recommendations are most appropriate to African scholars and Africans. Thiong'o asserts that "Language as culture is the collective memory bank of a people's experience in history (of history or of existence)" (http://ngugiwathiongo.com/, Accessed on December 31, 2017).

Thiong'o's view clearly shows the central role of language in human experience of the world. It also puts in context the condition for the possibility of relating to human world (by way of science and technology as tools for discerning the purposefulness of the world) for advance human development, especially beyond the glaring limitations of African colonial experience and genuine self-independence. The prospect of self-independence in light of post-colonial world can only be credible with the emergence of individual Africans who express themselves in African language of theirs. African peoples, authors, writers, and scholars should rise above writing African literature in European language. Thiong'o considers this situation as saturated with an "Afro-European" bias on African consciousness and thinking. The consequences are that in losing one's language, one loses 'memory of who one is', 'the memory of his/her being', the memory of his/her language, etc. There is a lot of power politics about language as the content of memory. (For instance, the change of name of Community is a way of wiping out the authentic-ness of a people, of wiping out the day-to-day mode of living of a people as part of their experience of the world). Through the rejection of African language, for publication, and for education of African people, the Africans were dis-membered or disconnected from their culture or identity or being as well-being. (There ought to be a linguistic connection, language is the keeper of memory).

Through the agenda of global development by implication, the globalization of one particular language culture of Europe. It could be any particular language of Europe that undermines the potency of other languages. However, in Thiong'o view, it is a different thing for a Swedish person accepting a second language (English, in this case) in order to improve oneself and connect with other people. But the case of the African is totally difference. The new language (English or French or Portuguese, etc.) was introduced to dis-organise the African person or mind. In most colonized communities of Africa, a familiar indigenous language was denigrated and rejected in order for peoples in these communities to "acquire a new language completely." It is like acquiring a new soul, a new understanding rather than a cross-pollination of ideas for the sake of the emergence of a better and integral humanity or genuine well-being. Considering the historical background, and how globalization is currently fashioned, it is difficult to convince African aware of any colonial narrative of African experience of his/her world and relationship among the colonizers and the colonized, globalization is a hard pill to sell, especially because of the in-balance in interest, well-being, and power.

Globalization and Language

Thiong'o is of the view that no matter how globalization is marketed, it is a globalization of the 'inequality of power.' (http://ngugiwathiongo.com/home/) (Accessed on December 31, 2017). The current idea of globalization is only an agenda that is directed towards Western/European development, which is a continuity of the 15th-19th Century industrial exploration solely aimed at the good of Europe and the New World, and based on the 'blood of African bodies.' (Ibid.) The point that is central above is the 'trust' issues on how true the current global development agenda? How free of African 'blood' or 'pain' is this era of global development is? The past and current politics of globalization is dented by what Thiong'o calls the 'the politics of memory', 'the memory of language', and 'the memory of African being' that has been purposefully erased. This purposeful tragic 'past'-of dented memory- has or is unfortunately the 'beginning' of African memory, especially for the emerging new African people of the 21st century.

There can be no development, peace or empowerment without authentic express-ability of oneself in one's own language of thinking. Any globalization project-done in any chosen European language-is another form of neo-colonization, which is not a way of genuine development or peace.

Colonization, Mono-linguistic World or Globalization

Colonization or a mono-linguistic world or globalization is a linguistic violence. In any society the predominance of violence- including linguistic violence- negates the authentic possibility or conditions for true development or peace. There is physical, economic, political, psychological or emotional violence as other ways of control. The association of African language with pain, violence, dirt and barbarism means a denigration of the African being of existence. Thiong'o considered this mode of association as 'passing on' the psychology of failure and defeat among African on how they should see African language (relate to psychologists Pavlov and Skinner on rewarding and rebuking actions/acts). There are two attitudes: This attitude of a language as a language of failure verses the language of reward, of enlightenment/success. The attitude on the language of failure and the psychology of denigration of Africa language of concept development is automatically passed on to generations of Africans for over 400 years. The time is very significant for the emergence of distorted African consciousness among Africans. There is now a normalization of an abnormal. There is no being that develops itself by denigrating itself. No being authentically exists in normalized abnormality. There is no peace is a distorted being (un-peaceable being). One has to check on the linguistic balance of power, in terms of ownership and control. In this context of search for development is anti-thetical to peace or development. Equal give and take is a condition for peaceful existence and sustained existence anchored in creative imagination. Creative imagination is ontologically tied to language and the ability of peoples to linguistically define and develop themselves. Without creative imagination there cannot be any true development, even from the point of conceptualization or formation of ideas leading to development. If the language of conceptualization of the world is foreign, unfamiliar or unknown to the indigenous people (if the language is not autochthonous to the people), then that situation alone defines a fatalist purpose for self-hate/self-divorce, and a distortion that is anti-self-development. The fatalistic logic (Thiong'o's) of the usage of Africa language determines the distorted content of science and technology associated with African identity and utility (or usefulness). So far, in the history of thought, English or French or Portuguese (include any other known colonial European languages) has been seen as the measure of academic excellence and social/political development and well-controlled economy. Economic control or political control is not complete without the colonization of the mental universe of the African people. Language as culture is the tool for accessing and transforming nature for human well-being. One of the ways of addressing this role of language and its healthy interaction with other languages, without the in-balance of power, is through translations or hermeneutics or interpretation (my reading of Gadamer as well as Thiong'o).

In Thiong'o's analysis, translation is the language of all languages. It is the language that all languages try to express. (This is 'inner language' in Gadamer's view). No language is capable of being better than another in expressing the content of its worldview. Each language is a way of expressing the universality in reality-that is the inner language. Each language expresses this inner language in its own way. Mono-lingualism distorts the idea of globalization as development. Every language has something to give every other language. There is an eternal and continued conversation between languages. Such a conversation affirms the equality of interlocutors. Unfortunately, colonization via a global mono-language advances the crisis of mental conditioning of the African people, which can never lead to true development among Africans. What we have is a replication of Afro-European intellectuals (intellectual community) in the interest of the West or Europe/North American new world. In speaking another foreign language (other than their indigenous languages) and through colonialism, the situation makes it possible for Africans to intellectually negate themselves. According to Roger Ariew and Eric Watkins, "it follows that men who use language are able to abstract or generalize their ideas" (Ariew (2009), p. 441) for the capacity to language is the capacity to ideas. There is no genuine development or peace for one who negates oneself. To know all the languages of the world without knowing one's own is enslavement (https://www.youtube.com/watch?v=5AnwONzPEGA, Accessed on January 1, 2018).

Like Gadamer, Thiong'o's views ought to be hermeneutically and ontologically understood, especially as a new horizon for understanding the world--(as our common context of illumination and content of consciousness.

We are the World! We live in our common World of Consciousness!)--in the context of meaning and new meanings.

A new meaning implies a new horizon which is constitutive of the nature of understanding and the understanding of hermeneutical situation. Each view of the world is only a positive contribution to understanding the 'world in itself,' and not really about understanding in totality being-in-itself. Our worldview is not a perfect or comprehensive experience of the world-in-itself. It is open to other worldviews, especially when confronted by a better understanding. It could also come through an individual person's insight in the internal expression of one's understanding of one's truth. Every cultural world has its own experience of the world-in-itself and not any one of these worldviews is a totality of reality itself. There are fundamental conceptual differences between the cultures of the world. No one culture solely possesses the key to the totality of truth through understanding or captures an all-time truth in the progress of history. Openness is part of the progress of history. As we acquire more historical experience we are open to the fact of choosing between defensible beliefs and advancing an authentic global ethics guided by the ethics of authenticity. The continued emergence of this self-consciousness should be at the basis of a global ethics of authenticity (Professor Charles Taylor) and genuine global development, especially if there can be no true global development without an authentic self-consciousness and disclosure.

For an authentic self-consciousness and disclosure, which is actualized in development and elementary features of basic peace, Africa needs an African language to communicate their understanding of culture, society and development. Without an effective language, one will continue to be "an outsider" to/about issues of one's well-being (in one's own world). To be developed is to be inherently true to oneself. Development is almost impossible without the sense of the authentic self, which is to be oneself. It is to be authentic to one's existence. It is to be oneself inside-out. What we have within the narrative of development is that Africans (including some of the most educated and probably those in diaspora) are outside themselves. There is a distortion that is within. It is what John Henrik Clark calls the distortion of African "frame of mind."

From an African philosophical perspective, Africa has lost most of these cultural awareness and spiritual well-being because of many years of distortion---arising from colonialism, slavery, neo-colonialism, globalization, etc. The generations of African people have been lost in the mode of thought. Unlike the gradual development of what is essentially considered as Western Philosophical Thought, what we see as African Philosophy is distorted, patched-work, filled with doubts about its authenticity and originality.

African Mind and African Philosophy

This mind in question cannot hold things together. It is a mind that understands superficially the intricacies of self-advancement, especially among the sea of progressive societies. It is a mind that is at home with ego worship and lack of well-grounded perception of genuine and selfless progress as articulated by Frantz Fanon.

Fanon's view on the distortion of collective 'consciousness' will be buttressed in this section. He is of the view that assimilation of the African lies at the root of distortion of self-consciousness. The claim to a sort of philosophies of black superiority is not the panacea to mental or conscious liberation of African people. The project of awakening the collective consciousness is one that must be done through a clear concept of a critical revolutionary humanism (different from the familiar integral humanism peculiar in Jacques Maritain's socio-political philosophy---see some of my reflections on Jacques Maritain recently published volume 30). It is an intellectual revolution of consciousness, of their dignity and of claim to their land (considered here in the richness of the beautiful earth, Nature as the 'fundamentum' or 'suppositum' of existence). Without the image of the land or the idea of the land, the African person or being is incapable of having a basis to rise-up from. I consider this point in the interpretation of "indigenous, native, autochthonous"—from the land, native to the land, etc.). Possessing the land, arising from the land is the first step to decolonizing the dignity of persons, especially the African. In Fanon's view, I consider or relate it to Adam Smith's moral sentiment or the natural sentiment as one that is available to all human beings. Fanon was not interested in subjugating the White or the Western in order to lift-up the African. His revolutionary approach is integral in recognizing the role of our common humanity in human development and global peace. Of course, the situation of the restoration of the African person's dignity is in the philosophy of negritude, which is not an exclusivist philosophical approach (but rather should be seen from a jointly exhaustive sense) of common –human-belongingness/well-being. This negritude is ordered to overcome the alienation of the other –which brings to the light the conflict between true development and deplorable alienation. The alienated has no access to dignity, to loss access to dignity is to lack the capacity to development, without development one is distorted and peace-less or without peace. Peace is development, and peace breeds development. Europe's interest in their development by way of the destruction of the other as uncivilized, brutish, inferior is at the basis of our global crisis that is reflected in Africans perpetually losing their language to express the world.

African 'Perpetual' Poverty and Authentic Reconstructed Development

I consider Walter Rodney's work as an essential text in understanding African poverty and the conditions for African development. The impoverishment of Africa has been a long process. Some anthropologists and historians/sociologists suggest as 4 million years of suppression history or of civilization, including the 4 centuries of slavery that so close to 15 million young people left Africa for the New World.

The African person having been conscientized or made conscious of his/her situations and plights begins to make a proper decision and distinction between his/her problems and non-problems. Having been enlightened and informed of the genuine problems at stake, after retrospection and knowing his/her primordial position in history and understanding of life, then knowing the present misinformation, miseducation and cultural alienation and mistake moves forward into the future for authentic symbiotic reconstruction and development. "Each cultural tradition expresses it way in the language that carries this tradition (Schmidt (2000), p. 3). This could be interpreted in light of Hegelian triad of construction, deconstruction, and reconstruction.

It is construction because before the arrival of European colonizers Africans had a way of life, a system of doing things, for instance, economic, cultural, religious and socio-political activities (philosophy of life or culture of existence). The African person had cultural values that helped in forming his/her way of life and determining his governmental or administrative system. Oliver Onwubiko, using comparative studies, identified these cultural values like: sense of good human relationship, sacredness of life, sense of hospitality, sense of respect to elders, a sense of time, and sense of community life (Onwubiko, O. A, (1991), *African Thought, Religion and Culture*, p. 13.)

Community life depicts communalism as an economic system. Brotherhood/sisterhood and extended family system in human relationship are other reflections of this community life. With the community, there is the sense of the Infinite God and polytheism in gods, sense of time from a poly-chronic point of view of doing two to three things within a given period of time.

Under deconstruction, we talk of the colonial face of Africa. At this period the European colonizers, traders and industrialists and the European missionaries landed in Africa and formed the "force of change." They distorted, deformed, defiled, and obliterated almost all African cultural heritage and values on the altar of their self-called barbarism. They tagged African cultures 'barbaric', 'primitive, and ''paganish,''brutish,' (uncivilized in an attempt to facilitate their claim that Africa has no civilization).

The deconstruction function started culturally by replacing communalism with the European free enterprise individualism or capitalism, spiritualistic nature of Africa for materialism and atheism. The colonizers made obsolete the African poly-chronic view of time for their clock time which was successive rather than simultaneous, e.g., the African woman could be cooking and at the same time cracking her palm kernel. A woman participating in a meeting could be peeling the melon seeds. This is part of African philosophy of life and time. The colonizers introduced indifference as against brotherhood/sisterhood and exaggerated African human relationship as full of 'tribalism' and 'nepotism.' But these problems were European terminologies that emerged after the scrambling of Africa and introduction of warrant chiefs. Through her education, colonialism introduced Western ideologies and values which were a misfit for the typical African and could only succeed in de-culturalizing the African, dividing his/her unique personality and mentality and throwing him to the valley of degraded humanity.

The next is reconstruction, created by a genuine interposing and intermingling of African good values and qualities alongside European good values and cultures, after extricating and extirpating both cultures of negative qualities. But this reconstruction function is to be done by the African, who has been conscientized, enlightened, enwisdomized and as such intellectually revolutionized.

The African elites or intelligentsia should be concerned in this solution if it is going to be successful. However, all of us cannot be at the helm of affairs at the same time. Kwame Nkrumah equally accepted this point by advocating the alliance of African intellectual revolutionaries, with the ideals of the masses for liberation and auto-development: "Intelligentsia and intellectuals if they are to play a part in the African Revolution, must become conscious of the class struggle in Africa, and align themselves with the oppressed masses." (Nkrumah, K (1970), *Class Struggle in Africa*, p. 40).

The purpose of these intellectuals is to ally themselves with the oppressed and impoverished African masses, make them understand that we have to define our history and ourselves, by refusing to be Eurocentric and Europhilias and turning to Afrocentric, from the perspective of reconstruction development policy of our culture, economy, political and social aspects. This would help to prevent present and further subservience to any form of colonization and economic backwardness (echoed in the words of Fanon in terms of political teachings).

Africa has an additive culture which is resilient by being able to accept new and old cultural elements of other cultures. African culture is also dynamic because it can produce changes from within its own people, an indicative of activeness and dynamism. (Onwubiko, O. A (1991), *African Thought, Religion and Culture*, p. 115). We need to have authentic symbioses of African and European good values after a proper re-evaluation, knowing fully well that no person is an island, and that we cannot individually become perfect, a 'utopic' African society or African continent. Perfection or wrong understanding of 'perfectness' is part of the cause of Plato and Aristotle's failures –for they thought of creating a perfect society but failed to accomplish it. Also, Napoleon, Hitler and other people of notoriety in Western history attempted to create a 'perfect society' but they all failed because they 'failed' to recognize the fact that what is perfect admits no change for the better. Thus our priority would be to create a possible better world, an African world, through our possible ingenuity and innovativeness by reconstructive development through dialectic of thought.

All through history, any country or continent that has risen from grass to grace, either culturally, economically, politically, technologically or otherwise had these through a reconstruction policy or scientification of their society. They brought in new ideas to the good ones they originally had for their own development. Such was the case with North Korea, China, Japan, etc. These countries were like the present African countries (and continent) but towards greatness they moved through a reconstructive policy of development. Basil Davidson had this to say about Japan, for they absorbed all the good values in Western culture for their own development, they created a point of view of the world strictly their own, and defined their history according to their taste. Davidson observed: "Japan had remained independent, standing on this independence Japan had been able to look to the West and gradually take from the West whatever might be useful, rejecting what was not useful." (Davidson, B. (1993), *The Black Man's Burden*, p. 40). Further on, Davidson expatiated on this reconstruction development which Africans should take as solution in spite of the four centuries of awful history of degradation, deprivations, and alienations which form the African experience: "Japan was able to accept 'Westernization' on its own terms, as its own speed and with its own reservations, ensuring as far as possible that new technology and organization were assimilated by Japanese thinkers and teachers." (Davidson, B. (1993), p. 42).

Such was the development of a people like the present impoverished and almost hopeless Africa. Through their (Japan) able leaders and enlightened or conscientized masses, the Japanese made history and determined their destiny. In the 19th Century Japan, already mentioned above, Japan realized hers through her 'meyi' elites and China through Mao, Ho and Che. Russia equally had this under Peter the Great and his czarist elites in the 18th Century. These people and their intelligentsia saw things and reality from their own separate interest and defined their destiny and future. With regard to the idea of reconstruction development or what Nkrumah called 'to digest the elements in Africa, and develop them in such a way that they fit into the African personality', Chinweizu Ibekwe was ad rem in re-echoing that: "You must discover, destroy or turn to your own use any such devices…we have to shake up reform, destroy or adopt for our independent purposes whatever institution and attitudes our conquerors planted among us." (Chinweizu, I. (1978), p. 493). Here, further, Chinweizu suggests the need for resolution of careful appraisal, to decipher what is relevant for this reconstruction development and equally destroy by discovering truly the Trajon horses of colonial imperialism and capitalism in our mist as we move to keep Africa on her feet and re-establish African reconstructed culture, values and ideals. No longer shall we be culturally alienated through Western education system. No longer shall we allow Africa to be the economic reservoir of the European world or serve the external interests of the so-called world markets which is the avenue of European manipulation of African economic productivity and exploitation of African economies.

The world markets have been formed to protect European capitalistic interests. Thus, there is a radical need of breaking off from the international capitalistic system and the so-called foreign aids which are exploitatively selfish and only allow incidental socio-economic development in Africa. When Africa economically concentrates on her internal development by giving off maldevelopment traits and establishing revolutionary stable leaders, then the new Africa would emerge. The New Africa which would be anti-colonialistic, anti-expansionist, economically and politically equipped to keep-off all intruders or further colonialist attempts and subservience. We have to conclude this with the words of Fanon "we must turn over a new leaf, we must work out new concepts and try to set a foot a new man" (Onwuanibe, R (1982), p. 115).

White Civilization and Western Missionaries

On the European missionaries' attitude to our religious beliefs and system and culture, Mike Ojike observes this cultural inferiorization with himself a living example of the European scheme of education:

> I mocked my father's religion as 'heathen,' thinking that this was inferior to the white man's. It will take decades, perhaps a century to re-educate the African into holding a proper balance between his culture and that of the West. He has been terribly (been) miseducated (Ojike, M, (1946), pp. 68-69).

With the distortion of African culture, civilization and education, the African essence-Being-with-and –for-others was destroyed and African man and woman became depersonalized and thingfied because no people can exist without the culture which forms the core or soul of her/his intellectual, social, economic development. The African became, by this, alienated of his/her cultural heritage and capabilities, especially language, pushed about by psychological imbalance that forced to accept European colonialism as the source of civilization to African continent.

Some European scholars hold this view that European colonialism brought development and civilization to Africa. Karl Jasper has it that Africa is in: "The age of the myth, the age of pre-history and pre-reflective thought… Africa, he said, is being brought into the mainstream of world civilization thanks to European civilization" (Nwala, T. U. (ed.) *Critical Review*, p. 5).

Some claimed that colonialism brought economic and technological development to Africa. But we must not fail to understand that Western cultures and the so called white or modern civilization brought in alien and un-acclamatizable values, systems, and cultures, which we see in terms of prevalent individualism, selfishness, property and capitalism, indifferentism and over all underdevelopment.

We can simply adduce that colonialism by its definition is contrary to the terms of civilization. For Ernst Cesaire colonialism and civilization are in infinite distance from each other. In fact, they are two parallel lines that can never meet. The so called 'civilization' is a disguised presentation of colonialism which Fredrick Lugard best explained as the energy and brain of Europeans, which cannot be expended for philanthropic purposes.

The destructions of African arts, culture, life-humanity via slavery is a true manifestation of European's desire to deny the civilization of Africa which ideally gave birth to Western civilization. However, African civilization does not define Western civilization as inferior. For as Johnann Goddfried von Verder would hold that civilization is subjective according to society. Thus, it is, not very meaningful to say that a society is civilized and the other uncivilized. Civilization is pluralistic in meaning. In attempt to hold it to a society or continent is anti-objectivity, untrue and subjectivistic. The fact then is there are civilizations but in order of precedence Africa takes the historic lead in civilization.

Thus we conclude by saying that, colonialism is a form of in-authentic existence, according to Martin Buber, for it disguised itself in the garment of civilization and exploited what is most human to African people, it blocked-up the possibilities and pace of African development (which should be an aspect of genuine global development). Civilization is positive, progressive in meaning, but colonialism is oppressive, violently exploitative, and hypocritical in meaning and action. Thus, if colonialism is actually civilization, the deplorable situations of Africa presently would not have been. As such Africa would not have been in such a mess after her contact with Europe of 'civilization' for about 400 to 500 years of economic, religious, cultural and political interactions and technological contact. Jean Paul Sartre, conscious of this false position of European colonialism and colonialist apologists and the missionaries, vividly remarks that his fellow Europeans were no civilizers nor true faithful missionaries but exploiters, dominators, history destroyers and under-developers. He notes: "You know well enough that we are exploiters. You know too that we have laid hands on first, the gold and metals, then the petroleum of the 'new continents', and that we have brought them back to the old countries. This was not excellent results, as witness our palaces, our cathedrals and our great industrial cities…" (Fanon, F. (1968), *The Wretched of the Earth* (Preface), p. 25).

Colonial Alienation (Language and Alienation)

Alienation from its etymology means "to make something another's", to take away. It is a social cum political problem that affects the individual's psychologically by throwing him in-balanced, disordered, depressed, into loneliness and unprogressive based on the psychological quagmire involved.

Great philosophers like Hugo Grotius see this alienation from a socio-political point of view as the transfer of sovereign authority to another person. Such also was the sense Thomas Hobbes in the Social Contract understood alienation as a denial of one's right of self-governance to a sovereign authority (another). John Locke equally supported this view on alienation. Jean-Jacques Rousseau, in his linguistic origin, understood alienation as "Renounce," to give out or sell but in a light of understanding for the common good of the state unlike colonialism and her own alienations. The effort of laying hands on what is another's was sustained through colonial alienation and self-abnegation. Marx or the Marxists saw alienation from socio-economic point of view by questing for the liberation of man, of the alienated man from economic determination and estrangement by the division of labour and technological development.

Influenced by this understanding of 'Alienation', philosophers like Richard Onwuanibe, Frantz Fanon, and Kwameh Nkrumah would see or apply alienation to the exploitative relationship that existed between colonial Europe and colonized Africa, which resulted to what Eric and Mary Josephson would better describe as: "…an extraordinary variety of psycho-socio disorders, including loss of self, anxiety states, anomie, despair, depersonalization, rootlessness, apathy, socio-disorganization, loneliness, atomization, powerlessness, meaninglessness, isolation, pessimism and the loss of beliefs and values" (Eric and Mary J. (1962), p. 12).

Thus alienation leads to inner, psychic violence, disorder and torturing which implicitly and explicitly expresses itself in the overall external aspect of one's existence by being depressed, indifferent to development and the cause of liberation, in active just like the spirit of racism which also created psychological degradation to the Africans which was worse than hunger and famine. Walter Rodney remarks: "Colonialism created conditions which led not just to periodic famine, but to chronic undernourishment, malnutrition and deterioration in the physique of the African people…" (Rodney, W (1982), p. 258.)

The European colonizers went about with psychological alienating and degrading propaganda to inferiorize and stupefy the African person and alienate him/her from his/her cultural milieu, socio-political cum geographical environment into the Western culture. Thus the African identity was exiled and lost in psychological depression and decay.

Colonialism created false myth to present intellectual, socio-political awareness in the African to justify colonial exploitation and perpetual domination. Africans were indicted by colonizers as beasts, incarnate of sexual potency, emotionally unstable, low Intelligence Quotient (IQ). These poignant myths according to Onwuanibe made the African to be in-authentic to himself/herself and to be overdetermined from outside or without, by the colonial powers. Richard Wright also observes that: "Not only had the Southern Whites not known me but, more importantly still, as I had lived in the South I had not had the chance to learn who I was. The pressure of Southern living kept me from being the kind of person that I might have been. I had been what my surroundings had demanded, what my family, conforming to the dictates of the Whites above them, had exacted of me, and what they Whites had said that I must be. Never being fully able to be myself…" (Wright, R (1980), p. 284.)

The Africans were tele-guided with the myths built to exploit and under-develop them. Policies like Assimilation and Association developed by both French and British governments and capitalists were to deprive the African of his/her aboriginal culture, values and languages which are his/her human qualities for the pursuit of happiness.

Summarily, the humanity of the African was denied and distorted. The project of African Westernization, in my view, was aimed at obliterating African linguistic world and Africans' peculiar frame of mind in relation to religion, philosophy, socio-cultural life and their world of existence, and finally, the obliterating effect left Africans with a socio-politically assumed 'psyche' of diminished capacity to reason. (Anozie, S. U. (2017). "Jacques Maritain's Interpersonal Relations and African Philosophy of Personhood/Community," p. 97.) His/her political struggle for liberation was trampled upon, creating a divided personality. But the fact is once the African regains himself/herself from the futility of alienation, he would go back to his original position.

Capitalist Neo-colonialism

In this chapter, colonialism has been understood as a system of oppression. Having understood colonialism as system of oppression, exploitation and the exportation of African economies and wealth to the metropolitan 'mother' countries, suffice it then to posit 'neo-colonialism' as a system or factor of facilitate or perpetuate colonial cum capitalist domination of African countries by European capitalists and colonial 'super powers.'

Neo-colonialism literarily means 'new' method, strategy or modern system of continued colonialization on the merely theoretically pronounced independent states of Africa and the yet-to-be-independent states. With the greedy quest of the capitalistic states of Europe to assault Africa in all, especially economically, they planned out new systems to continue their plans of under-developing and frustrating the possibilities of development in Africa. This gives us a prelude to understanding neo-colonialism as system to continue the endless list of inhuman crimes on African people and their economy by control of their political, economic and social ideologies and by manipulating African values. As we pointed out earlier, one of these approaches is through language, and the rejection of African capacity to language, to reason and logos.

Neo-colonialism is one on the list of factors that have maimed and ruined African developments. Unlike the colonial period when Europeans were physically among the African people, planning and executing methods and policies for African exploitation and plunder both on human and material, natural resources. This time they (colonizers) are far from us and still tele-guide us with their agencies, policies and through her so called 'economic advice and assistance'. Thus Nkrumah echoes this in these words: "As long as the government of less developed countries remains in the hands of colonial administrators, their economies are set to a pattern determined by the interests, not of the indigenous inhabitants but by the national beneficiaries of the ruling country" (Turok, B. (1987), pp. 33-34.) Or the "reactionary leaders who neglect the ideal general interest and welfare when they come into power and thus become instrument of suppression on behalf of the quasi-gone colonials who they represent as the hidden hand of colonialism." (Nkrumah, K. *Consciencism* (1964), pp. 100-102.)

On one hand, African reactionaries leaders go about deceiving the African masses as 'liberators' but on the other hand, exploiting the economies of the African states and nations, recruiting foreign 'experts' in economy and political hypocrites as political advisers' and acceptance of selfish foreign investments and aids. Nkrumah's observations are: "It is the indigenous bourgeoisie who provide the main means by which international monopoly, finance, continue to plunder African and to frustrate the purposes of the African Revolution" (Nkrumah, K. (1970), p. 63.)

With monopolistic-capitalist foreign aids and assistance, the colonial elements gave selfish advices, and adapted conditions that these capitals to be used in patronizing their own European industries rather than the indigenous local industries. With this system colonial Europe controls our major economic and mineral resources, industries, banks, currency, etc. for their own development.

Also, the alarming political conditions of African states after independence are soaring. African has had the greatest number of coup de 'tat and change of governments which stagnate the pace of real development and eliminate able-bodied people, intelligent visionary revolutionary leaders of Africa, leaving African policies into the hands of their colonial sponsored 'puppet leaders.' These leaders support the colonial exploitative and monopolistic-capitalist interest and policies. Such was the case of Patrice Lumumba, Kwame Nkrumah, and Maummar Gaddafi and others assassinated or intimidated African revolutionary leaders or persons who had good intentions for African unity and development. My position at this point does not mean that these African leaders were spotless or had no administrative defects. But there is no political guardian, no connoisseur.

Further on the issue of coup de' tat, situations of guerrilla attacks or coup de 'tat were not seen in areas controlled by European administrators. Nkrumah was not ignorant of this obvious fact after analyzing the actual situations and causes of political instability in Africa by pointing accusing fingers on European capitalist colonizers: "Imperialist aggression has expressed itself not only in coup de 'tat, but in the assassination of revolutionary leaders, and the setting up of new intelligence organization." (Nkrumah, K. (1970), p. 48.) And so, unless as Ntalaja of Zaire would suggest, Africa liberates herself from European rule for the "second Independence," she will continue to be a reservoir of Colonial European resources and be perpetually underdeveloped. Reactionary African leaders must never forget that if the compromise on the true interest of African history and humanity will judge and condemn them.

It is now a categorical imperative that the African must accept A. M. Babu's advice of rejecting foreign investments, move for mental decolonization (Rodney, W. (1982) *How Europe Underdeveloped Africa*, pp. 312-315), which implies that liberation of Africa from imperialist capitalist dominations whether political, social, economic and cultural (linguistic). Without these done, Africa will continue to be deceived and ruined into the dungeon of darkness and perpetual tales of woes by colonialism, neo-colonialism and underdevelopment.

Responsible Critical Proposal

Our duty in this work is to provide a viable formative proposal after critically elaborating and articulating the plights and predicaments of the African continent brought on her by the selfish capitalistic European colonial power. European inhuman atrocities, planned genocide of human slavery and gourmand drilling of African rich resources for Europeans' economic glorifications are well recorded. Having come to this stage, it is now a stage of decision, a stage of re-evaluation and deliberation on what system and scheme to adopt to free the African Being with-and-for-others and her continent from the shackles of colonial impoverishing imperialism, exploitations and these woeful tales of underdevelopment and the possible death of a continent.

The onus is ours to make critiques for a mature viable proposal for a radical re-africanization of our already violated, massacred, Eurocentric-formed personality and polluted-mentality cause by European colonialism (not totally distinguished from globalization). Our radical germane proposal is one, of intellectual revolution in ideological conscientization where the masses are educated, to actually understand themselves and their problems and move out to solve them. And without this done we will continue to roam in ignorance and point accusing fingers on non-problems. The other proposal is authentic reconstructed development, having been enlightened, the African is able to sieve out / rehabilitate good values of typical Africa to harmonize them with good European values, for no continent can claim a perfect possession of all good values. We must be out to accept good values and ideologies for our own benefit without compromising the liberation and decolonization of Africa, our continent.

Intellectual Revolution in Ideological Conscientization (a way to global development)

Our main interest here is to first understand ideological conscientization which is the bedrock of intellectual revolution for African liberation. The liberation and decolonization of Africa must essentially come from within, from individual person to national discovery. It is an ontological epistemological consciousness and self- recovery or reflection method for authentic liberation.

Conscientization, etymologically put, comes from the Latin word "conscientio"-"to know deep down." According New Catholic Encyclopedia, Volume 4, 'conscientio' is contrasted to 'in alio scientio' –implying knowing oneself together with other things or object. It is on this note that conscientization is seen as the awareness or self-consciousness of one's condition, predicaments or position at a particular point in time. Influenced by this common parlance of understanding of conscientization, Steve Biko defined it then as: "…a process whereby individuals or group living within a given social and political setting are made aware of their situation…conscientization implies a desire to engage people in an emancipatory process in an attempt to free one from a situation of bondage." (Biko, S (1978), p. 31.)

With Biko, we understand that the major and the worst problem an individual person or a group of people would have, is to be ignorant of their positions, their original position, and the cause or causes of their present plight. Some may find the cause of the present plight to that of imposition of concepts and categories of domination. In Tsenay Serequeberhan's words, "The discourse of African philosophy…is a reflective and cultural effort to rethink the African situation beyond the confines of European concepts and categories." (Serequeberhan, T(1991), pp. 22-23.)

It is only when one recognizes his/her initial position of freedom which he/she is presently lacking that he/she proceeds to search for solutions. And conscientization is that solution to self-awareness or rediscovery. Thus conscientization is a pedagogical process of arousing critical self-consciousness of the oppressed, the exploited, the humiliated and that is the African person of original position: freedom, dignity, equality, decency and progressive development.

For an authentic ideological conscientization, the African masses are to be educated to understand the problems at stake so that they do not pursue shadow for reality. And the problem at stake is that European colonialism is the bane of Africans development (even world development) because it massacred, conquered and impoverished the African continent of her human and natural resources necessary for her political, economic, and technological development. Worst still, to prevent African discovery of his/her bondage, the European colonizers via her Western education corrupted the thinking and sensibilities of the African and filled him/her with abnormal complexes (Rodney, W(1982),

How Europe Underdeveloped Africa, p. 273), mal-educated the African, deadened his/her intellectual capabilities and polluted his/her mentality. It is to this that Fanon calls for political education of the masses for enlightenment and self-consciousness: "To hold a responsible position in an underdeveloped country is to know that in the end everything depends on the education of the masses, on the raising of the level of thought, and on what we are too quick to call 'political teachings'." (Fanon in Onwuanibe, R (1983), p. 107.) Fanon's political education is same as Ngugi's calls for decolonizing the mind. Decolonizing the mind is a negative way of suggesting intellectual awakening or arousal. Nkrumah consented to Fanon's 'political teaching' by advocating for the education of the masses which initiates self-discovery and self-consciousness in the African. Nkrumah observes: "The basis of a revolution is created when the original structure and conditions within a given society have aroused mass consent and mass desire for positive action to change or transform that society." (Nkrumah, K (1973) *Class Struggle in Africa*, p. 80.)

Conscientization calls for instructing and creating a conscience that embarks on the quest for liberation from colonialism, neo-colonialism or exploration as a whole and a search for ways to put these to an end. Every Tom, Dick, and Harry should be involved: the illiterate Africans, the quasi-literate or elites and the bourgeois, whom Fanon identified as 'ignorant' and incomprehensive' because they allow themselves to be used by the colonizers to perpetuate their (colonial) plans of underdevelopment and dehumanization.

This ideological conscientization calls for self-consciousness or awareness. For the Igbos of Southeastern part of Nigeria have it that "Onye n'amaghi ebe mmiri bidoro mawaya, agaghi ama ebe o machara ya"- "He who does not know where the rain started beating him, will not know where it stopped," and suffice it to add "such a person is not worthy of being sheltered if he runs into a neighbour for shelter." (Igbo Proverb.) This boils down to the fact of freeing our people from ignorance of the facts of our problems and predicaments and missing our true target--which is the liberation and establishment of truly developed Africa. Through ideological conscientization the African is freed from his/her ignorance, white-washed mentality. It is what Chinweizu calls "delusion of freedom" and be conscientized on the need for common cause of ideal liberation of Africans and Africa.

Ideological conscientization becomes a prelude to intellectual revolution which taken in globo would involve social, political, economic and cultural discovery and ethical revolutions. Having understood him/herself through self-discovery the African reasserts him/herself by determining the pace of his/her political cum economic development and destiny. Thus, in what may be related to Africa, Albert Hirschman, an economist in respect to Latin America, would opine that: "…it is also…this 'conquest of decision centers' which were previously in foreign hands, and a new ability to strike out on one's own economically, politically and intellectually. For this reason, the quest for development is also a quest of self-discovery and self-assertion and thus comes to be indissolubly to a new nationalism." (Gerassi, J (1965), p. 398.)

Intellectual revolution would also involve correcting some of the ideas of our revolutionary leaders, who erred in the course of delivering the message of African liberation and development, like Mugabe, Gaddafi, Lumumba, etc. who relied and hoped on the intervention of the United Nations in Congo situation, forgetting that the United Nations is a property of the 'Great' European Nations who were indifferent to colonialism and imperialistic capitalism. We are correcting them not that we are for excessive moral conquest either or conscientious objectors who reject military functions or violence, but because having critically evaluated the use of revolutionary violence as a solution, is to the detriment of the African people. For Africa, in attempt to do this, must surely suffer the loser and the vanquished. In the light of this, Onwuanibe was right when he observed that: "When one is frustrated by the use of violence, one often reacts by trying to frustrate the frustration or counter it by more violence, and violence perpetuates, unless one comes to realize that it is unavailing in the face of greater violence." (Onwuanibe, R (1983), p. 60.) As we know, violence only begets violence. Violence without intellectual revolution stays as at the level of mere destruction.

Africa is bound to lose its humanistic potentialities in violence or war. Also according to Onwuanibe revolutionary violence would lead to institutionalizing violence and it degenerates into license for violence is more excessive in the hands of those who are fighting for freedom and this is not the spirit of the African person, who knows where he/she is going. For now, the European or Western scientific technology is too vast for the African technological comparison and challenge.

Summarily, ideological conscientization leading to intellectual revolution is a basic factor in the self-consciousness and self-reassertion of the African for authentic liberation from colonial exploitation and decay. This self-consciousness exists for itself and, for itself, determines its future developments as Hegel would also hold. By this ideological conscientization and intellectual revolution the African knows his/her problems and sets out to solve them properly, especially by recognizing and using his/her indigenous language in expressing the world or understanding of the world.

Conclusion

So far we have been able to establish how Africa look at Global Development and how some significant historical events have made Africa feel about Western categories and conceptual frame work on global development. Real development is an integrative project. It is a duty for all. Development means peace, world without peace is not a developed world. That is how African people understand global development and would participate in determining the direction of this global development.

We have also established that European colonialism is the bedrock of African un-progressiveness, dehumanization, exploitation, economic backwardness and intellectual darkness. Colonialism, at its emergence, distorted, deformed and obliterated African culture, language and values, and ipso facto, destroyed the original African linguistic understanding and view of life, to establish European own culture and ideologies which facilitated the continued exploitation, subjugation and underdevelopment of Africa. Thus, all boil down to the fact that European colonialism is the bane, the cause, of the woe and the ruin of African development. This includes the distortion of African history as well as the creation of a Eurocentric linguistic African personality, imbedded with confused values through colonial educational system. Incidentally, the colonial education system has not done Europeans the best alone, but also aroused the sense of political liberation and emergence of scientific intellectualism among the vibrant African scholars and philosophers, who quested for the struggle for freedom and self-determination.

It is now African peoples and their scholars' onus to wake-up from this dungeon which European colonialism and her degradations have thrown them into, and redirect our history and ideas. This can only be done by conscientization (awakening from self-immolation or self-distortion) of the masses of Africa, educating them for the needs of dedicated reconstruction of Africa in all ramifications, to create a new, free African people and continent. In line with this view, Fanon would say: "Let us decide not to imitate, let us combine our muscles and our brain in a new direction. Let us try to create a whole man, whom Europe has been incapable of bringing to triumphant birth." (Fanon, F (1968), p. 252.)

We have to follow this clarion call of Fanon, Thiong'o, Nkrumah, etc. We need to follow a new course of action and creation of new ideology or ideologies based on the facts of our concrete African experiences in all these five centuries of inhuman subjugation and economic/cultural mal-developments. One of these new courses of action is to conceptualize the globalization that is different from a Euro-centric notion of development. Another course of action is to reject every attempt at the fatalist gesture of an incapable African language of thinking or the preferential option for a mono-linguistic world of our common existence.

Thus for economic reconstruction, we have to break-off from European international capitalist market and system, which for all these years have extracted our enormous resources and deceived us by positing underdevelopment in Africa. We should not allow Europe or the New World to shade from us the true cause of African underdevelopment and un-progressiveness. It is nothing but European colonialism and her unholy, inglorious devices for African collapse-as this project would affirm.

We have to create an integrated economy oriented to the needs of Africans as defined politically by the African people and intelligentsia. Anything short of that will be incomplete and incompatible to our aspiration for political, economic and cultural autonomy (Chinwezu, (1978), p. 286.)We advocate the need of dedicated reconstruction process policy which could be effective when Africans know their present by looking into the past and knowing the future by looking into the past and present. Such are the proposals that can liberate us for now from European Colonialism-the bane of African development and to in-state economic, political and cultural re-evaluated values, synthesized from the good African cultural/ideological values and the good European culture and ideologies which some of them are truly based on our interest, determination and pace. Chinweizu, by way of conclusion put it thus, "[U]ntil we snap our necks out of their braces and face forward, and realize that our preoccupation ought to be with future until we define our future the way we, not they want it, there not be even the possibility of creating... Africa." (Chinweizu, (1978), p. 498.)

Bibliography

Anozie, S. U (2017). African esotericism with a concentration on the Igbos. In *Spirituality and global ethics*. Edited by Mahmoud Masaeli. UK: Cambridge Scholar Publishing.

-------- (2017). Jacques Maritain's interpersonal relations and African philosophy of personhood/community. In *Maritain Studies* (Volume XXXIII). Edited by Nikolaj Zunic. Published by the Canadian Jacques Maritain Association.

Ariew, R and Eric Watkins. (2009). *Modern philosophy: an anthology of primary sources*. Indianapolis: Hackett Publishing Company, Inc.

Biko, S. (1978). *I write what I know*. London: Heinemann Books.

Chinweizu, I. (1978). *The west and the rest of us*. London: Nok Publication and Nigeria Ltd.

Davidson, B. (1993). *The black man's burden*. Ibadan: Spectrum.

Fanon, F. (1968), *The wretched of the earth*. Trans. Constance Farringhton, New York: Grove Press.

Gadamer, H. (1975). *Truth and method*. New York: The Seabury Press.

------------(2004). *Truth and method*. Trans. Joel Weinsheimer and Donald G. Marshall, London: Continuum, 2nd rev. ed.

------------(1976). *Philosophical hermeneutics*. Trans. and ed. David E. Linge. Los Angeles: University of California Press.

Gerassi, J. (1965). *The great fear in Latin America*. New York: Collier Macmillian.

Josephson, Eric and Mary (Eds.) (1962). *Man alone: alienation in modern society*. New York: Bell Publishing Company Inc.

Merleau-Ponty, M. (1964). *Signs*. Evanston, Illinois: Northwestern University Press.

Nkrumah, K. (1964). *Consciencism*. London: Panaf Books Ltd.

-----------(1970). *Class struggle in Africa*. New York: Lawrence Hill and Co.

Ojike, M. (1946). *My Africa*. London: Blandford Press.

Onwuanibe, R. (1983). *A critique of revolutionary humanism: Fanon*. USA: Warren H. Green Inc.

Onwubiko, O. A. (1991). *African thought, religion and culture*. Enugu: Snaap Press, Vol. 1.

Rodney, W. (1982). *How Europe underdeveloped Africa*. Ikenga Publication Nigeria.

Schmidt, L. K. (Ed). (2000). Language in a hermeneutic ontology. In *Language and linguisticality in Gadamer's hermeneutics*. Ed. Lawrence K. Schmidt. Maryland: Lexington Books.

Serequeberhan, T. (Ed). (1991). *African philosophy: the essential readings*. New York: Paragon House.

Chapter 9
African Hermeneutics of Illuminating Consciousness The Intercultural Problem of Language and Hermeneutics

Stanley Uche Anozie

(The College of the Humanities (Religion), Carleton University, Ottawa, Ontario, Canada, 2018)

Abstract. This work is simply set to relate Hans-Georg Gadamer's approach to hermeneutics with African philosophical reflections and narrative texts that 'capture the emergence' of African illuminating consciousness. The intercultural problem of language strictly focuses on the written tradition (literature) and the *linguistic* implications of African narrative texts like Chinua Achebe's use of English language in *Things Fall Apart*, and why Igbo African language could have been better used in advancing African intellectual consciousness. Each language is able to communicate meaning through dialogue rather than in the use of exact words or similar words in translations. There is understanding in the act of dialogue itself. The intercultural problem of hermeneutics addresses understanding the hermeneutical meanings in Achebe's Igbo African (tragedy) narrative, without focusing solely on *language* (linguistic re-presentation) but also on *meaningfulness*, *hermeneutical re-presentation* and the *communication* of *communitarian* understanding of African tragedy (of losing their frame of mind) as part of African hermeneutics of self-consciousness or African intellectual/intercultural experience communicated through a Western culture/colonial language agency in Achebe. The continued emergence of this self-consciousness should be at the basis of a global ethics of authenticity (Professor Charles Taylor), especially if there is no morality without an authentic self-consciousness and disclosure.

Keywords: African, Hermeneutics, Illumination, Consciousness, Language, Proverbs, African philosophy, Gadamer, Achebe, Clarke, Intercultural.

Introduction

Gadamer's hermeneutics bears on my conception and articulation of African hermeneutics leading to what I term as African hermeneutics of illuminating consciousness. Simply put, it is about Africans' articulation of their experience of the world through their own conceptual scheme and language. This is especially so because of the claim of the universality of hermeneutics with regard to language and understanding as core matters in African thought (ontology and epistemology). I dialogue with Achebe's crucial fictional text as a classical manuscript of African thought in relation to Gadamer's philosophical hermeneutics. I equally make references to views of some scholars on African thought. These scholars include Professors John Henrik Clarke, Yosef ben Jochannan, Ivan van Sertima, John Murungi, etc.

As we recognize in hermeneutics, dialogue involves listening to other views, especially if they are foundational views in the development of understanding. I use relevant Gadamer's hermeneutical principles to articulate some hermeneutical themes from Achebe's text to better understand African hermeneutics/illuminating consciousness of themselves and the world, especially in relation to African experience of communal tragedy (imposed on her through Western Colonization and control of the faculty of understanding/consciousness, especially the consciousness of the self that arises through communication, language and hermeneutics). I apply the philosophical treasure of illuminating consciousness in relation to understanding of Igbo African *Chi proverbs (*in *Things Fall Apart*) as an ontological aspect to depict the depth of African hermeneutics and the philosophical insight of African notion of *Chi*. For one to clearly understand some of the *Chi proverbs*, one needs to decipher the usage of *Chi* with its ontological and epistemological interpretive implications. The interpretive connections between Gadamer and Achebe in this essay are to develop and advance a 'unique' understanding of African hermeneutics within the universality of hermeneutics project. It is especially so with regard to African hermeneutical thought in written texts and oral communication, as contents for 'illuminating' consciousness and interculturality.

Interculturality is a common feature of most multicultural societies and is of a peculiar philosophical interest in a post-colonial world (I use post-colonial advisedly since the dominant characters of colonialism are significantly determinant even in a globalized multicultural society). That is the situation of the intercultural problem of language because both of the parties (European and African) need to make sense of what the other person is communicating. It is not merely an issue of having a translator or an interpreter, but making sense of the 'inner meaning' or the illuminating 'otherness' of reality that has been communicated through another language.

I now take a brief look at Gadamer's philosophical hermeneutics and the claim of universality of hermeneutics as the framework for addressing African hermeneutics and her illuminating consciousness in view of an integrated-globalized ethics.

Gadamer and African Hermeneutics: Colonialism and Language

Gadamer's main task is to focus on the hermeneutics of language. His goal is to understand the act and language of communication in which the truth of being is genuinely understood. It means hermeneutics is about our experience and how we understood our experience of being through language. In this sense, we are focusing on the ontological constitution of understanding through language and its relation to beings. The universality of language in the understanding of reality is fundamental and central in hermeneutics. In Gadamer's theory language is present in every human endeavor. It is all-encompassing (as part of our consciousness).

Language (not any particular language) is the realm of consciousness and common understanding. This kind of situation of common understanding during conversation/dialogue must have taken place between traditional Africans in Nigeria and the European colonizers (who could not speak or understand the inner meanings of the local African languages) in Achebe's text. I use "European colonizers" in a broad sense to include 'colonization of thought', 'colonization and control of civilization', 'colonization of self-consciousness' of the 'other' in order to denigrate the other person as incapable of critical thinking, perpetually unphilosophical, or being non-philosophical (relate to Theophilus Okere's non-philosophy). In the present, for Africans to be understood by Europeans, and vice versa, there ought to be an intercultural approach (the context for dialogue) to hermeneutics because of the problem of language as means to addressing the general problem of understanding. Some consider this problem in the context of hermeneutics as the intercultural dialogue between people of different thought history/horizons, historical consciousness, cultures, and languages. This common intercultural problem of understanding has continued to be an important part of hermeneutics in general that needs to be addressed through what has been referred to as dialogic hermeneutics. In this critical dialogic context, Gadamer provides the framework to address these difficulties. Some of these difficulties are: what happens with our different languages if we must understand each other? How does genuine comprehension of inner meaning and understanding take place without further misunderstanding and misrepresentation of any people? Within the context of African people, one has to bear in mind the intellectual concerns about Joseph Conrad's *The Heart of Darkness* in a colonial intercultural situation at the background of Achebe's *Things Fall Apart* narrative. Another aspect to this intercultural problem of language, as part of the problem of the understanding, is the criticism by some African scholars against Achebe's *English* literature (non-African language literature.)

Achebe learned the use of English language (mastered it as some say) as a foreign language. He, through his narrative, recognized the fact that English language is a language of colonial empowerment within his cultural world and that he had no choice but to use it as such. Achebe had Igbo language as his original language but was compelled through colonial policies to acquire a new language (English) in order to communicate the understanding of his African world. In Gadamer's view, an author's inability to use an original or native language or language of the homeland should never be seen as a hindrance to the narrative of non-African or African worldviews, especially because we exist and express ourselves within a language (of being) and that language-every language for that matter-has the capacity for the universal hermeneutical task of understanding and transmission of illuminating consciousness of a culture/civilization.

Gadamer's theory of language, in addressing this one problem of understanding, introduces a form of language revolution into philosophy. The use of language goes beyond a phenomenological method of experience to a conscious hermeneutical reflection on everyday existence and the worldviews of cultures. For him, our understanding requires us to integrate the temporal aspects of human experience, whether as past, present or the future in ways that provide meaning (through conceptual schemes) and reveal the reality of language in the world of human experience.

Human experience of the world brings to light these inseparable time structure of experience but limited relations in understanding. Meanwhile, although our perspectives are given pre-reflectively, our understanding is limited because of the limits of our language. Language discovers the unknown but it is not *a means* of representing a truth already known. In this way language is not reduced to the status of mere tool of understanding. There is no extra-linguistic relation with the world.

Gadamer further explains that language is not an object or something that we use and reject after it has done its service. We do not find ourselves as consciousness over against the world, i.e., as a tool of understanding in a wordless condition. Our knowledge of ourselves is linguistic and it is essential to our being human. It ought not to be seen as an object for it is in essence *what we are*, i.e., *our* language and it *speaks us*. When Gadamer says that *language speaks us,* it implies that our language of existence (any language) is capable of expressing our worldviews. As human beings who have languages, we are spoken to through our respective languages. Gadamer accepts that language and understanding are inseparable structural aspects of our being-in-the-world. Language is not an optional condition of understanding. Through the language we use, the objects of our concern appear to us, depending on the world already disclosed to us.

Following Gadamer's discourse about the disclosive quality of language and his claim about the universality of hermeneutics, I think, it is possible and pertinent for Achebe to express African reality in African language since language, any language, is inseparable from reality. Achebe does not use African language *per se* in pursuing his *African* narrative task. His view and use of language generate some hermeneutical difficulties in the translation and contemporary reading of his narrative literature. Each language is appropriate for hermeneutics because each language uses its exact words to communicate understanding in its very way. A language *can* have a suitable or appropriate word that uniquely describes an object within its cultural world.

In Gadamer's opinion, every language is able to say whatever it wants to say. But according to African scholars and linguists, language *only* better says whatever it says within its cultural milieu of understanding. A language may say whatever it wants to say, but it does not communicate meaning to other person who is not able to understand that particular language (a linguist argument.)

How will one know that a language has effectively communicated a particular meaning when one does not understand or use that language to express understanding? Gadamer's response is that it is only in dialogue, although it seems to us that our language does a better job at representing our reality. This is why in some of the examples of Igbo proverbs in Achebe one still has to provide some explanations or transliterations for a non-Igbo reader in order to fully disclose meanings in the text.

The disclosure function of language is of importance to hermeneutics. Language reveals the world around us and does not focus on itself but through language our subject matter or reality is understood. Language discloses reality and reality does influence language. Language strives to press beyond the limits of established conventions while it discloses reality. The question that is often raised by African scholars and linguists is: was Achebe justified in using English language since he is only using it to make his culture (his subject matter)- African worldviews understood? One recalls that English language at this time was an important language within Achebe's world. He describes his approach as communicating through worldly accepted–language, a domesticated language. Achebe uses a new approach to language that presents African world via a mediated agency. According to Gadamer, there is no problem with using another language. Meanwhile, one has to recall that Gadamer, for this research, does not only provide a hermeneutical *framework* but he also provides an *optimistic platform* and *a meeting point* to advance the interpretation/understanding of the other (i.e. an African other.) In providing a framework, Gadamer does not argue against the justification for choosing English language since reality could be accessed by any language, but he justifies the universal capacity of language-any language for that matter-to be used in the task of hermeneutics.

On Achebe's second concern, one has to recall that in *Things Fall Apart* it was clearly noted that the colonial English language was a privilege matter or a socio-political matter. Those of Achebe's age bracket and above who could not express themselves in English or in Europeanized African way were considered illiterate people. Using English language was a tool to foster acceptability and belongingness to a colonial world with colonial 'philosophy' of imperialism (The English colonizers used the policy of 'Association'—that means that the colonized maintain some of their cultural practices and identities while the colonizers occupy the positions of administration in their Euro-African economic relations. The French used the policy of 'Assimilation'—that means that the colonized are meant to become part of one French cultural identity by adopting French language and culture. It is the 19th and 20th Centuries' policy of expanding French culture in their colonies. The attempt by Achebe confirms the ability for any language to apprehend any cultural reality. Nevertheless, I argue that Achebe's use of English language to present African worldviews (in an effort to avoid misrepresentation) does create an intercultural problem of language, especially following a history of colonial misrepresentation, misunderstanding and purposeful philosophical hegemony.

Without the purposeful effort for domination and philosophical hegemony, language is the mirror through which we look at the worldviews of a people. Achebe's usage of English language somehow denies Igbo language and African people the opportunity to genuinely present African thought, epistemology, ontology, and worldviews to other cultures. Achebe's approach takes away the opportunity for African language to develop its possibilities and suitably transmit its nuance of reality, especially in a colonial and post-colonial world. Every hermeneutical theory is not merely a linguistic theory but also an ontological theory for understanding 'being' and 'truth' for African people, African experience and the development of African languages.

Every language certainly has the capacity to communicate reality but a specific language is most suitable for the specific people it belongs to as part of their life-world. This point goes to support the understanding that the language of a people reflects the reality of the people in question. It means that to avoid using an African language creates some nuance challenges (that can be overcome through dialogue) in reflecting African worldviews in some specific contexts. For instance, to translate *Umuofia* as "people of the bush or people of the forest" does not truly capture the inner meaning of that name and it could be derogatory for the native speakers of Igbo African language. In *Things Fall Apart*, Igbo names like "Ikemefuna" (meaning--May my strength not be lost), "Okonkwo," (meaning--A male child born on *Nkwo* market day)[352] "Nneka" (meaning--Mother is superior or precious), etc have deeper hermeneutical implications or bear hermeneutical weight in understanding the context and the specific message in the text. No good English transliteration will suitably capture the philosophical meaning without drowning the precision and clear points these names make in the narrative or text. Another good example is Achebe's proverb: "Whenever you see a toad jumping in the broad daylight,

---

[352] The Igbo people have four days in a week. There are four market days: Eke, Orie, Afor and Nkwo. Children are named according to the market day they were born or because something very significant happened around that time of their birth or because wishes are fulfilled. When one is not aware of these situations, it is possible to misinterpret the inner meaning of the names.

then know that something is after its life." The Igbo language rendering of this proverb is: *Awo anaghi agba ọsọ ehihie n'efu.* The English translation of it in the text does not bring out the deeper meaning and the philosophical depth of this proverb or help a non-Igbo person/reader to appreciate its hermeneutical purpose in that part of the narrative.

The 'toad' (*Awo*) in the context of the proverb above stands for man in his ontological and existential situation. The toad has to move/run/jump because there is an urgent situation (life and death, important issue.) Ralph Madu translates it in as: "The nocturnal toad does not run during the day in vain" (Madu, 1996, p. 217). One could consider Madu's translation as closer to the inner meaning of that Igbo proverb than Achebe's. But none of these captures, in my view, the coded meaning of the proverb in the situation under consideration. This is why in my later analysis of this proverb it has a precise hermeneutic meaning as 'urgency or importance' based on the contexts and the subject matter of the discussion in Achebe's part of the text). The argument is that the promotion of indigenous African language in Achebe would have enabled the indigenous language, through writing, gain its "true ideality" (Gadamar, 1975, pp. 352-353) and its true intellectual quality. The capacity of every language to have intellectual quality means that each language is able to philosophically express its world in its own way, independent of how other cultures perceive reality. As noted, in every language there is a unity of thought and reality. When that truth which is being communicated to us is not well uttered then more harm is done than good. It means that African people and their languages lose more because of lack of development of their own philosophical linguistic heritage. Now, if the issue is on the 'truth for us', then it ought to be what 'the truth we wish to communicate to others is all about', i.e., Igbo African experience of truth given to the rest of the world (The *de re* and *de dicto* distinctions). It is about what we mean to communicate and not what the languages of the 'reader', 'hearer' or 'listener' will like us communicate to him/her. What determines the content of communication is the subject matter or reality of the speaker or writer and not the reader or listener. 'Listening' involves overcoming your own negative prejudices and socio-historical conditions in order to understand the truth of what has been presented to you as it was intended, and more.

Gadamer is not after a discussion on linguistics but on the intended meaning, the inner constitution of understanding by language as such. This is part of the essential meaning of the universality of hermeneutics that is grounded in 'within language.' The reality in question is the 'reality' that is found *within* or within the *inner* language. As I earlier noted about Gadamer, there are the outer word and the inner word (logos or language.) It is in the inner word or language that the universality of hermeneutics is understood. It is in the inner universality that all these particular languages and different people (different cultures) are able to communicate meanings that are also truly understood. This view recalls the history of philosophical hermeneutics and the claim of the universality of hermeneutics in which Plato, Aristotle, Augustine, Husserl, etc were of great importance to Gadamer. In Greek thought: λόγος προφορικός (*logos prophorikos*) and λόγος ἐνδιάθετος (*logos endiathetos*) are essential parts of the understanding. The *logos endiathetos* (inner word) describes this inner constitution that makes it possible for our thought to be united in the description of the same reality despite our different languages and diverse worlds. To possess a language is to possess a world. Since we possess language in a linguistic world, then we have a world of existence to describe (There is no model paradigm for a description of the world). Igbo language (as an African language) necessarily describes a world of its own—an Igbo African world, a world of its experience, a world of its consciousness that should not be dictated by any form of imperialism. Any form of imperialism (including philosophical) will distort the universality of language.

African Hermeneutics of Illuminating Consciousness: without Colonial and Philosophical Imperialism

Is there a time of great awakening for all humanity in African Philosophy? Is there any time for a total awareness of the world or the illumination of the self as an essential aspect of the world? I do not see this in African world philosophy and spirituality. There are reasons to see or understand revealing moments or temporary ritualized celebratory experiences in Igbo African new yam festivals, in age-grade programs, etc (Anozie, The Paradox, 2017, pp. 263-266). Life or 'living' is a process. It is a holistic process of self-disclosure or self-understanding, which we consider as the core meaning of illuminating consciousness. The whole person does not transition into a 'one-time' illuminating consciousness. It is a gradual process, unless we are talking about the illumination coming from the experience that the elders in a village/community will tend to share. The elders are considered to have lived long enough (lived through the self-revealing process) to connect to spirit ancestors, in terms of relationship to the world, as we are in a process of living or the process of becoming.

African authentic self-discovery is the end result of a process of living/becoming. It is simply what comes at the summit of life or end of life (one's life as well as our community's life-I am cautious to use our collective lives). It is not what the young person can conclusively say is certainly accomplished. Authentic self-discovery is the actualization of the full-ness of one's becoming/being or the meaning of one's existence as much as we can know it. Self-discovery or self-consciousness is within the mandate of human epistemic prowess or faculty. Belonging to various age groups of the community is an indication of what the stages of this illumination could be. This is what I have called the luminary progress in my works: *'The Paradox of Non-Violent Religions and Violent Cultural Practices'* and *'African Esotericism'* (through Okonko, Ekentensi groups, etc) (Anozie, The Paradox, 2017, pp. 258-266). Much of these luminary processes leading to conscious illumination have been denigrated, distorted, discarded into the garbage-bin of colonial amnesia and selective memorial of history and historicity (philosophical imperialism), without being truly challenged to excel.

From an Igbo African philosophical perspective, Africa has lost most of this cultural awareness and spiritual well-being because of many years of distortion---arising from colonialism, slavery, neo-colonialism, globalization, etc. I think this is what Professors Clarke and Sertima refer to as the distortion of African frame of mind. The generations of African people have been lost in the mode of thought. Unlike the gradual development of what is essentially considered as Western Philosophical Thought, what we see as African Philosophy is distorted, patched-work, filled with doubts about its authenticity and originality.

Frantz Fanon's work is also a good area to find the implications or effects of this psychological damage or imperialist distortion. Fanon reflects on the 'Black Skin, White Mask' phenomenon-the phenomenon of lack of the authentic self. At the heart of some African intelligentsia is the replication of Western Philosophy according to the approval of the Masters—Colonial Masters! But truly, there is nothing to justify that these world philosophies must be 'mono-cultural.' The visions of reality should be variedly considered because of our diverse conditions of being or lifeworld: "African consciousness in the first two decades of the century was further fed by a variety of sources….The governments were mostly white…"
(http://www.unesco.org/culture/caribbean/pdf/ghc_onlinechapter_vol5_chap6_en.pdf)

African Illuminating Consciousness and John Murungi's Reflections

Scholarship is part of the politics of control/imperialism. The tradition of European/Western imperialism in relation to the quality of African Philosophy has been long and negative. There is the paralysis of African Philosophy. We have to find a proper grounding of African Philosophy. We have to avoid a 'philosophical agenda' imposed on us. The focus must be for an African audience. We have to overcome a form of philosophical welfa-rism. No human being is a stranger to the concept of humanity or human-ness. We need to challenge the trend of current philosophy which is the trend of the direction of consciousness (unto truth and unto falsity).

Falsifying the Content of Philosophizing and Colonizing 'Reason'

The falsifying the content of philosophy is a continual phenomenon. Philosophizing is dwelling in the open-ness of critical thinking. One has to avoid a false reflection or fabrication of Africa's philosophical content. The problem of African Philosophy is a problem against philosophy in general. Colonial education distinguished itself by denigrating or excluding Africa. It holds that Africa is 'philosophically barren' in order to promote 'Eurocentric philosophy.' According to Samuel Oluoch Imbo, "the real African has been distorted by Western scholars beyond recognition…European narratives rendered these African stories primitive and barbaric" (Imbo, 2002, p. 2). At the background of such purposeful ontological forgetfulness (which is a systemic approach to encourage the loss of consciousness) of about 4 million years of African historicity, metaphysical Africanity, and African civilization (Imbo, p. 2). This purposeful forgetfulness is in tandem with European colonization of reason as a way of emphasizing a monopoly of philosophy/philosophical culture (via monoculturality).

Colonization of Reason as Monopoly of Philosophy (Mono-culturality)

Reason is considered a unique faculty that distinguishes human beings from all other animals. However, this capacity to rationality is never attributed to African people as it is *for* Europeans and possibly other assumed 'hierarchies of civilizations before Africa.' The agents of religions were contributive to this agenda of colonization of mind. Of course, some patches of individual Europeans have stood against this current of colonization of reason.

Philosophy does not imply 'universal conditions' of philosophizing. We cannot eliminate any people, culture, or race from doing philosophy. According to Okot p' Bitek, there are African scholars who failed to provide quality illumination on African Philosophy because their materials of thought were dictated by the audience—European audience. Bitek includes names like Jomo Kenyatta, John Mbiti, Willie Abraham, Koffi A. Busia, J. B. Danquah (Imbo, 2002, p. 2). In my view, some true African philosophers paid a price or betrayed the trajectory of African philosophical narrative because of the iron-hand influence of colonialism and mono-culturalists' ideology. Imbo considers the emergence of such African scholars as the emergence of "Indigenous Apologists" (Imbo, 2002, p. 4). This also impacted on most well-meaning Westerners in experiencing (authentic intellectual confrontation) true African Identity and Philosophy (Imbo, 2002, p. 3). Some of the African scholar apologists bought into "faddish aping" (Imbo (2002), p. 4) of Western scholars and their agenda (Western theories of African societies).

Western scholars and social anthropologists solidified this dichotomy of reality and primitivity, barbarity of Africa and the nobility of Europe. Social anthropologists became the 'handmaid' of colonialism, power, and civilization decimation of the African Mind. This made it possible for the West to overlook 'genuine' African identity and reality and what African is capable of offering (a preconceived model of society) (Imbo, 2002, p. 3). This is in line with "imperialist historiography" programmed to see and present Africa in an unfortunate light (Imbo, 2002, p. 3). The mind-set was determined to do a bad job of "pathological dichotomous framework" (Imbo, 2002, p. 3). My task, like Imbo's, is to resuscitate African illuminating consciousness as the emergence of "African Truth."

African Hermeneutics of Illuminating Consciousness in Oral and Written Traditions: The Emergence of "African Truth"

Hermeneutics deals with understanding the utterances of people, and not only written texts. Most African traditional societies depend on oral tradition in communicating their worldviews. For Gadamer, an oral tradition is deficient in carrying out the real hermeneutical task. But written tradition provides the wholeness necessary in interpretation. Written tradition is consistent, reliable, durable, and so expresses the wholeness in history which is part of the universality of hermeneutics. Achebe's written narrative accomplishes important hermeneutical tasks of providing consistency, reliability and durability while expressing and correcting some of the misrepresentations of African hermeneutic of illuminating philosophical worldviews.

African hermeneutic of illuminating consciousness recognizes the good qualities of both written and oral traditions. Africans wrote. Africans used oral traditions too! What is handed down as tradition could be orally given through repetitions in forms of stories, myths or texts that are clear and easy to investigate. While oral tradition is repetitive, written tradition realizes full interpretation because of the consistency of subject matter. In oral tradition one loses some of the qualities of communication preserved in human history and the loss of the continuity that one gets from the effective use of memory. In a typical oral tradition as well as in a written tradition society the power of memory is undeniably crucial in re-presentation and interpretation of worldviews, and transmission of tradition (oral and written.)

In African tradition, it is important to observe the advantage or role of oral tradition. The spoken words could be better interpreted following emotional elements, tone, and circumstance. This ability to use the spoken words also relates to the 'creative personality' of the person using a particular language to communicate meaning of a people's worldview/consciousness. This point underscores my concern that Achebe has problems with using English rather than Igbo language for expressing Igbo African consciousness in literature. The content and nuances of literature are primarily transmitted through the language of the people, i.e. the language of their daily lives. Some of Achebe's English narrative lines do not adequately represent exact Igbo African worldviews, for instance in his transliteration of some Igbo proverbs, the presentation of the notion of *Chi* as merely individual fate in understanding tragedy, etc.

Despite these difficulties, Achebe accepts that literature is one of the best ways to unravel the true cultural and philosophical/illuminating consciousness of his people through narratives. In Gadamer's supportive view, such literature is necessary in the development of reading consciousness which leads to an effective historical consciousness and the continuity of illuminating consciousness. Now one could critically apply this understanding to what advantages a written Igbo African/any African language literature would have been to the development of an enlightening consciousness among African scholars and students. Had this been the case with Achebe's text (in Igbo language), then our hermeneutical task will be purely and directly on it as the continuity of memory (for Africans). In another way, it is not only the continuity of memory and transmission of illuminating consciousness but also what Gadamer refers at the acquisition of *full sovereignty* as against philosophical imperialism/dominance.

African full sovereignty from/against philosophical imperialism and hermeneutical tasks are parts of African illumination worldviews, especially its traditional, social, religious, linguistic, cognitive, ontological and philosophical truth at the core of *African Hermeneutics*. African Hermeneutics is part of the ongoing inquiry for understanding and disclosure of meaning in the African world (African truth). In light of Achebe's work, it is an attempt at the communication and preservation of the original history of a people within its original context. The cultural and historical context of any literature is important in understanding its meaning. However, this does not require a mere *reconstruction* of the past. I will now take a look at the application of hermeneutics to African tragedy of philosophical imperialism.

Application: Understanding African Tragedy of Philosophical Imperialism

Achebe's view of African tragedy has a hermeneutical challenge which demands dialogue and understanding. It reflects the sense of tragedy as Clarke and Sertima consider the gamut of African loss of consciousness (sense of the self). It is a tragedy of its kind for cultures to co-exist in a way that a culture dominates and determines the quality of the existence of the other cultures. This dominance could also be seen in philosophy and civilizational considerations. The imperialists' traits were shared through philosophical reflections and systemic erosion of the African mind/consciousness. In my view Achebe was not so direct in pointing these traits out, especially considering the conditions of publishing his work—*Things Fall Apart*. However, this tragedy, as the loss of self-consciousness is revealed by way of 'inner meaning'--through philosophical hermeneutics and conscious illumination. May I apply some hermeneutics in African consciousness via language and *Chi* proverbs?

The Hermeneutics of African (Igbo) *Chi* Proverbs in Achebe's Narrative

The Igbo are known to express themselves with craft by using wise sayings. Their speech patterns give them the ability to use many short phrases to address sensitive issues among them. Proverbs could be used to make discussions short or to prolong discursive negotiations. It could also be used to make understanding difficult for the uninitiated or keep discussions among the elders' forum. Proverbs could be used to present literal thoughts and non-literal/complicated thoughts that are best said in not very clear manner (with hidden meanings.) This makes proverbs to be described as having 'coded message' or deeper meaning beyond the surface words. This is what makes the Igbo a proverb-using people.

In the text, Achebe notes, "Among the Ibo [Igbo] the art of conversation is regarded very highly, and proverbs are the palm-oil with which words are eaten" (Achebe, 2009, p. 7). That means narratives in Igbo culture go with a style of speaking and through wise sayings. In the narrative, the proverbs capture the cultural and linguistic heritage of the Igbo in words that must be explained through careful interpretive approach.

In chapter fourteen of the text another proverb is used. It says, "[I]f a man said yea his *chi* also affirmed" (Achebe, 2009, p. 7). This proverb illustrates the double aspects of human existence. The double aspects are the divine and the human aspects of existence. For a person to accomplish anything in Igbo worldviews he/she must live in accord with his/her destiny or fate. It involves an unpredictable aspect which implies that a person has to first accept that he/she is capable of accomplishing a task before one's *Chi* (personal god or guardian) concurs with the same task.

A further discussion of the role of *Chi* in Igbo African worldviews is necessary because of *Chi*'s place in the proverbs and in the events that happen in people's life. A subtle but important distinction here is that *Chi* is started with a capital letter to associate it with Igbo religion (as respect to the divine or a higher being.) However, I will retain the use of *chi* (with small letter) as in the text. They both mean the same thing. For the Igbo, according to Christian Anieke, *Chi* is an important concept in traditional society. He adds, "*Chi* can be defined as personal destiny, or personalized providence, of the individual which shapes their history and destiny. Some people see *Chi* as a divine emanation from God which is responsible for the individual's fate or destiny" (Anieke, 2008, p. 34). The complexity of meanings about the specific role of the *Chi* is still present in the above statement. But *Chi* involves element of both fate and faith (personal duty blessed by one's *Chi*), in terms of the support one receives from the gods in order to succeed in one's individual task. It is in this sense that *Chi's* role could also imply the task of a mediator. One's relationship to the

Supreme Being (God) is determined by one's relations to his/her *Chi*. *Chi* is only an individual relationship, rather than universal, there could be a lucky person (with a good luck *Chi* (*Chiọma*)) or even a bad luck person (with bad luck *Chi* (*Chiọjọọ*)). This reminds us about the place of predestination and freewill in Igbo traditional world. In relation to the above, there are other proverbs among the Igbo that affirm predestination. For example: *Onye kwe ma chi ya ekweghi, o ga-egbu onwe ya?* (If one says yes and his/her *Chi* disagrees, should one commit suicide?) While presenting the Igbo proverbs in Igbo language above, one recalls the argument in the earlier part of this paper that English language translation or transliteration of Igbo proverbs and narratives hindered the communication of their true inner meaning. The essence of the *Chi* proverbs in the narrative is to sharpen the image of the hero (Okonkwo) and clearly presents the depth of his struggles [with fate.] This same situation is reinforced through other *Chi* proverbs (in chapter fourteen) when Okonkwo returned to his community after his exile of seven years. Achebe's text presents it thus: "Clearly his personal god or *chi* was not made for great things. A man could not rise beyond the destiny of his *chi*" (Achebe, 2009, p. 131).

Some Other Proverbs and their Meanings in Achebe's *Things Fall Apart*

Here are some of them used by Achebe in the text:

- "[T]he sun will shine on those who stand before it shines on those who kneel under them." This proverb suggests the levels of considerations that the gods grant to people and their status.
- "If a child washed his hands he could eat with kings." A child shapes his own destiny. It means a well-groomed person succeeds or grows to enjoy with kings or the company of successful people or people of honor.
- In chapter one the proverb states, "He who brings *kola* brings life" (Achebe, 2009, p. 6). Kola nut is a caffeine-containing African nut (of evergreen trees of genus *Cola* –it is native to tropical rainforest of African) eaten before or during discussion. It has a bitter taste and is regarded as a stimulant to reduce the effects of hunger and fatigue. The presence of kola affirms the formal beginning of a gathering or meeting of the community. It is an essential edible in Igbo ceremonies. It is also used as a sign of welcome to guests in homes. Kola is interpreted as life-giving

fruit. It is believed that from the seed springs out life–a living tree. In Anieke's view, "kola is 'a force that unites the living, the dead, and the supernatural forces in one place'. Therefore, to bring kola is to express a wish for unity with supernatural forces and with fellow human beings; in other words, to bring life" (Anieke, p. 108).

- In chapter three the text states, "an old woman is always uneasy when dry bones are mentioned in a proverb." The incident surrounding this proverb helps recall to Okonkwo the story of his father's laziness. Okonkwo is sensitive to certain symbols, objects and images used in community discussions. It also means when something worry us, anything said relating to it keeps us on the edge or nervous.
- In chapter three the proverb says, "[T]he lizard that jumped from the high iroko tree to the ground said he would praise himself if no one else did." It means sometimes self-praise is acceptable. We live for ourselves. The *iroko* tree (Chorophoria excelsa) is commonly seen in west coast of tropical Africa. It is a hardwood, tough and dense of mostly brown color. It is also called *African Teak*.
- In chapter eight the proverb says, "A child's fingers are not scalded by a piece of hot yam which its mother puts into its palm." Okonkwo uses this to justify his killing of Ikemefuna and why the Earth goddess ought not to punish him. If a higher being demands a tough task from a person, then the task does not hurt the person.
- "If I fall down for you and you fall down for me, it is play" (Achebe, 1958, p. 51). This is the proverb people introduce in negotiations as to demand compromise and mutual understanding or mutual considerations.
- Another proverb says: "as a man danced so the drums were beaten for him"- meaning that what dictates success is from a world outside an individual or beyond and only the beyond that determines the nature of success of an individual.

Igbo proverbs could have multiple applications and interpretations at a time. There is no one proverb that provides the 'total picture' of a situation. Each proverb speaks or answers from a perspective while it gradually unfolds in meaningfulness.

The Unfolding of History and African Illuminating Consciousness

Our experiences and understanding of the world are the essential part of development of the universal history of Being (Consciousness, Being is

Consciousness of Itself). This progress is through the historical dialectics of thesis, antithesis and synthesis in African becoming and in Gadamer's Hegelian view. For Gadamer, the experience of Europe of his time and the need for European integration is part of history. It is in this similar manner that the experiences of the process of emancipation and end of imperial rule in former colonial countries under Europe are part of history (especially for African scholars and the recovery of a distorted history as part of the re-claim of consciousness). Every worldview or every perspective/horizon of reality is required in the effort to arrive at the disclosure of meaning or truth from a horizon. Every cultural perspective is a horizon. A horizon is a limited range of vision and it requires the emergence of new horizons (the horizon of our conscious world).

Achebe brings in a critical and constructive way the cultural encounter (an aspect of African illuminating consciousness) could take place by focusing on the positive elements for the progress of our universal existence. It is not just for the Africans to see but for the European to reappraise their philosophical and anthropological comprehensions of African world and its truth of understanding. Although Achebe's cross-cultural interactions narrative lays many emphases on the perspective of an Igbo African person, it also lays a general foundation for further hermeneutical inquiry in philosophic capacity of the African mind that radiate consciousness through a dialogic consensus (as part of an emerging authentic global ethics). There is always a continual merging of the different worldviews or horizons, including the old and the new; the familiar and the unfamiliar or alien (aspects of the reflections of consciousness).

Gadamer and Achebe: Effective Historical Consciousness (World Consciousness and Self-consciousness)

Gadamer recognizes the importance of hermeneutical situation as a principle of hermeneutics and as part of the conditions of understanding. The consciousness of the hermeneutical situation is, according him, important in true understanding of a text or document. The question about the importance of one's 'horizon' and historical consciousness in hermeneutics is sometimes variedly understood. Gadamer analyzes historical consciousness, historical situation and the issue of horizon. When one possesses a horizon, it does not really imply the acquisition of a historical situation. These (the possession of a horizon and a historical situation) help make the task of hermeneutics a comprehensive endeavor in which the truth of understanding and meaning are achieved. Our historical consciousness is self-evident to us since we are historically attuned in our pursuit of an African truth.

The main difficulty for African scholars is in the *re-presentation* (not reconstruction) of this African historical situation and experience in a way that does not do justice to the totality of truth of African worldviews and understanding. However, sometimes, when this happens, it does not necessarily mean that such consequent misunderstanding or misrepresentation is purposely intended by a writer. The reality of African historical situation and its illumination is among the things we make use of in hermeneutics rather than attempt to neglect or overcome it. One cannot overcome that which is an essential structure or constitutive of one's being and the understanding of one's existence/reality. Even one's historical situation could be interpreted as part of human facticity. It is the context or condition in which we are found, dialogued or conversed with. Effective historical consciousness or effective history (*Wirkungsgeschichte*) is part of the general encounter that leads to productive conversations or dialogue. This is really what Achebe's project is all about: the recovery of the history of influences or awareness of history of effects that make it possible for renewed understanding of his African world.

World Consciousness: One World, Many World-views

I think that there is at least one serious criticism: Achebe had constraints of colonialism (linguistic colonial effect or purpose philosophical imperialist tool) to write in the language of the colonial masters. His use of English language is part of welcoming the dictating and dominating cultural views that negatively influenced the representation of African worldviews. This criticism, I think, is what Gadamer forestalls (knowingly or unknowingly) when he considers every language as capable of reflecting every worldview or suitably translates it. Language itself has a universal character to communicate the reality of its world. His views ought to be hermeneutically and ontologically understood, especially as a new horizon for understanding the world (our common context of illumination and common content of consciousness. We are the World! We live in our common World of Consciousness!)--is the context of new meanings.

A new meaning implies a new horizon which is constitutive of the nature of understanding and the understanding of hermeneutical situation. Each view of the world is only a positive contribution to understanding the 'world in itself,' and not really about understanding in totality being-in-itself. Our worldview is not a perfect or comprehensive experience of the world-in-itself. It is open to other worldviews, especially when confronted by better understanding. It could also come through individual person insight in the internal expression of one's understanding of one's truth. Every cultural world has its own experience of the world-in-itself and not any one of these worldviews is a totality of reality itself. There are fundamental conceptual differences between the cultures of the world. No one culture solely possesses the key to the totality of truth through understanding or captures an all-time truth. Openness is part of the progress of history. As we acquire more historical experience we are open to the fact of choosing between defensible beliefs and advancing an authentic global ethics guided by the ethics of authenticity.

Conclusion

Achebe's narrative literature presents us with difficult concerns of self-awareness (read as African condition, reflected in Clarke and Sertima's loss of African Mind or Consciousness and Murungi's philosophical imperialism). I highlighted on what was lost or the negative implication of African narrative in English language following the arguments of African scholars that African language ought to be used *first* in communicating African hermeneutic of illuminating consciousness and life-world/truth. However, Gadamer strictly argues that everything could be said through language and in its inner unity is their *interpersonal and intercultural* dialogue deeply present. His approach is ontologically and hermeneutically based. The quality of hermeneutics is dependent upon the language of dialogue: a written language or an oral language. As gain or advantage, written language has more consistency, reliability and un-changeability that is important in hermeneutics or the understanding of meanings. It has also helped in the communication of new meanings present in Achebe's narrative. Certainly, the English language hinders the ability to effectively communicate the subtle uniqueness of illuminating ideas present in African Philosophy and Hermeneutics (as intended by Achebe without making it fuzzy or veiled). Hermeneutics is not an abstract theory. It associates with understanding our life experiences and our life-world's truth in an intercultural world, and even more in an integrally globalized world.

References

Achebe, C. (1958). *Things Fall Apart*. London: Heinemann.

---------- (2009). *Things Fall Apart*. Canada: Anchor Canada edition.

Anieke, C. (2008). *Problems of Intercultural Communication and Understanding in Achebe's Representation of the Igbo and Their Culture*. Enugu: Mbaeze Printing Press.

Anozie, S. U. (2012). Human Rights and Terrorism: The Niger Delta oil war. In M. Masaeli (Ed.), *Morality and Terrorism: An Interfaith Perspective*. Orange County, California: Nortia Press.

----------(2017). The Paradox of Non-Violent Religions and Violent Cultural Practices. In M. Masaeli and R. Sneller (Eds.), *The Root Causes of Terrorism: A Religious Studies Perspective*. UK: Cambridge Scholars Publishing.

---------- (2017). African Esoterism with a Concentration on Igbo tradition. In M. Masaeli (Ed.), *Spirituality and Global Ethics*. UK: Cambridge Scholars Publishing.

Bujo, B. (1998). *The Ethical Dimension of Community: The African Model and theDialogue between North and South*. Nairobi: Pauline's Publication Africa.

Gadamer, H. (1975). *Truth and Method*. London: Sheed and Ward.

----------(2004). *Truth and Method*, trans. J. Weinsheimer and D. G. Marshall. London: Continuum, 2nd rev. eds.

Imbo, S. O. (2002). *Oral Traditions as Philosophy: Okot P'Bitek's legacy for African philosophy*. USA: Rowman & Littlefield Publishers.

Irele, F. A. (2009). Introduction. In F. A. Irele. (eds.). *Things fall apart Chinua Achebe: A Norton Critical Edition*. NY: W. W. Norton and Co, Inc.

Madu, R. O. (1996). *African Symbols, Proverbs and Myths: The Hermeneutics of Destiny*. New York: Peter Lang.

[i] Asari Dokubo made some incendiary comments before the recently concluded presidential election in Nigeria. He threatened the whole nation on the re-election of President Jonathan.

[ii] I think about the troubling role that Movement for the Actualization of the Sovereign State of Biafra (MASSOB) has taken up by threatening war and violence in the Southeastern States of Nigeria. There are reports of arrests and intimidations of law abiding citizens by members of the group. This new role disrupts the group's original purpose of existence (as a peaceful group).

www.ingramcontent.com/pod-product-compliance
Lightning Source LLC
Chambersburg PA
CBHW072144290426
44111CB00012B/1970